# MOLTMANN

## Messianic Theology in the Making

Richard J. Bauckham

Marshall Pickering

Marshall Morgan and Scott
3 Beggarwood Lane, Basingstoke, Hants RG23 7LP, UK

Copyright © 1987 Richard J. Bauckham
First published in 1987 by Marshall Morgan and Scott Publications Ltd
Part of the Marshall Pickering Holdings Group
A subsidiary of the Zondervan Corporation

ISBN 0–551–01566–7

Text Set in Linotron Baskerville by Input Typesetting Ltd., London
Printed in Great Britain by Camelot Press Ltd., Shirley, Southampton.

# CONTENTS

# PREFACE

I first read *Theology of Hope* in April 1973, and I remember that first reading as one of the most exciting theological experiences of my life. I do not know many times I have reread it since, in the course of teaching Moltmann's theology and in preparing this book, but it has proved, along with Moltmann's later work, a source of constant stimulation and inspiration for my own theological thinking. For this reason, as well as because of the blindingly obvious fact that this book would not exist without his massive contribution to contemporary theology, I owe Jügen Moltmann himself a very considerable debt of gratitude, greater than prefaces usually record.

My thanks are also due to many other people. Paul Gale lent me his home in Suffolk for that cold, wet week in 1973 when I first read Moltmann. Serious planning of the book began when Paul Avis offered me the opportunity of publishing it in the *Contemporary Christian Studies* series. Many of my students at the university of Manchester, to whom I have introduced Moltmann's theology during the past ten years, have encouraged me by their enthusiasm for it and, not least by asking difficult questions, have contributed to the thinking behind this book. Stephen Williams read the first draft of much of the book and made valuable comments. Finally, the book is dedicated to Tony Lane, with whom I have enjoyed many theological conversations in which questions of interpreting Moltmann have played a major role. He was also prominent among those who, over several years, kept asking me when my book on Moltmann would be finished, until, like the unjust judge in the parable, I could no longer put off writing it.

Richard Bauckham
University of Manchester
March 1987

# FOREWORD BY JÜRGEN MOLTMANN

In the last twenty years numerous articles, dissertations and theses on particular aspects of my theology have been published, but this study by Richard Bauckham is much the most comprehensive and thorough work on that stage of my theological journey which is defined by the books *Theology of Hope* (1964), *The Crucified God* (1972) and *The Church in the Power of the Spirit* (1975). Bauckham not only gives an account of the content of these books and summarizes the various ideas; he also goes into the movement of the ideas and shows the coherence of the arguments. In this way he brings to light the concealed methods I have used. He demonstrates the consistency and coherence of the thought even where I myself had the feeling of being led by spontaneous inspiration or of only being carried back and forth.

Every study of a theologian and his theology is like a *mirror*. In many cases one looks into the mirror and realises at once: I know all this already. In other cases one looks into the mirror with astonishment, because one does not recognize oneself at all and asks oneself anxiously whether this is due to oneself or to this peculiarly dim mirror. But there are also mirrors in which one recognizes oneself better than one had known oneself before. From these mirrors one learns something new about oneself and one's theological career, and one is glad of this revelation of the hidden motives and methods in one's thought. Richard Bauckham's work has been this kind of mirror for me. It has given me clarity about the theological path on which I have not so much travelled as been led. I am grateful to him for this.

I must stress this because theology for me has never been a neutral scientific study or an objective doctrine, but an existential experience, which must be personally suffered, digested and understood. I have seldom desired or produced these *experiences of theology* myself; they have usually come upon me unexpectedly, so that I had to see how I could cope with them and live with them. I have dealt with the theological experience of God not only individually, but always collectively as well: my individual biography has been painfully affected by the collective biography of the German people during the last years of the Second World War and during a long imprisonment afterwards. The individual experiences of my faith and my theology are embedded in my generation's collective experiences of guilt and suffering. The 'question of God' first came to me during the fire-storm which, in July 1943, reduced my home town of Hamburg to rubble and ashes: Why have I survived this? And then with the uncovering of the German crimes at Auschwitz and Maidanek: How can one live with this?

In the theological works in which I have tried to come to grips with these experiences of God, I have practised a kind of *experimental theology*. This is at its heart a theology in discussion and dialogue with the God who thrusts experiences of himself irresistibly upon one. It therefore became for me, more unintentionally than intentionally, a risky kind of theology, i.e. a theology which seeks God and the assurance of his nearness by means of daring and vulnerable theses. Wilhelm Dantine of Vienna once called my theology a 'daring theology' – an observation which hit the mark, because theological thinking without the security of tradition, dogma or authorities really does become a risky and adventurous undertaking. Jacob, who wrestled all night with the angel of God and emerged from this encounter with a lame hip but also with a blessing, has always been for me the model of a true theologian.

Experimental theology is also *dialogical theology* and theology open to the world. Only solitary theologians cocoon themselves like silkworms in their own systems and persuade their 'disciples' that there is no home outside the cocoon. But theology in dialogue is theology engaged in the struggle for the truth, which liberates, and in opposition to nihilistic ideologies, which oppress. So dialogical theology cannot be timeless or without location. It must often forego correctness in order to be concrete. It cannot afford balance, but must take sides and speak onesidedly. Its intention is not to satisfy itself, but to make a contribution to the healing of everything in church, culture and creation. For me theology is alive, not in the well-defined 'schools' of Barth, Bultmann or Tillich, but in movements, dialogues and conflicts.

In those 'schools' extensions of the thought of the 'master' were developed. In the dialogues and conflicts of our generation one exposes oneself to others, to those who are different and quite often hostile, one comes to know one's limits, one is given new questions and must strive for answers which have no precedents in the tradition. Richard Bauckham has examined skilfully and in detail my continuous dialogue with *Ernst Bloch* and the 'Frankfurt School'. He has also highlighted, to my surprise, my closeness to *Albert Camus*. Besides the early Christian-Marxist dialogue, the dialogue with Jewish thought has always been important to me. Again and again, when seeking orientation, I have reached for Franz Rosenzweig's *The Star of Redemption*. The development of the political dimension of Christian theology has brought me into partnership with the theologians of the Third World. Just as they were inspired by the 'theology of hope,' so I took up suggestions from the 'theology of liberation' of Latin America and the *'minjung* theology' of Korea. Christian theology must reach out beyond the limits of its own culture, if it is to be ecumenical and not lapse into the narrow provincialism which threatens European theology at the present time.

The theological method which I used in the three books can be described as: *the whole of theology in one focal point*. In *Theology of Hope* hope, from being an object of theology, became for me the subject of theology. To think theologically out of hope means to see the whole of theology in the light of the future of God. In *The Crucified God* the whole of theology came together for me in the focal point of the cross, and in the perspective of the crucified Christ I learned to understand God and humanity in their common suffering. *The Church in the Power of the Spirit* is by comparison not so strongly concentrated into one perspective, because ecclesiology has to deal with many different themes. But the pneumatological view of the church led me to correct the onesided Christocentrism of Reformation theology and the theology of Karl Barth. Of course, this method gives rise to onesided emphases and exaggerations, but one also sees things which one had not seen before. And for me those three books were the means of theological discoveries and adventures of that kind. If one reads them together, the 'onesidednesses' of each to some extent correct each other. However, I decided then not to go on using this method of concentrating the whole of theology into one focal point, but, conversely, to present *my own part as a contribution to the collective whole of theology*. In my series of systematic

'Contributions to Theology', which began in 1980 with *The Trinity and the Kingdom of God* and continued in 1985 with my Gifford lectures on *God in Creation*, I have given up the method of focussing on one focal point at a time and am attempting to contribute my limited understandings to the great conversation of theology about the times of history and the places of the earth. What are important to me are not the immediate, short-term questions, but the longterm problems of theology, because the big theological decisions have longterm results for good or ill.

Richard Bauckham's work confines itself to the first and probably larger part of my theological endeavours. This is wise. The critical questions which he formulates at the ends of his chapters do justice to my arguments and are therefore justified. I will respond to them in my next book, on Christology. A 'foreword' is after all only a word *before* the real speech and should point to the main substance which follows. In this sense I now give Richard Baukham the chance to speak. I was delighted to be his first reader.

[Jürgen Moltmann]
Tübingen, 20 September 1986.

# INTRODUCTION

In view of the fact that Jürgen Moltmann has probably had more influence worldwide than any other Protestant dogmatic theologian alive today, studies of his work are surprisingly few. This book aims to fill a gap by providing an introduction to two decades of Moltmann's work: the period 1960–1979, which includes his great trilogy *Theology of Hope* (1964), *The Crucified God* (1972) and *The Church in the Power of the Spirit* (1975). These three major works are naturally the focus of study, but Moltmann's many minor works from the same period also help to fill out the picture and enable the development of his thinking to be plotted and explained. Very often they prepare for, relate to, or expand on the three major works, and so will be used in this study largely for their bearing on the themes of the trilogy. Some account will also be given of the main influences on Moltmann's thought, though in a way that complements, rather than repeats Douglas Meeks' valuable account of Moltmann's theological background.[1]

This study breaks off on the threshold of Moltmann's second series of major works, a projected five volumes, of which the first two, *The Trinity and the Kingdom of God* (1980) and *God in Creation* (1985), have so far appeared. To this new series of 'contributions to theology' Moltmann gives the overall title *Messianic Theology*. Since he now regards the earlier trilogy as preparatory work for this new series, it seemed appropriate to entitle the present study *Messianic Theology in the Making*. The second series differs from the first principally in being a series of studies of particular topics (the doctrine of God, creation, Christology, eschatology, and theological method), whereas the trilogy really consists of three different perspectives on the whole of theology. *Theology of Hope* is not a study of eschatology so much as a study of the eschatological orientation of the whole of theology. *The Crucified God* is a 'theology of the cross' in Luther's sense, an attempt to see the crucified Christ as the criterion of Christian theology. *The Church in the Power of the Spirit* complements these two angles of approach with a pneumatological and ecclesiological perspective.

Another way of distinguishing the three angles of approach would be in terms of the dialectic of cross and resurrection which lies at the heart of Moltmann's theology. *Theology of Hope* works from the perspective of the resurrection of the crucified Christ, *The Crucified God* from the perspective of the cross of the risen Christ, and *The Church in the Power of the Spirit* from the perspective of the working out of that dialectic in the history of the Spirit. Thus in the trilogy Moltmann evolved a coherent theological vision in three complementary perspectives. This now provides the foundation on which he can build in the form of more detailed studies of major doctrines. To end this study between *The Church in the Power of the Spirit* and *The Trinity and the Kingdom of God* is therefore to recognise the only natural break in Moltmann's theological development.

This book is intended primarily as a guide and an aid to the reading of Moltmann's work. It therefore concentrates on explaining the central ideas which structure his theology, showing their development and coherence across the range of issues with which he deals. This inevitably leaves no space for the discussion of important specific areas of Moltmann's thought, such as his anthropology, or of his detailed attention to particular issues in Christian praxis, such as medical ethics, violence and non-violence, and human rights. Furthermore, the focus of the study is on careful exposition of Moltmann's thought, which must precede critical engagement with it. Where criticisms of his work are discussed, this is usually for the sake of understanding it more accurately or to show how his thought takes certain criticisms on board as it develops. But the aim is certainly not to encourage an uncritical response to Moltmann's work, which would be contrary to his own view of the open, provisional and dialogical nature of theological work (TKG xi-xiv).[2] The aim is rather to facilitate the reader's own dialogue with Moltmann's theology.

# 1
## THE EMERGENCE OF THE THEOLOGY OF HOPE IN DIALOGUE WITH ERNST BLOCH

*Theology of Hope*, first published in 1964 when Moltmann was thirty-eight, not only established his reputation as a major theologian, but has undoubtedly been one of the most influential theological works of the post-war period, both in the West and in the Third World. Its importance lay in the fact that it was not a contribution to a particular area of theology, but opened up the whole subject-matter of theology to a dimension which twentieth-century theology had generally played down: the dimension of hope for the future of the world. It might equally well have been called a theology of the resurrection, since the future it addressed was the future of the risen Christ and its theological heart was an interpretation of the resurrection of the crucified Christ as divine promise for the future of all reality. Its eschatological perspective was therefore Christologically grounded and at the same time orientated to the future of this world in which the cross of Christ stood. It opened theology simultaneously towards the future and towards the world. By renouncing a purely individual or other-worldly eschatology and insisting that the resurrection of Christ projects a universal eschatological horizon for this world, Moltmann's theology of hope brought the eschatological future to bear on the immediate temporal future of society. It understood the Church in its mission to the world as an agent of eschatological unrest, charged with keeping society on the move towards the coming Kingdom of God. As a theological turning towards the future and the world it aimed at a practical turning towards the future and the world on the part of the churches.

**The context and origins of the theology of hope** 'Every theology undoubtedly has its historical context' (EH 44). *Theology of Hope* appeared in the midst of 'the outburst of hope' (CF 107) which characterised the 1960s, both in Western society generally and in German theology. In Europe and North America it was a period when an open future seemed to offer unlimited possibilities in every area of life. Technological optimism projected a future of unblemished material prosperity and growth, a sense of liberation from traditional mores raised expectations of personal fulfilment, and hopes ran high for the realisation of civil and political liberties, not least in some of the countries of Eastern Europe, where a new humanistic Marxism was emerging prior to its later repression. In retrospect the secular optimism of the 1960s looks like a temporary social mood or even a 'psychic epidemic',[1] but at the time it could seem as though hopeful turning to the future was *the* characteristic of modern humanity: 'The humanity of this modern age is fascinated only by the future, i.e. by that which has never been'.[2]

The optimistic mood of the 1960s certainly contributed to the success of *Theology of Hope*, but it would be a mistake to dismiss Moltmann's theologically grounded doctrine of hope as a mere reflection of a transient secular mood. As he pointed out, looking back on *Theology of Hope*'s context in the 1960s, 'the context is not yet the text. If one knows the historical context of a theology, it does not necessarily follow that one knows its specific text' (EH 44). Insofar as *Theology of Hope* establishes a theological connection with the future-orientation of modern society, the connection depends on the longterm facts of large-scale historical change in modern times, rather than on the all too optimistic fascination with change in the 1960s. Insofar as *Theology of Hope* bases Christian hope on the cross and resurrection of Christ, it provides resources with which Christian hope can surmount, without illusion or resignation, the 'crisis of hope' (GEB 10) which has set in since the end of the 1960s in Western societies.

That not only Moltmann, but also a number of other German theologians were developing future-orientated theologies from the late

1950s into the early 1960s, must presumably be attributed to a conjunction of the Zeitgeist with inner-theological developments. These included the continuing failure of previous systematic attempts to take up the undeniable eschatological orientation of biblical theology in a satisfactory way, and the continuing failure of theology to engage in a critical, rather than accommodating, way with the realities of contemporary secular society. Consequently there emerged what some at the time called a 'school of hope',[3] including Gerhard Sauter, Johannes Baptist Metz,[4] and Wolfhart Pannenberg, who was developing his eschatological theology at the time when he and Moltmann were colleagues at Wuppertal (1958–61).[5] However, although these theologians interacted quite closely with each other's work and Moltmann borrowed ideas especially from Pannenberg and Metz, each was pursuing his own distinctive line of theological development. The different directions in which they moved after the 1960s already have roots in the origins of their respective interests in the future.

Douglas Meeks has expertly traced the origins of Moltmann's theology of hope in the influence of his teachers Otto Weber, Ernst Wolf, Hans Joachim Iwand, Gerhard von Rad and Ernst Käsemann, with whom he studied theology at Göttingen from 1948.[6] Moltmann, of course, learned much from Karl Barth's theology, whose uncompromising Christocentrism had served the needs of the Confessing Church during the War and now spoke to the experience of those who, like Moltmann, came to the lecture halls from the prisoner of war camps.[7] That theology is based on God's self-revelation in his Word in the biblical history and has its determining centre in the cross and resurrection of Jesus Christ are the methodological convictions which link Moltmann's work with Barth's, though he came to differ from Barth in opening both to an eschatological perspective. This eschatological perspective Moltmann gained in the first place from Weber, and then from the Dutch 'apostolate theology' of A. A. van Ruler and J. C. Hoekendijk, to which Weber introduced him. Moltmann's own testimony is that it was in reading van Ruler in 1957 that he first realised that Barth had not said all there is to say in theology (UZ 9; EG 11). From this school of Reformed theology, Moltmann learned to think of the Church as constituted by its mission to the world in the service of the coming universal Kingdom of God. In this perspective, theology becomes, as it always remained for Moltmann, a servant of the

Church's mission to the world with a view to God's universal lordship. Over against Barth's theology, this was to give Moltmann's theology its openness to the world and to the future.

Into this perspective, Moltmann was able to integrate the concern for social ethics, for the Church's missionary responsibility in the sphere of public society, which he first learned from Ernst Wolf. He was also one of the first theologians to pay serious attention to the work of Dietrich Bonhoeffer, and early in his career wrote two important analyses of Bonhoeffer's thought.[8] He shared and learned from Bonhoeffer's Christological approach to social ethics and the secular world, even though, once again, these concerns were to be transfigured in his own work by the eschatological perspective.[9]

It is Iwand's theology which Meeks calls 'the single most important source for what is new and unique in Moltmann's theology.'[10] From Iwand Moltmann learned, among other things, how to appropriate Hegel's interpretation of the modern experience of the absence of God in relation to the godforsakenness of the crucified Jesus and Hegel's idea of a dialectical historical process of reconciliation corresponding to the dialectic of cross and resurrection.[11] By opening up Hegel's dialectic eschatologically, Moltmann was able to see the cross and resurrection as an event of universal eschatological promise in which Jesus was identified with the godforsakenness of all reality in hope of the eschatological resurrection of all reality. This Hegelian inheritance, via Iwand, was to be the key to Moltmann's development of an eschatology based on the contradiction of the cross and resurrection of Jesus.

Gerhard von Rad and Ernst Käsemann, Moltmann's teachers in Old Testament and New Testament theology respectively, provided the basis for his eschatological interpretation of biblical theology. From von Rad he learned to read the Old Testament as the history of God's promise,[12] and from Käsemann he learned to see the apocalyptic orientation of primitive Christianity as decisive for New Testament theology. The biblical chapters of *Theology of Hope* (II and III) demonstrate how far biblical scholarship contributed to the distinctive features of the theology of hope. It was Old Testament scholars, van Rad and later W. Zimmerli, R. Rendtorff and others, who led the trend away from Bultmann's unhistorical understanding of revelation, and it was Käsemann who led the 'apocalyptic renaissance' of the 1960s,[13] finding in New Testament apocalyptic, with its expectation of

God's lordship over the world, the way to break out of his teacher Bultmann's subjective individualism. Thus the pressure from biblical scholarship to overcome the dehistoricising of eschatology which had characterised most twentieth-century German theology was mounting, and it was in the conjunction of these biblical theological influences with his systematic theological concerns and, eventually, with Ernst Bloch's philosophy of hope, that Moltmann found the way to do theological justice to biblical eschatology. At the same time he found the futurist eschatology was not, after all, a liability for contemporary theology, but precisely the means by which theology could open itself in critical relationship to the reality of the modern world.

Many of Moltmann's early theological writings, including his doctoral dissertation and his *Habilitationsschrift*, written under Weber's direction, were on the history of Reformed theology, with a particular interest in the federal and salvation-historical theologies of the seventeenth and eighteenth centuries, and culminating in his study of the Reformed doctrine of predestination and perseverance.[14] In these works, Moltmann's preference for an eschatologically orientated history of promise, as the theological concept most faithful to the biblical revelation, is already clear, and in *Theology of Hope* (69–74) Moltmann acknowledged the value of this older tradition of salvation-historical theology and its nineteenth-century legacy, even though it cannot be simply adopted into the modern intellectual context. His debt to Calvin's understanding of Christian hope, which again is explicit in *Theology of Hope* (18–20),[15] also emerges in his work on Reformed theology (PP 43–44).

From about 1959 these converging influences and concerns began to take the systematic shape of Moltmann's theology of hope.[16] But the catalyst for this development, which enabled him to fit everything else into place, was the Marxist philosophy of Ernst Bloch (1885–1977). An examination of Moltmann's relationship with Bloch's work will provide us with the most illuminating route into Moltmann's thought.

**The theology of hope as parallel to the philosophy of hope** Although the theology of hope was in Moltmann's thoughts long before he read Bloch,[17] there is no doubt that from about 1960, when the theology of hope was taking shape in Moltmann's writings, he was deeply influenced by Bloch's work.[18] Moreover, although this influence was most important in the 60s, to some extent he has kept up a critical dialogue with Bloch's philosophy throughout his career.[19] In a ninetieth-birthday tribute to Bloch in 1975, he admits having learned theology from Bloch, even though it was far from the atheist Bloch's intention to teach theology (GEB 90). Moltmann has certainly not made an uncritical use of Bloch's philosophy (RRF 152) and disclaims being a follower of Bloch (EG 11), but his critical theological dialogue with Bloch has been as important as any other single factor among the many which have shaped his theology.[20]

The most important of Bloch's many works, *Das Prinzip Hoffnung* (The Principle of Hope), though largely written during his exile in the USA in the 1940s, was first published in a complete edition in 1959, and Moltmann read it soon afterwards. The effect was remarkable. He read it while on holiday in Switzerland, and 'the beauty of the Swiss mountains passed me by unnoticed' (EG 11). His first meeting with Bloch, and a discussion which went on far into the night, followed in 1960 (GEB 63), not long before Bloch, who was finding his position as Professor of Philosophy at Leipzig an impossible one in view of official opposition to his unorthodox Marxism, decided to settle in the West and, in 1961 at the age of seventy-six, accepted a chair at Tübingen. Thenceforth, as 'the Magus of Tübingen', Bloch enjoyed an extraordinary reputation as a champion of humanistic Marxism against the repressive Soviet variety and, not least, a catalyst for new developments in German theology in the 1960s and for the Christian-Marxist dialogue which blossomed in the 1960s. This atheist philosopher, fascinated with religious themes[21] but sharply critical of Christian theology,[22] became so influential in theological circles in the 1960s as to be dubbed by some 'a twentieth-century Church Father' (GEB 91). When Moltmann himself moved to a chair of systematic theology at Tübingen in 1967, his personal contacts with Bloch increased, but by that time Bloch had already made a major impact on his thought.

Reading Bloch's comprehensive philosophical treatment of the theme of hope helped Moltmann formulate a plan for supplying the remarkable lack of a comparable Christian theological treatment (UZ 10). All the threads in his thinking which were to contribute to *Theology of Hope* suddenly came together 'like a pattern for a tapestry' (EG 11). It is as a Christian theological *parallel* to Bloch's philosophy of hope

(UZ 10; EG 11) – indebted to it, but also in critical distinction from it – that Moltmann's theology of hope is, from this point of view, best understood.

Moltmann has, of course, read and interpreted Bloch from the point of view of his own interests. There are other angles from which Bloch's work can be viewed, but it is as a 'system of theoretical messianism' (in Walter Benjamin's phrase) that Moltmann has understood Bloch's work (GEB 11–12). It is from this point of view that we shall attempt to understand, first, Moltmann's indebtedness to Bloch and, secondly, the points at which his criticism of Bloch leads him in a different direction.

Bloch developed an ambitious, highly experimental and original utopian philosophy, which both takes up Marxism into itself and transcends the 'orthodox' Marxist tradition.[23] It is a philosophy orientated to the future and the new, an attempt to write philosophy in the future tense as 'theory of what needs to be.' Seeing the world as an unfinished process, it systematically rejects any concepts which tie the world down to what it already is and joins instead in the world's journey towards its truth which has not yet come into being. Bloch's philosophy is a thought experiment in relation to an experimental world, a world radically open to a still undecided future, a world which can therefore be shaped by human activity. The aim of Bloch's philosophy is not a merely theoretical interpretation of the world as it is, but a 'theory-praxis' which sets goals and identifies the possibilities for Marxist revolutionary activity to change the world, and therefore helps open the world up to a successful outcome. It conceives the world as open to the achievement of utopia and itself aims at utopia.

Bloch's philosophy of hope provided Moltmann with important materials for his parallel project of a theology of hope. In the first place, Bloch provided Moltmann with a view of reality as open to the future and therefore with a set of concepts and categories with which to articulate a Christian eschatological understanding of reality, much as Neo-Platonism provided Augustine and Aristotelianism provided Thomas Aquinas with philosophical categories which they took into the service of their theologies. Moltmann claimed that Bloch's philosophy of hope is the most appropriate philosophy for articulating an eschatologically orientated Christian theology (PT 174).[24] This is not to say that Bloch's philosophy passed unchanged into Moltmann's theology, any more than Neo-Platonism remained itself in Augustine's theology or Aristotelianism in Aquinas'. As we shall see, Moltmann's theological dialogue with Bloch produced significant refunctioning of Blochian concepts as they passed into his work. But an extensive debt to Bloch is clear throughout Moltmann's work in the 1960s and extends far beyond his occasional explicit references to Bloch. When he speaks, for example, of '*docta spes*' (TH 36), '*homo absconditus*' (TH 91), of humanity's 'permanent non-identity in historical terms,' of the 'advancing front line' of the present, of the 'explosive effect' of hope (HP 172), of Christ's resurrection 'into that as yet undetermined future realm ahead of us' (TH 212), of the 'tendency' and 'latency' of the resurrection event (TH 203, 211–13, 216, 225), of 'the "leap" into a different quality,' (FC 16), of the fact that 'all things . . . do not yet contain their truth in themselves' (TH 223), of the 'successful world experiment' (RRF 36), of 'a totality of new being' (TH 223, 226) – all these phrases, and many more, are echoes of Blochian language and Christian eschatological uses of Blochian concepts.[25]

Bloch provided Moltmann with ways of thinking about reality as open to the new future and to the ultimate *novum* of the *eschaton*. He did so by means of the subjective and objective aspects of his philosophy of hope: his anthropology of hope and his ontology of 'not yet being'. Humanity, for Bloch, is *homo absconditus*, an open experimental being, who has not yet found his true being, whose true identity is not yet decided but will come about as humanity transforms itself and its environment in search of the fulfilment it lacks. Thus to be human is to have a utopia ahead, to be always on the move towards something else, to live in dreams and fantasies of the future, to be always striving for a desirable future. To be human is to hope. In *Das Prinzip Hoffnung* Bloch assembled a kind of encyclopedia of evidence of the human utopian consciousness from history, religion and culture. But it is essential to Bloch's philosophy that utopian hope is not just a subjective feature of human consciousness: it corresponds to the ontological possibilities of reality. Here Bloch is constantly concerned to deflect the tendency to limit the world's possibilities to the actual possibilities of the world as it is now. The world is not a closed reality whose possibilities are determined from the beginning and merely unfold. The world is full of real, but not yet actual possibilities, that is, possibilities whose conditions have not yet fully emerged. Such possibilities may or may not become actual possibilities in the future. They can only be anticipated in leaps of the hopeful imagination, but motivated by such imaginative hope human activity can help bring about the dialectical leaps of history in which such possibilities become actual. Thus the openness of human hope to new possibilities and the ontological openness of reality to new possibilities combine to enable human intervention in the experimental process of the world, in order to move it in the direction of a humanly successful outcome.

Bloch's correlation of hope and ontological possibilities requires that hope is not just a subjective projection, but a real anticipation of utopia. Human imagination is informed by the not yet actual possibilities which are developing in the forefront of the process. This being so, and because reality is open to the development of the radically new which has never yet been (the *novum*), Bloch takes seriously the 'utopian excess' of human religion, art and daydreams, in which utopian possibilities, which have not yet appeared as actual possibilities, are anticipated. The *novum* is never wholly new: it preappears in anticipation. On the other hand, it is not confined to its preappearances, but comes as the unexpected fulfilment of what has preappeared. The future can be anticipated, but it cannot be foreseen. The final *novum*, the eschatological utopia, cannot be detailed, since it can only come about through the future emergence of new possibilities, but it can be experimentally projected as the ultimate goal of the direction of the process, to be realised through human work and planning. Nor, of course, can utopia be guaranteed, since for Bloch the world is not teleological in the sense of having a preordained end, but genuinely open, a world experiment, whose final result may be 'everything or nothing' (cf PH 193–194). Hope must therefore be 'militant optimism', which is open to 'hazard', but boldly takes hold of the open possibilities of the future in order to realise the 'utopian excess' of the hopeful imagination. On this basis, Bloch is insistent that the limited economic and social objectives of traditional Marxism must be transcended. In the light of a future in which more will become possible than can now be envisaged as possible, the utopian hopes of the religious traditions of humanity can be inherited by the 'meta-religion' of Marxist philosophy, so that its theory-praxis can aim towards the elimination of all alienating conditions in humanity and nature, towards the solution of the riddle of the world process, the total meaning of which is not yet decided, towards the 'home of identity' in which both humanity and nature find their self-identity and mutual identity.

The attraction of this way of thinking for a theologian who wished to reinstate Christian eschatological thought as concerned with the radically new future of this world, should be clear. Instead of the closed universe of traditional metaphysics and mechanistic science, whose future possibilities are already settled, Bloch's philosophy offered Moltmann a view of the world as open to the fulfilment of human hopes for the radically new. To a limited extent, therefore, Bloch's anthropology of hope and his ontology of the not yet provided, for Moltmann, the presuppositions about humanity and the world to which the biblical message of hope in the promises of God corresponds. Statements of promise, which contradict present reality, cannot be shown to be true by their correspondence to reality as it now is (TH 18), but precisely for this reason they *do* correspond to the reality of an unfinished world which is open to the future. This is not very clear in the argument of *Theology of Hope* (but cf. the very Blochian passages on pp. 25, 91–92, 288–89), for reasons which will emerge later in our discussion, but it is much clearer in two of Moltmann's most Blochian essays: 'Religion, Revolution and the Future' (RRF II) and 'Where There Is Hope, There Is Religion' (EH II: the title is a quotation from Bloch). In these essays Moltmann endorses the main elements in Bloch's philosophy, as outlined above, and especially in the latter it is clear that these are the presuppositions for the theology of hope and even, in some sense, 'verify' the biblical religion of hope (EH 20). It is to man as a 'creature of hope,' who can be defined only by his direction towards the open future, and to the world as 'an open creative process,' a *laboratorium possibilis salutis* (Bloch's phrase taken up by Moltmann), that the divine promise comes. 'With the experiment "man" and the experiment "world" God has joined a hope' (EH 27). This correlation of Christian hope with the nature of humanity and the world, according to Bloch's philosophy, is not only significant for the credibility of Moltmann's theology. It also provides a basis for cooperation in shaping the future, not only between Christians and adherents of other messianic religions, notably Judaism, but also between Christians and non-religious movements of hope, especially Marxism.

As well as a concept of the openness of the world to the future,

Moltmann found in Bloch a clue to the way in which Christian eschatology could relate the expectation of an ultimate future to hopeful activity for change in the present. For Bloch the true function of utopia, the *novum ultimum*, is to be not an escapist dream, but a critical, motivating perspective on the present. Prevailing ideologies which sanctify the status quo are countered by the utopian imagination which shows up the inadequacies of the present and arouses hopes for really new possibilities. Such hopes become 'creative expectation' (Bloch's term, taken up by Moltmann: TH 335) which enables people to identify and grasp the possibilities which are emerging at the front of the process, so as to transform the present in the direction of the anticipated utopia. The ultimacy of a utopia which is conceived as 'everything', the most that human hopes can conceive, has a positive value in this process. By leaving the maximum possible space for more and better still to come, it keeps hope always on the move, never able to rest content with limited objectives and achievements, not susceptible to the 'melancholy of fulfilment', but productive of always fresh, flexible and revisable expectations for the penultimate future (cf. RRF 16). In a very similar way Moltmann sees the ultimate hope of Christian eschatology in intimate connection with the proximate hopes for immediately achievable changes, both stimulating and relativising them (TH 33–34). This, of course, depends on his locating the *novum ultimum*, not in some heavenly beyond, but (like Bloch and also like early Christian eschatology) at the end of the temporal future of this world, so that the proximate hopes of history lead towards it. This enables Moltmann to turn around the traditional Marxist complaint that Christian eschatology, by offering imaginary consolation for present misery in another world, makes people content with and so supports the status quo in this world. Just as Bloch sees the religious utopias of the past truly coming into their own in a humanist Marxist theory-praxis directed to their future but thoroughly worldly reality, so Moltmann sees the Christian eschatological hope coming into its own in a genuinely revolutionary Christianity which takes up and carries further the historical movements of human hope (TH 34). There is, however, a difference. Bloch's utopia will be a human achievement in collaboration with the immanent possibilities of the natural world, and so each intermediate *novum* in history is a real step on the way to the *novum ultimum*. For Moltmann, only God brings about his final Kingdom, and so the hopeful activity of people in history anticipates, but does not bring nearer, the eschaton itself.

These correspondences make Moltmann's theology of hope a parallel to Bloch's philosophy of hope, not only in its actual contents, but in its general conception of itself. Bloch's philosophy is 'theory-praxis', in the spirit of Marx's famous eleventh thesis on Feuerbach: 'The philosophers have only *interpreted* the world in various ways; the point, however, is to *change* it.'[26] Bloch's philosophy is an 'open system' which aims towards a truth which, in large part, has not yet appeared. It is therefore as unfinished, as revisable, as the world itself, but its real test comes in praxis, in its own participation in the world's transformation, in giving people a 'handlehold' by which they can grasp and shape the process. Similarly, Moltmann echoes Marx's dictum: 'The theologian is not concerned merely to supply a different *interpretation* of the world, of history and of human nature, but to *transform* them in expectation of a divine transformation' (TH 84). Eschatological thinking turns theology into a provisional, hopeful and praxis-orientated theory of what needs to be:

> in the medium of hope our theological concepts become not judgments which nail reality down to what it is, but anticipations which show reality its prospects and its future possibilities. Theological concepts do not give a fixed form to reality, but they are expanded by hope and anticipate future being . . . They are thus concepts which are engaged in a process of movement, and which call forth practical movement and change (TH 35–36).

The verifiability by correspondence to existing reality, which theology of hope necessarily forfeits by its turn towards the future, is replaced by the test of world-transforming praxis (cf. RRF 138; HD 180). If the purpose of Bloch's philosophy of hope is to promote Marxist revolutionary praxis, the purpose of Moltmann's theology of hope is to promote the revolutionary praxis of the Christian mission.[27] Again the parallel permits a dialogue and a degree of critical cooperation between the two.

**The theology of hope in divergence from the philosophy of hope** The heart of the attraction of Bloch's work for Moltmann is probably only reached when we remember that Bloch was 'a Marxist with a Bible in his hand' (RRF 15), and that it was to the 'messianic passion' hidden beneath the 'outer garment' of the principle of hope that Moltmann really warmed (HD 174).[28] The congeniality of Bloch's philosophy for Christian eschatological thought is not simply coincidental, but corresponds to the fact that biblical messianic religion was one of the sources of inspiration for Bloch's own work, and, in Bloch's view, the primary historical source of the tradition of utopian thought which Marxist philosophy has inherited and must further inherit. 'The eschatological conscience came into the world through the Bible', Moltmann was already quoting from Bloch (PH 221) in 1960 (HP 124; also quoted in MHO 19; EH 31; CG 99; GEB 26), while to Bloch's remark that it is difficult to wage a revolution without the Bible, Moltmann added that it is even more difficult not to bring about a revolution with the Bible (EH 6). The explosive messianic power of the Bible is what both the atheist Bloch and the Christian theologian Moltmann, partly through Bloch's work, discovered when they saw the future-orientation and eschatology of biblical religion not as dead cultural history, but as full of still available hope. While Moltmann follows few of the details of Bloch's biblical interpretation, Bloch's general project for a Marxist philosophical 'inheritance' of biblical messianism certainly helped inspire his parallel project for a contemporary theological development of biblical messianism. Whereas the theological tradition found futurist eschatology embarrassingly hard to stomach, the Marxist philosopher showed that precisely this futurist eschatology gave the Bible its revolutionary power still in the twentieth century. Admittedly, this power had not been very apparent in the history of the Church, because, according to Bloch, Christianity's eschatological consciousness was suppressed when, from Constantine onwards, it became a state religion, an ideology of the status quo, and Moltmann accepts Bloch's verdict that for most of the history of Christianity the revolutionary potential of eschatological thinking was realised only by the heretics and fanatics, like Bloch's hero Thomas Münzer (PH 496–515; TH 15, 25).[29] This, however, was precisely Moltmann's point: that biblical eschatology leads to criticism of the status quo and to movements for change (TGT 204).[30] It was no great surprise that a Marxist philosopher should see its potential taken up in Marxism, while a church and a theology accommodated to the status quo could make nothing of it.

For Bloch,[31] religion is alienating when it projects a divine lord 'above', whose theocratic absolutism eliminates human freedom and stabilises the world as it is. But the messianic stream of biblical religion, which originated when Moses led a band of rebellious slaves out of oppression in Egypt and projected a God 'ahead', is liberating. It expresses a spirit of revolt against the present state of affairs and a departure from the present towards the open future. In the religion of Moses and the prophets, 'God' is functionally a symbol for hope (the *Deus spes*), for the promise of the Kingdom. In this religion, taken up and embodied preeminently in Jesus, the real utopian content of religion emerges most explicitly, since 'what men expressed in the hypostases of the gods was never anything other than *longed-for future*' (PH 1191–1192; quoted RRF 153). Thus, whereas Bloch takes it for granted, with Feuerbach, that God is a projection which must be resolved into its human content, he holds that the really central element in religion is a projection *into the future*, which cannot be resolved into humanity as it is but must be maintained in the form of the utopian hope for 'everything'. The religious hope of the future Kingdom, because it points beyond every merely social utopia, even the classless society, needs to be, not suppressed, but inherited by a Marxist 'meta-religion'. This will carry through the 'exodus out of God', out of the transcendent God 'above' into the 'God hope', which was already taking place in biblical messianic religion.

We are now in a position to appreciate the crucial points at which Moltmann's early theology moves through a critical dialogue with Bloch into a different path from Bloch's. They arise out of the question whether biblical eschatology is *adequately* inherited in Bloch's 'meta-religion' or whether it does not still require a *theology* of hope (RRF 152–53). Moltmann's major criticisms of Bloch revolve around the related questions of God and the resurrection of the dead.[32]

In his dialogue with Bloch's atheism Moltmann clearly found some of the most important aspects of the question of God involved, because Bloch's is not a shallow Enlightenment atheism but an atheism which appreciates both the alienating and the liberating functions of the idea of God in religious history, and seeks both to overcome the former and to appropriate the latter. Because Moltmann shares, to a considerable extent, Bloch's recognition of the alienating effect of certain forms of the religious consciousness and his desire to overcome them, he is prepared to go a long way in interpreting Bloch's atheism positively as an 'atheism for God's sake' (RRF 153; EH 31, 39; MHO 28; CG 252).[33] Since atheism is always relative to the particular form of theism which it rejects, Bloch's atheism can be justified insofar as it is a rejection of a repressive Christianity which allied itself with political domination against human freedom (GEB 70–71). It is an atheism which can help Christians to dethrone the false gods projected in humanity's own image, and to realise, following the Mosaic prohibition of images, that all concepts of God are at best provisional and must not halt the movement of transcendence towards the God whose unmediated presence at the end will surpass all historical images of him (EH 39–40; RRF 153; HD 180–82; cf. HP 108). 'There is an atheism which is negative theology' (MHO 28). But just as there is a repressive theism whose god suppresses human freedom, so there is also a repressive atheism, which projects the state authorities and their ideology into the space vacated by the overlord god 'above' and proves at least as inimical to freedom, as Bloch knew to his cost (GEB 71). The question is whether the exodus from these repressive theisms and atheisms is to be led by the liberating God of hope or by 'the God hope' (Bloch's *Deus spes*). Are they, in fact, functionally equivalent, so that messianic religion can be adequately inherited by Bloch's militant utopian atheism and must be so inherited, if it is to follow its own liberating logic?

Moltmann questions whether Bloch's understanding of the future as immanent transcending or 'transcending without transcendence' (PH 210)[34] provides an adequate ground for hope.[35] In Bloch's materialist philosophy 'the ever fruitful womb of matter' is the source of all the possibilities which arise in the process, even though, because the process is open, not deterministic, this does not mean that they are all present at the beginning. The new possibilities of the future arise out of the tendencies and contradictions of the present. But then hope is a means by which reality is, so to speak, continually pulling itself up by its own bootstraps. The ground for hope's continual transcending of present possibilities must lie within hope itself. Moltmann's question is whether without real transcendence, without the transcendent power of the future which arouses hope, hope can be as hopeful or reality as open as the religious hopes, which Bloch's system claims to inherit, require (GEB 26–27; RRF 154–59).

Moltmann presses this question in terms of the power of hope, in Bloch's system, to overcome the power of the negative in history. For Bloch, the negative, in the form of lack or inadequacy in the present, is the driving force of the process, which proceeds dialectically as the negative is negated and the 'not' taken up into a 'not yet'. Thus, for example, lack of freedom is overcome as in contradicting it hope grasps the not yet actual possibility of freedom. But such a dialectic only overcomes the negative insofar as it has the possibility of becoming a 'not yet'. It cannot overcome 'the abyss of nothingness into which all being sinks' (Hegel). At the point where all possibilities of humanity or nature run out, in hopeless suffering or in the face of death, it offers no negation of the negative (EH 34–35). Immanent transcending can awaken hope for new possibilities in the area of not yet being, but not in the area of 'no-longer-being' (DTH 220).[36] This, however, was precisely the area in which biblical eschatology emerged, in that where all earthly possibilities were swallowed up in nothingness, it became possible to hope in the God who creates out of nothing, who gives life to the dead and calls into existence the things which do not exist (Rom. 4.17). Precisely the point which Bloch's principle of hope cannot reach – the resurrection of the dead – is the foundation of Christian eschatology (RRF 160). This radical hope for the negation of the absolute negative can only arise in connection with real transcendence, as hope in 'the power of a future which proves itself creative over against total nothingness' (EH 35). Bloch's world, full of possibilities as it is, has regions over whose doors the sign, 'Abandon hope, all ye who enter here,' still hangs (GEB 57). It is not open enough because it is not open to the really transcendent God of hope whose possibilities are unrestricted and who can therefore abrogate even the *nihil* itself in an attained *totum* (RRF 161; GEB 61–62; cf GC 91–92).

Bloch himself fully realised that in inheriting religious hopes Marxist utopian philosophy could certainly not confine its expectations to the negation of negatives in the economic and social spheres of life. He knew that death is the 'strongest anti-utopia' (PH 1103), and tried to find a truth in the religious hopes of life beyond death.[37] This was his notion that the 'core' of human existence, the hidden identity of humanity which has not yet emerged in the process, is beyond the reach of death precisely because it has not yet come to be and so cannot pass away. The individual's best intentions, which are nearest to this 'core', contribute to its emergence and in this way give a kind of immortality to the individual who has learned to submerge himself in his solidarity with the working class. Moltmann's criticism of this view is illuminating. He finds it inadequate in the same way that belief in the immortality of the soul (as distinct from resurrection) is inadequate. It holds that while the husk of reality must be abandoned to death, there is something, the not yet actual core of existence, which remains beyond the reach of death. But this does not take the real deadliness of death seriously, unlike hope for resurrection as God's new creation of life out of absolute death (RRF 165–70; EH 37–38).[38]

For Moltmann, this point is of great importance, because only hope for precisely the transient earthly and bodily reality which must perish makes possible real *love* for bodily and earthly life and love which is prepared to expend itself in suffering and death. With hope in the God who raises the dead, one does not have to cling to one's identity against the threat of losing it, but can lose one's life in self-giving love for others. One does not have to deny the full reality of death, but can endure its full deadliness in love (TH 31–32, 91; RRF 169–70; HD 185–86). And whereas Bloch's principle of hope seems to Moltmann to be hope available only to those who are active in the vanguard of progress towards a better future, hope in the God who raises the dead makes hope available to the suffering and the dying (GEB 58; RRF 17), while hope in the God who raised precisely the crucified Jesus means loving solidarity with society's victims for whom progress offers no hope (FC 17). 'If God creates what is new out of nothing, then the poor, the abandoned, and the dying are closer to him than are the efficient and militant heroes of the revolution who helped mankind' (RRF 18).[39]

Within this disagreement about the resurrection of the dead there is therefore emerging an even more serious disagreement between Moltmann and Bloch over a theology of the cross,[40] which was to take Moltmann in *The Crucified God* further from Bloch than he was in *Theology of Hope*. However, for the moment it is important to notice how the disagreement over transcendence and resurrection corresponds to fundamental features of the argument and content of *Theology of Hope*. Precisely those elements in the Christian hope which 'resist being succeeded by the "meta-religion" of *Das Prinzip Hoffnung*' (RRF 152) are constitutive of Christian hope in *Theology of Hope*. Christian hope is by definition hope in the God who raises the dead, and looks from the promise given in his raising of the crucified Christ towards the future which will correspond to this. In echoes of Blochian language Moltmann indicates that Christian hope arises precisely and only at the point where the *Creator ex nihilo* has transcended precisely those boundaries of life which Bloch's principle of hope fails to cross:

> To believe does in fact mean to cross and transcend bounds, to be engaged in an exodus. Yet this happens in a way that does not suppress or skip the unpleasant realities. Death is real death, and decay is putrefying decay. Guilt remains guilt and suffering remains, even for the believer, a cry to which there is no ready-made answer. Faith . . . can overstep the bounds of life, with their closed wall of suffering, guilt and death, only at the point where they have in actual fact been broken through. It is only in following the Christ who was raised from suffering, from a God-forsaken death and from the grave that it gains an open prospect in which there is nothing more to oppress us, a view of the realm of freedom and of joy. Where the bounds that mark the end of all human hopes are broken through in the raising of the crucified one, there faith can and must expand into hope (TH 19–20).

From one point of view, which is largely only implicit in the text, chapters II and III of *Theology of Hope*, in which Moltmann traces the development of the biblical eschatological hope, are an attempt to show that the Old Testament idea of God and the New Testament witness to his raising Christ from the dead are such essential components of Israelite and early Christian hope that it cannot be continued or inherited without them (cf. GEB 27). For the reader familiar with Bloch's terminology and ideas, the implicit countering of Bloch's position occasionally rises to the surface of the text, as when Moltmann insists that the Kingdom of God – one of Bloch's own terms for the *eschaton* – must be understood as the lordship of the God who raises the dead, and therefore not a kingdom which can arise from the immanent possibilities of the process or which can be reduced to a kingdom without God:

> The sole Lord of the kingdom is the God 'who has raised Jesus from the dead' and therein shows himself to be the *creator ex nihilo* . . . His future does not result from the trends of world history. His rule is his raising of the dead and consists in calling into being the things that are not, and choosing things which are not, to bring to nothing things which are (I Cor. I.28). This makes it impossible . . . to conceive the kingdom of God 'without God' and to resolve 'God' himself as the 'highest Good' into the ideal of the kingdom (TH 221).[41]

Moltmann is once again insisting that, as he put it elsewhere, the biblical religious hopes from which Bloch's messianism arises surpass the eschatological goal into which he wishes to lead them (GEB 27). The thrust of Moltmann's interpretation of biblical eschatology is that the *God* of hope is the necessary presupposition for the liberating exodus from *all* forms of oppression and alienation and cannot be adequately replaced by human hope and the immanent possibilities of the world alone.

Also distinguishing his position from Bloch's is Moltmann's frequent insistence in *Theology of Hope* that Christian hope is not simply directed to an open future full of all kinds of possibilities, good and evil, but 'sets out from a definite reality in history [the raising of Jesus] and announces the future of *that* reality, *its* future possibilities and *its* power over the future' (TH 17, my italics; cf. 192). This is what distinguishes eschatology from utopianism (TH 17, 20). Usually Moltmann's use of Blochian terminology in *Theology of Hope* describes not the world in its general openness to the future, as it is anyway, but the *effect* of the promises of God and the raising of the crucified Christ in opening up those new possibilities which lie on the way to the fulfilment of the promises (e.g. TH 85, 103, 203).[42]

Moltmann's insistence on real transcendence removes one difficulty in Bloch's system: the difficult notion that the objective but not yet actual possibilities inform the utopian imagination by preappearing in it and thereby arouse hope which can move towards actualising them.[43] Because for Moltmann it is God, as the transcendent power of the future, who creates the new possibilities of the future, the mediation between these and hope can be effected by his promise. On the other hand, the introduction of transcendence creates a problem which Bloch did not have to face: how do the new possibilities which God creates relate to the immanent possibilities of the world? Moltmann needs to be able to argue that while the world cannot produce these possibilities, it is open to them. It cannot transform itself, but it is 'transformable' (TH 288). Thus it cannot be 'a rigid cosmos of established facts and eternal laws' (TH 92). It must be more like Bloch's unfinished world, 'full of boundless possibilities for good and for evil' (TH 289), but even more open than Bloch's world: 'open to the resurrection of the dead' (TH 92). Yet in *Theology of Hope* the relation between immanent and transcendent possibilities, between the future that is not yet and the future that is created out of nothing, is not properly established, and is somewhat obscured by the indiscriminate use of Blochian language to describe both.[44]

After the 1960s Bloch's influence on Moltmann's work becomes much less obvious, but there are reasons for supposing that Moltmann's continuing dialogue with Bloch's thought still had a role behind the scenes. Moltmann could not develop a theology of the cross without implicitly attempting to deflect Bloch's frequent and bitter attacks on any such theology.[45] He could not face the challenge of Auschwitz to theodicy without some memory of Bloch's characteristic debating epigram: 'One does not have to be a theologian in order not to comprehend Auschwitz. One does not have to have a *theologia crucis* in order to comprehend it' (GEB 59). Although Job himself is notably absent from Moltmann's discussions of the problem of suffering,[46] something of the spirit of Bloch's Job, the protesting atheist Job, 'the rebel who had trust in God, without believing in him' (AC 122),[47] hovers with Ivan Karamazov, another Blochian hero (MHO 66–67), around the argument of *The Crucified God*. As for Bloch's Jesus, 'the supreme model of another world in which there was no oppression and no lordly God' (AC 136), whose dying cry expressed 'the most utter of all abandonments' (AC 257), he is not, despite resemblances, really the Jesus of *The Crucified God*, but the latter could be read as his partly polemical counterpart. In spite of Moltmann's plausible claim to have left Bloch's philosophy of hope behind at this stage of his work (CG 5), the theodicy problem in *The Crucified God* still has Blochian dimensions.

# 2
# FROM THEOLOGY OF HOPE
# TO POLITICAL THEOLOGY

**The structure and method of *Theology of Hope*** The heart of the argument of *Theology of Hope* is the eschatological interpretation of the resurrection of Jesus in chapter III. Moltmann's famous claim that 'from first to last, and not merely in the epilogue, Christianity is eschatology, is hope' (TH 16) is a claim about the meaning of the event on which Christian faith is based: the raising of the crucified Jesus from the dead by God (cf. TH 165–66). It is this event which makes Christian faith eschatological and which determines the nature of the Christian eschatological hope. Hence 'Christian eschatology is at heart Christology in an eschatological perspective' (TH 192). Moltmann's early theology is no less Christocentric than Barth's, but it differs from Barth's in the extent to which all Christology becomes necessarily eschatological. For Moltmann, the raising of the crucified Christ means that he has a future towards which faith in the risen Christ must be directed, and therefore 'all statements and judgments about him must at once imply something about the future which is to be expected from him' (TH 17). 'The primitive Easter faith teaches us that Jesus is always intelligible only in relationship to his future. Through the guidance of hope, we learn to understand him' (HP 171). Thus the Christological eschatology or eschatological Christology of chapter III is Moltmann's central theological proposal in *Theology of Hope*.

Moltmann's claim that the Christ-event is only properly understood within an eschatological perspective is supported, in chapter III, by the claim that the Christ-event must be understood against its Old

Testament background. The facts that Jesus was a Jew and that the God who raised him from the dead was the God of Israel make the Old Testament 'a necessary presupposition' for Christology (TH 141). Consequently, Moltmann sees the Old Testament history of promise as the background against which the New Testament's eschatological interpretation of the Christ-event becomes intelligible and normative for Christian faith. This is why the discussion of Old Testament theology in chapter II forms an essential preliminary to the treatment of New Testament theology in chapter III.

In the argument of chapters II and III two theological categories emerge as the key biblical theological categories which control Moltmann's interpretation of Christology and eschatology. They are an understanding of divine revelation as *promise* and an understanding of history as *mission*. The two themes are closely related. Inevitably, they lead Moltmann, beyond the sphere of biblical theology, into dialogue with other understandings of divine revelation and other understandings of history. The former takes place in chapter I, where Moltmann takes issue with other views of revelation in modern German theology and adumbrates the proposal which is set out more fully in chapters II-IV. This debate about revelation explains the fact that whereas, as we have noticed, a dialogue with Bloch is only implicit in *Theology of Hope*, Moltmann's explicit dialogue partners, especially in chapter I but also recurrently throughout the book, are Karl Barth, Rudolf Bultmann and Wolfhart Pannenberg, who supply both the major alternative understandings of revelation and the alternative theological views of history in relation to revelation. But Moltmann is not content to dialogue with theologians. In chapter IV he develops his Christian understanding of history in debate with modern secular historiography and philosophy of history in their attempts to come to terms with the modern experience of history as continual revolutionary crisis.

Finally, in chapter V, Moltmann reflects on the kind of role for the Church in modern society that is involved in his proposed understanding of the mission of the Church within the perspective of the future of the risen Christ.

This outline of the structure of the argument of *Theology of Hope* can also show us how the book corresponds to Moltmann's view of the nature and method of Christian theology. For Moltmann, the determining starting-point for Christian theology must be the biblical history of revelation: 'Christian theology speaks of God with respect to the concrete, specific, and contingent history, which is told and witnessed to in the biblical writings' (FH 1; cf. RRF 203), and therefore: 'Without biblical theology . . . theology cannot be Christian theology' (EH 7). This means that theology moves *from* the unique events of the biblical revelation, which culminate in the history of Jesus, *to* the universal significance of this revelation for all people and all reality (cf. TH 141–44, 194; HP 76, 215). It should not, as theology has so often done, begin from certain general ideas about God, the world or human existence, supposed to be accessible to all people, and strive to make the biblical revelation intelligible and universally relevant to all people by interpreting it in the light of these universal concepts (cf. HP 5). This method is inappropriate because it inevitably allows alien concepts to control the meaning of the biblical revelation. In particular, it tends to suppress the eschatological character of the biblical revelation because it requires the revelation to correspond to general ideas derived from what reality is like now, instead of allowing the revelation to open up the prospect of a different future of transformed reality. Not even the *question* of God as general human experience raises it should control our hermeneutics. Rather, the biblical revelation must be understood in its own terms and allowed to raise its own questions (TH 95).[1] Its universality does not consist in its correspondence to universal presuppositions about reality, but consists in its eschatological claim to project the universal future of all reality (HP 21–22). It is not that the God about whom all people ask anyway is revealed in the particular history of Jesus, but that the God who reveals himself in the history of Israel and of Jesus reveals himself in the resurrection of Jesus as the God of all people and the Lord of all reality. Theology's movement from the particular to the universal will therefore be its involvement in the movement of missionary history from the resurrection of Jesus towards the universal, eschatological lordship of Jesus.

The eschatological direction of the biblical revelation therefore provides Christian theology with its own path from the particular to the universal, and in chapters II and III of *Theology of Hope* Moltmann is following that path. But this does not at all mean that Christian theology makes no contact with general human experience or other views of reality. Christian theology claims universality on its own terms – on the basis of a Christological eschatology – but in doing so it relates itself to all reality, whose eschatological future it seeks. The universal questions which people ask about the nature of God, the meaning of the world and the meaning of human life, are not dismissed, but they are taken up and redirected within the comprehensive eschatological perspective of Christian theology (TH 192). Instead of being questions which, in being put to the biblical revelation, control its interpretation, they must themselves be questioned by the biblical revelation and find themselves set within a different context: that of a world open to the future lordship of Jesus Christ.

In other words, Christian theology, because of its claim to universality, must enter a critical dialogue with other interpretations of the world and human experience. Its eschatological horizon opens it to the world and at the same time gives it the task of opening the world to its future. Thus theology, claims Moltmann, 'must overcome its limitation to church, faith and inwardness in order to search, together with all others, for the truth of the whole and the salvation of a divided world' (HP 206). Because of its eschatological perspective, which makes theology a *theologia viae* (RRF 207), open to the future, it does not already know all the answers, but it does know that the questions must be directed towards the all-inclusive future of Jesus Christ (cf. TH 33). This gives it the ability to enter a real dialogue in which it can learn without detriment to its faithfulness to its biblical starting-point. Only if the biblical revelation is allowed its autonomous ability to question all other approaches to reality can Christian theology be a source of different perspectives and radical change in society, but equally it can only be this if it brings its biblical perspective into dialogue with other approaches. Critical dialogue is the alternative to the irrelevance that results both from theological accommodation to prevailing views and from theological isolation within an ecclesiastical ghetto (cf. HP 31; FH 157). In critical dialogue theology becomes the missionary theology of a church directed towards the open future of the world.

Although Moltmann's emphasis on theology as dialogue increased with time (cf. EH 12–13, for a strong statement from 1971), the principle is already operative in *Theology of Hope* and explains chapter IV, in which Moltmann engages with the modern experience of history as reflected in historiography and philosophy of history. The principal aim of this chapter is to show how the eschatological tendencies of these approaches, which in one way or another seek an end of history within history, can be transcended in a Christian missionary understanding of history which keeps history on the move towards the eschatological horizon of the resurrection.[2] Secular historicism and Christian traditionalism alike try to suppress the movement of revolutionary change in which the modern experience of history consists and to close off the open future which it implies. But a hermeneutic of Christian mission, which recalls the revelatory events of the past as events of promise for the future, will meet the modern experience of history not by suppressing it but by giving it eschatological direction. Much of the secret of *Theology of Hope*'s contemporary relevance lies hidden in the rather technical discussions of chapter IV.[3]

In Moltmann's view Christian theology 'proves' itself not in correspondence to reality as it is, but in opening up future prospects for reality and initiating movement towards these (TH 89, 94). This must be done both theoretically in dialogue with other approaches to truth, as in chapter IV, but it must also be done practically. It is entirely essential to Moltmann's conception of theology that it serve the church's missionary praxis in the world. Hence the concluding chapter of *Theology of Hope* raises 'the question of the concrete form assumed by a live eschatological hope in modern society' (304). Here Moltmann shows how the theology of hope becomes concrete in critical opposition and creative expectation, which enable the church to resist accommodation to society and to keep society on the move towards the future Kingdom.

**Revelation as promise**  Moltmann's understanding of Old Testament theology is dependent on a typology of religions, which is also basic to the whole of *Theology of Hope:* the contrast between epiphany religions and the biblical religion of promise (TH 42–43, 95–102; EH 16–19). The crucial feature of an epiphany religion, for Moltmann's argument, is that it is anti-historical: it finds the meaning of life not in historical change but in contact with changeless eternity. Such religion was characteristic of the nature religions of Canaan with whose influence Old Testament religion was in constant tension. Its experience of the divine corresponds to the ever-recurring cycle of the seasons: the gods 'appear' in the seasonal festivities and guarantee 'the eternal return' in which life is renewed through contact with primal time. Thus the stability of a recurring order is protected against the meaningless chaos of history. The appearance of the divine, in such a view, Moltmann calls 'the epiphany of the eternal present.'[4] Its purpose is to grant correspondence with and participation in the timeless world of the divine. Essentially continuous with such nature religions was the Greek philosophical view of reality, according to which the essence of things is the eternal present of being behind the transitory appearance of history (EH 17). In both cases, history is meaningless transience, while the true divine reality in contact with which people seek their true reality is a timeless presence. Because of the influence of Greek philosophy on the Christian theological tradition, even into the twentieth century, the contrast between epiphany religion and the religion of promise serves Moltmann as a key not only to the Old Testament but also to conflicting views of revelation and eschatology in Christian theology (TH 28–30; chap. I *passim*). Wherever revelation and eschatology are interpreted with reference to the eternal in the present, rather than with reference to the temporal future, a theological equivalent to epiphany religion is to be seen. It is therefore very important that in chapter II Moltmann establishes that the Old Testament roots of Christian faith lie in Israel's adoption and maintenance of a religion of promise rather than an epiphany religion.[5]

Israel's religion was originally a nomadic religion. By contrast with the gods of agrarian religion, who guarantee the recurring cycle of nature, the God of a nomadic tribe leads his people in their journeyings to new places and new experiences and is trusted to bring them to a future goal. The peculiar character of Israelite religion originated, not from this nomadic religion as such, but from 'the fact that the Israelite tribes took the wilderness God of promise with them from the wilderness, along with the corresponding understanding of existence and the world, retained them in the land amid the totally new experiences of agrarian life, and endeavoured to undergo and to master the new experiences in the land in the light of the God of promise' (TH 97).[6]

In Israel, therefore, revelatory appearances of God were understood as occasions for divine promise, and revelation acquired a quite different significance for Israel as compared with the epiphany religions: 'Here Yahweh's revelation manifestly does not serve to bring the ever-threatened present into congruence with his eternity. On the contrary, its effect is that the hearers of the promise become incongruous with the reality around them . . . The result is not the religious sanctioning of the present, but a break-away from the present towards the future' (TH 100, cf. 102). Here Moltmann finds the religious-historical origin of the characteristic theme of *Theology of Hope*: that revelation as promise does not correspond to, but contradicts present reality.

It is important to notice, as Morse points out,[7] that Moltmann's contrast between 'the epiphany of the eternal present' and 'the apocalypse of the promised future' (TH 57), as alternative concepts of revelation, does not deny God's presence in the latter case. In the former he is present as 'eternal presence', but in the latter he is present in his promises (RRF 211). The crucial distinction is that in the former God is known in abstraction from history, whereas in the latter he is 'one who makes possible for the very first time the feeling for history in the category of the future' (TH 100).

This can be understood in the light of Moltmann's careful explanation of the concept of promise in seven points (TH 102–6):
(*a*) A promise announces the coming of a reality that does not yet exist. In the case of the divine promise, this future reality need not be a conceivable development from the possibilities of the present, but is what is possible for God.
(*b*) The promise initiates a history which leads to its fulfilment, and by arousing people's hopes for this fulfilment it involves people in its history and thus gives them a sense for history.
(*c*) The history initiated by the promise has a definite direction towards the promised fulfilment. Thus the promise creates a sense of past and future, dividing reality 'into one reality which is passing and can be left behind, and another which must be expected and sought.'
(*d*) Because it announces a future reality, the promise stands in contrast to the reality which is open to present experience and seeks a different reality which will correspond to it.
(*e*) Between the giving of the promise and its fulfilment is an interval in which people may live in hope and obedience or in resignation and disobedience. This distinguishes the promise from fatalistic predictions.

(*f*) Since it is God who gives the promises, it is God in his freedom and faithfulness who is trusted to fulfil them. This means that fulfilment is not a matter of implementing a prediction to the letter, but can contain elements of surprise and novelty.

(*g*) The promises to Israel were not left behind in Israel's history, through fulfilment or disappointment, but were constantly reinterpreted in a wider sense. In an 'expanding history of promise' each fulfilment left an overplus of promise pointing to further fulfilment, since a reality wholly corresponding to the God who gave the promise was never reached.[8]

Since this sevenfold characterisation of the meaning of promise is foundational for Moltmann's whole argument in *Theology of Hope*, several observations on it may be made. Although much of it is indebted to Walther Zimmerli's essay, 'Promise and Fulfillment',[9] it is notable that point (*d*) is not explicit in Zimmerli. Moltmann draws out this implication because it anticipates the dialectical understanding of promise which emerges more fully later in the book. By contrast with statements which describe existing reality and whose truth is therefore tested by their correspondence to existing reality, promises 'must stand in contradiction to the reality which can at present be experienced. ... They do not seek to illuminate the reality which exists, but the reality which is coming. They do not seek to make a mental picture of existing reality, but to lead existing reality towards the promised and hoped-for transformation ... In doing so they give reality a historic character' (TH 18). The point is that the promise, in contradicting this present reality, discloses not an eternal present, but a different future for this reality, whose changeableness thereby becomes not meaningless transience, but movement in a meaningful direction.

Also notable in Moltmann's explanation of promise in the Old Testament is the stress on the way in which the promise involves those who receive it in its history. This not only gives a sense of history as meaningful movement towards a specific future, but also adumbrates that sense of history as *mission* with arises out of the New Testament culmination of the history of promise. Finally, point (*g*) indicates briefly how Moltmann sees a process of interpretation of the promise leading from particular promises, such as that of the land, to the eschatological expectation first found in the prophets and developed in apocalyptic (TH 124–38). The eschatological promise is for a final future wholly corresponding to God, beyond which, therefore, no further overspill of promise can remain. The promise became eschatological in this sense when it was extended to the furthest conceivable bounds: to the promise of God's universal lordship over all nations, to the promise of his reversal of death, and (in apocalyptic) to the promise of the transformation of the cosmos itself. This unlimited promise, contradicting *every* negative feature of existing reality, forms the context within which the Christ-event is to be understood.

But how does promise reveal God? In his promises God is known not as a transcendental self beyond history, but as one who pledges himself to do things in history – to implement his righteousness, to accomplish his lordship in the world. He is identified as God in his faithfulness to his promises. This concept of revelation has two important implications. In the first place, it makes the history of this world a constituent of God's self-revelation (TH 114, 119), and so in contrast to all epiphany religion, God's self-revelation here does not abstract from history, but actually makes history. Secondly, the knowledge of God through this revelation has to be a knowledge which draws the knower into expectant trust. In the openness of history, God is known as the one who has proved faithful in the past and is trusted for the future. A promise cannot be proved true from its correspondence to the reality of the present, but insofar as it can prove itself does so in contradicting present reality (TH 18–19). 'It has not yet found its answer, and therefore draws the mind to the future, to obedience and creative expectation, and brings it into opposition to the existing reality which has not the truth in it. It thus provokes a peculiar incongruence with being, in the consciousness of hoping and trusting' (TH 118–19). Revelation as promise therefore calls for a particular kind of critical involvement in history: in New Testament terms, mission.

**The resurrection of the Crucified**   This concept of revelation as promise, established from the Old Testament, is Moltmann's hermeneutical key to New Testament theology, and as such it enables him to do justice to the decisive significance of apocalyptic eschatology in primitive Christianity in general, and in Pauline theology in particular, as Moltmann discovered it from the work of Ernst Käsemann. It is not that the Old Testament religion of promise finds in the New Testament a fulfilment in which it comes to an end. Christ is not the 'end of the promise', but 'its rebirth, its liberation and validation' (TH 145). The resurrection of the crucified Jesus was an event in which God, in raising one man already for the sake of the resurrection of all others in the future, confirmed and guaranteed his promise for the eschatological new creation of life out of death and his eschatological lordship over all things. The promise is still outstanding, but the resurrection of Jesus gives a new basis for confidence in its fulfilment. Moreover, in that the resurrection of the *crucified* Jesus means grace for the godless, the promise is released from any bond to the law and the election of Israel. It becomes unconditional and therefore universal in the sense that all may share in its benefit. Thus in Christ the promise is 'made true wholly, unbreakably, for ever and for all' (TH 147). This insistence that Christianity, no less than Old Testament religion, is faith in God's promise is not a denial that in Christ eschatological salvation is already present, but it is an insistence that it is present 'solely in the form of promise, i.e. as pointing and directing us towards a still outstanding future' (Käsemann, quoted TH 148). Accordingly, Moltmann finds in Paul's conflict with the enthusiasts at Corinth another form of the difference between eschatological faith and the non-eschatological epiphany of the eternal present, even if the latter takes on the form of a wholly realised eschatology (TH 154–65).

The Christological centre and basis of Moltmann's theology of hope is his understanding of the resurrection of the crucified Jesus as an event of eschatological promise. But at this point he enters the area of questions about the reality and meaning of the resurrection which have been one of the key problems of modern theology. The difficult sections in which he deals with these questions (TH 165–202) are of major importance for his work, as well as for the more general discussion of this topic. The core of his argument is that only within an eschatological view of reality as a whole, as open to the transforming possibilities of the divine promise, can the resurrection of Jesus have the significance which was constitutive for Christian faith in the beginning and still is.

The problem is that the questions we ask about the reality of the resurrection – did it happen? what does it mean for me? – necessarily arise out of particular modern views of reality, which are in fact alien to the New Testament's kerygmatic accounts of the resurrection. If we assume these views of reality to be unquestionable, then we can only hear or accept whatever elements of the New Testament's understanding of the resurrection can fit into them. On the other hand, it is possible to allow the view of reality from which we question the resurrection to be itself questioned by the resurrection. In Moltmann's treatment of the modern historical approach to the historical question of the resurrection (TH 172–82) and of the Existentialist approach to the existential significance of the resurrection (TH 182–90), he finds the early Christian understanding of the resurrection as eschatological promise rebounding on the interpreter and setting in question his view of the world, which in both cases rests on a presupposition of the fundamental similarity of all experience. On such a presupposition, the significance of the resurrection as an event of eschatological novelty, which by contradicting all present experience opens up a new future for the world, cannot be grasped. It presupposes instead an eschatological horizon of understanding, in which questions about reality are related to the promises of God. This does not mean that the questions we ask about the historical meaning of the resurrection and about its existential meaning are dismissed. It does mean that they receive answers which are not available within the modern views of reality from which they are asked, but which become available when these questions are taken up into the perspective of questions about the eschatological promise in which the resurrection properly belongs.

Thus, there is no question that for Moltmann the reality of the event of the resurrection itself must be affirmed as the basis of Christian faith and hope (TH 172–73), but it does not fit the modern concept of the historical which is based on analogy with present experience.[10] However, it is precisely the unparalleled nature of the resurrection which is its point. Precisely because it has no analogy in the history known to us, its significance is as an analogy to the *future* of all reality.[11] By contradicting and calling in question all other historical experience, this unique event becomes a 'history-making' event, which cannot be fitted into concepts of history which were formed without reference to it but itself creates a new understanding of history as subject to the eschatological promise of God (TH 180–81). In this case, however, the event of the resurrection of Jesus cannot be affirmed in the manner

in which the modern historian speaks of the past, 'in historical detach-
ment in the form of a report on a process complete in itself' (TH
188–89), but only in a combination of historical remembrance and
hope for the future. The event of the resurrection of Jesus in the past
entails his universal eschatological future. Therefore 'the only mode of
communication appropriate to the event must be missionary proclamation to all people without distinction – a mission which knows itself
in the service of the promised future of this event' (TH 189).

Thus it belongs to the reality of the resurrection that it cannot be
merely reported in a disinterested way. The Existentialist interpretation, allied to the form-critical approach to the resurrection narra-
tives, correctly saw that they were kerygmatic testimonies of faith.
But, in accepting the modern historical approach which excludes the
resurrection from history, the Existentialist interpretation confined the
meaning of the resurrection to the understanding of existence expressed
in the kerygma, and failed to see that the texts do not subscribe to
this dichotomy between factual and existential truth. They testify
rather to an *event* which because of its eschatological character required
universal missionary proclamation (TH 187–88). Thus the kind of self-
understanding to which the resurrection gives rise is a consciousness
of missionary vocation in the light of the promised future of all reality.
It sets believers in contradiction to present reality and openness to the
world and to the future (TH 195–97).

As well as engaging with these particular modern approaches to the
resurrection, Moltmann tries to characterise the total modern situation
out of which our various questions about the resurrection arise, so that
this total experience of reality may also be called in question by the
resurrection of Jesus. At 'the foundations of modern experience of self
and the world', he suggests, is the experience of 'the death of God'
(TH 167–68). By this he means, not necessarily all that was meant
by it in the 'death of God' theology of the 1960s, but that in modern
approaches to reality the idea of God seems no longer necessary. At
best it is optional. In the modern experience of self and the world God
is not required as an explanation or apparent as an inference. The
way in which Moltmann's theology of the resurrection encounters this
modern situation is barely indicated in *Theology of Hope* (168–72, cf.
84, 210–11), but it is a theme which contains the seed of significant
later developments in Moltmann's theology.

For its clarification, we need first to grasp the dialectic of cross and resurrection which is central to Moltmann's understanding of the resurrection as an event of eschatological promise. The dialectic of cross and resurrection means that Jesus, crucified and risen, has his *identity in total contradiction*. The cross and the resurrection represent total opposites:

> The experience of the cross of Jesus means for [the disciples] the experience of the god-forsakenness of God's ambassador – that is, an absolute *nihil* embracing also God. The experience of the appearance of the crucified one as the living Lord therefore means for them the experience of the nearness of God in the god-forsaken one, of the divineness of God in the crucified and dead Christ – that is, a new totality which annihilates the total *nihil*. The two experiences stand in a radical contradiction to each other, like death and life, nothing and everything, godlessness and the divinity of God (TH 198).

Yet in the resurrection appearances Jesus identified himself as the same Jesus *in* this total contradiction. The identity is not to be explained by reducing the contradiction, but by recognising that the point of identification lies in God who raised Jesus from death. It was not that Jesus was less than wholly dead or less than wholly raised, but the Creator *ex nihilo*, the God who raises the dead, created the continuity through this radical discontinuity (TH 200).

This dialectic which took place in the crucified and risen Jesus is the dialectic which is promised for the whole of reality. Jesus in his death was identified with the godforsaken state of the whole of reality, whose negative characteristics are fully recognisable in the light of the cross and by contrast with the resurrection. Jesus' resurrection is therefore the promise of God for nothing less than the new creation of all reality, for, in Hegel's terms, the negation of the negative (TH 211), the new totality annihilating the total *nihil* (TH 198). This central proposition of the theology of hope explains again Moltmann's concern, which we have noticed in the previous chapter, to assert a hope which depends on a really transcendent God. A hope which transcends the absolute nothingness of the cross can only be founded on the promise of the God who raised Jesus from the dead (cf. TH 221).

Further implications of this dialectic of cross and resurrection will emerge later. For the moment, we should notice that the death of God's Messiah was experienced by his disciples as his abandonment by God, and in that sense as a kind of 'death of God' (TH 210, cf. 198). Here we have only the seed of the thesis of *The Crucified God*, but it is enough to establish the connexion with the modern experience of the 'death of God', which Hegel called a universal Good Friday (TH 169). While rejecting Hegel's dehistoricising of the historical Good Friday (cf. DTH 224), Moltmann adapts his dialectic. The world in which 'God is dead', in which God's presence cannot be seen or inferred, is the world as the cross shows it to be.[12] But, then, Jesus' resurrection is 'the beginning and source of the abolition of the universal Good Friday, of that god-forsakenness of the world which comes to light in the deadliness of the death on the cross' (TH 211). The world in which God is apparent, the world which corresponds to God and proves God, is not the world as it is, but the new creation promised in Jesus' resurrection. Thus the Gospel of the crucified and risen Christ contradicts the modern experience of the 'death of God' in the way in which the promise of God always contradicts present experience. It does not deny the questionableness of God in the modern age, but by raising the question of God as a question about his future glorification in all reality, it makes present reality itself questionable (cf. HP 19). It opens the world in hope to the coming presence of God.

Consistently with this view, Moltmann interprets the traditional proofs of God and their modern equivalents as 'sketches for the future on the part of Christian hope . . . anticipations of the as yet unattained future land in which God is all in all' (TH 282; cf. 272–81; HP 22–26). In supposing that the reality of God can be perceived in or inferred from the present reality of the world and human existence, they are appropriate not to the present world, but only to that world for which faith hopes, in which God will be revealed in all reality. In this argument, it is not simply the *unconcluded* nature of present reality which requires God's self-revelation to be eschatological, as is the case for Pannenberg. Rather it is the suffering and godforsakenness of present reality which makes it incapable of revealing God. In distinction from Pannenberg, Moltmann holds the revelation of God to be not only eschatological, but *dialectical*.[13] God will prove himself in his new creation of this godforsaken reality. The loss of transcendence 'above' in the 'death of God' is made up not merely by a transcendence of the absolute future, but by a transcendent future which enters into historically productive conflict with the godless present. This last point will become clear in the next section.

**History as mission**  Christian eschatology, according to Moltmann,

> does not speak of the future as such. It sets out from a definite reality in history and announces the future of that reality, its future possibilities and its power over the future. Christian eschatology speaks of Jesus Christ and *his* future . . . Hence the question whether all statements about the future are grounded in the person and history of Jesus Christ provides it with the touchstone by which to distinguish the spirit of eschatology from that of utopia (TH 17).

In Blochian terms, which Moltmann refunctions, Christian eschatology seeks 'the tendencies and latencies of the Christ event of the crucifixion and resurrection' (TH 203), i.e. the divine intention for the future which is hidden in the cross and revealed in the resurrection. This does not at all mean that the Christ-event reveals some kind of plan of future history. Rather, in the total contradiction of cross and resurrection, there come to light promises of righteousness as opposed to sin, freedom as opposed to bondage, glory as opposed to suffering, peace as opposed to dissension, life as opposed to death: the negations of the great negatives, all encompassed by the promise of the presence of God as opposed to godforsakenness (TH 18, 203, 210–11). These are the direction in which the Christ-event points, but the knowledge of Christ's future is necessarily 'provisional, fragmentary, open, straining beyond itself' (TH 203). Because what is expected from Christ in his parousia is really *new* (TH 227–29), it must retain a large degree of openness. The concretisations of the future in the eschatological conceptions of each age are conditioned by the actual miseries of their time, against which they are directed, and must therefore vary (TH 215; RRF 102–3). New dimensions of the promised future come to light in the historical experience of the Church in every period,[14] but the general orientation towards the future of Christ remains constant (RRF 103; FH 45).[15]

In stressing that the eschatological future is the future of the event of promise Moltmann radically distinguishes the 'tendency' of this event from any conception of an immanent process of history into which the Christ-event might be fitted. The dialectic of cross and resurrection cannot be assimilated to any general dialectic of world history, because it sets the promise in total contradiction to world history, thereby creating its own dialectical process which can be resolved only in the new creation of all things (TH 225–27, cf. 221). In other words, there is an historical process which leads from the resurrection to the parousia of Christ, but it is a process created by the promise, which affects present reality by *contradicting* it (TH 86). 'As the future that is really outstanding, it [the parousia] works upon the present by awaking hopes and establishing resistance' (TH 227). There is no tension here, as Morse alleges,[16] between the idea that the promise creates history and the Blochian idea that the future creates history. It is the promise *as* announcement of the eschatological future which creates history: 'The promise which announces the *eschaton*, and in which the *eschaton* announces itself, is the motive power, the mainspring, the driving force and the torture of history' (TH 165). That the eschatological future affects the present through the mediation of the promise is only another way of saying this: 'In the promise, the hidden future already announces itself and exerts its influence on the present through the hope it awakens' (TH 18, cf. 139).

The *eschaton* is nothing less than the new creation of all things, and cannot therefore be the result of any trends of world history (TH 221). But it is God's recreation of *this world*,[17] just as the resurrection of Jesus is God's raising of *Jesus* from death. Moltmann's theology of hope hinges on this expectation, not of *another* world, but of the divine transformation of *this* world. Such an expectation, aroused by God's promise in the Christ-event, affects this world already. It does so initially by contradiction, by setting in contrast to present reality the promised future *of that reality* (cf. TH 222). Present reality therefore becomes, for those who trust the promise, 'not yet' what it can be (TH 164–65). It is seen as transformable in the direction of the promised

future, and believers in the promise are involved in seeking and acti-
vating the present possibilities of world history which lead in the
direction of the eschatological future (TH 288–89). Eschatological
hope, with its promise of universal transformation, thrusts believers
into the worldly reality for whose future they hope, but keeps them
unreconciled to its present condition, 'a constant disturbance in human
society', and 'the source of continual new impulses towards the realisation of righteousness, freedom and humanity here in the light of the
promised future that is to come' (TH 22). In this way, the promise
creates history in the form of the universal mission of the Church. The
theme of mission is the second main theme of *Theology of Hope*, relating
in this necessary, complementary way to the theme of promise (cf. TH
88–89). Nothing is more characteristic of Moltmann's theology of hope
than the insistence that Christian knowledge of God in Christ is a
hope for the future of the world which entails a call to universal
mission. It is *self-involving* and *world-transforming* knowledge, 'a knowledge that draws us onwards – not upwards – into situations that are
not yet finalised but still outstanding' (TH 118). In being both self-
involving and world-transforming this kind of knowledge also transcends the Kantian dichotomy of self and world, subject and object,
which has dogged modern theology. In the light of the promise, self-
understanding and world-understanding are correlated in the
missionary consciousness of solidarity with the world in hope and the
missionary impulse to self-expending love for worldly reality (TH 225,
cf. 48–50, 68–69, 91–92, 335–38; HP 213; RRF 219).

The effect of the promised future on the present is the element in
the structure of the theology of hope which, in Moltmann's view,
decisively distinguishes it from all other-worldly forms of Christianity.
It is therefore important to be clear how it happens. According to
Moltmann, the Christian is himself transformed by the Gospel message
which arouses hope in him, but in such a way as to involve him in
the Church's mission of world-transformation (cf. TH 328–29). The
dialectic of cross and resurrection controls Moltmann's account of both
aspects. Christians experience salvation now only in the form of hope:
'it is only through their hope that they here attain to participation in
the life of the resurrection' (TH 161). This also means that they
experience the promise of the resurrection under the form of the cross,
because the Christian 'is led by hope into the tensions and antitheses

of obedience and suffering in the world' (TH 161). He experiences in his obedience to the promise the contradiction between the promise and the present reality in which he lives. Thus the Spirit, who is the presence of the resurrection life of the future in Christian experience now, is experienced as the power to *suffer* in love and hope (TH 211–13; cf. HP 150). It is a favourite theme of Moltmann's that hope for God's new creation makes possible self-expending love which is prepared to suffer and die (cf. TH 32, 337–38; HP 196; RRF 58; and chapter 1 above).

However, if hope thrusts the Christian into the painful contradiction between the promise and present reality, it simultaneously thrusts him into the world. The contradiction arises from a hope for the world, for the whole of this worldly reality, which it exposes in all its god-forsakenness. The Christian's suffering is thus a loving solidarity with the whole of the suffering creation (TH 206; cf. HP 148), and a hopeful solidarity in expectation of the transformation of all creation (TH 223). Love and hope for the world involve the Christian in a movement towards world-transformation which has two moments: critical opposition and creative expectation (TH 118, 330; RRF 140). In the first moment, hope liberates the Christian from all accommodation to the status quo and sets him critically against it (TH 119, 222). In the second moment, it gives rise to attempts to change the world in the direction of its promised transformation, imaginatively grasping and realising the objective possibilities in the present which conform most closely to the coming Kingdom (TH 34–35, 288–90; cf. HP 183).

This last point is of great importance because it is Moltmann's strongest qualification, in *Theology of Hope*, of the dualism his thinking produces between this godforsaken reality and the Kingdom of God which only God's creative act at the *eschaton* can produce. This dualism functions in *Theology of Hope* to exclude the possibility of a process towards the Kingdom arising immanently out of present reality, but not to exclude a process created by the promise. On the contrary, Moltmann is maintaining precisely that the promise discloses for the world a wide open horizon of new possibility and sets in motion already a dialectical process of negating the present in order to create the future. It must be admitted, however, that Moltmann's brief references in *Theology of Hope* to the positive side of this process require further clarification.

Nor does *Theology of Hope* go very far towards putting the Church's mission of world-transformation into concrete terms. Chapter V is concrete enough in its account of the way in which modern industrial society, whose tendency is to stabilise itself, assigns to religion sociological roles in which the Church funtions merely to compensate for the dehumanised nature of public life and therefore helps to stabilise society in its present form.[18] By contrast with these roles to which society tries to confine religion, the true task of Christianity is to be the element in society which cannot be assimilated, which resists the stagnation of modern society and keeps it on the move towards a better future. But 'the concrete form assumed by a live eschatological hope in modern society' (TH 304) is very generally described (cf. TH 329, 338), and Moltmann himself later admitted that *Theology of Hope* left his readers without guidance when it came to the concrete questions of the praxis of hope (UZ 13).

**Problems and clarifications**   The dialectic of cross and resurrection, present reality and promise, constitutes the creative centre of Moltmann's early theology, but it also raises problems of interpretation. Both Alves and Pannenberg see it as 'a 90–degree rotation of the idea of transcendence of the early Barth.'[19] In other words, the wholly other God of dialectical theology, who in his Word breaks into the world vertically from above and negates everything human, becomes in Moltmann the God of a qualitatively other *future*, who in his Word of promise negates the human present. Moltmann substitutes a transcendent future for Barth's transcendent eternity, but the dialectic is otherwise similarly conceived.[20] Moreover, it is tempting to see Moltmann's theological development from *Theology of Hope* onwards as analogous to Barth's movement from his early stress on the wholly other God who contradicts human reality to his later emphasis on the incarnate God who identifies with humanity. Similarly, Moltmann moved from an early stress on the wholly future God who contradicts present reality to a later emphasis (in *The Crucified God*) on the incarnate God who identifies with the suffering of the present. There is certainly something in this parallel, but it should not conceal the fact that the relationship of God to created reality in *Theology of Hope* contains a decisive difference from that in dialectical theology. In *Theology of Hope* it is present reality which God in his promise contradicts, and his contradiction of it is part of the dynamic by which his promise creates history and moves reality towards its transformation into non-contradiction of or correspondence to God. The dialectic aims at resolution. When Moltmann claimed that the transcendent future is not 'wholly other' (*ganz anders*) but 'the wholly transforming' (*der ganz Ändernde*) (FC 11 = RRF 190; cf. HP 36; FC 30), he was borrowing the wordplay from Barth, but using it in his own way.

In evaluating Moltmann's dialectic and its effects in his theology, it is important to grasp the point of the 'identity in total contradiction' (TH 199) of the crucified and risen Jesus, and the corresponding relation between present reality and the promised new creation. The contradiction is total, *not* because this present reality is wholly evil – for in that case there could be no identity in the contradiction, only an annihilation of this world and its replacement by another (cf. RRF 14) – but because this reality is subject to sin and suffering and transitoriness and *ends in nothingness*. It has no immanent possibility of transcending its own tendency towards nothingness, and therefore it is only God who, in recreating it out of nothingness, can *give* it continuity *in* the radical discontinuity of death and resurrection (cf. TH 200, 221). God creates a qualitatively new future, but in his faithfulness to his old creation takes it up into the new (RRF 12–13). Moltmann's point in emphasising the *total* contradiction of cross and resurrection is to establish that the negation of the absolute negative of death is not an immanent possibility for human hope but only a God-given possibility for hope in the promise. But the God-given *continuity* in this contradiction is just as essential to his thought as the contradiction itself is. Without it there would be no sense in Moltmann's frequent claim that the hope of resurrection makes it possible in spite of death to love this reality which is subject to death.[21]

More problematic is what happens when the total contradiction of promise and present reality sets in motion a dialectic of *historical* change. Here Moltmann is concerned to understand the promise as a divine initiative which creates a human initiative for real historical change. What happens is that the promise gives the believer a critical distance from his present so that he can recognise its deficiencies and work to transform the present in the direction of the promised future. But since there is no question here of new creation out of death, the process of historical change cannot involve the *total* overturning of all existing conditions.[22] In transformations short of the *eschaton* itself, the dialectical process of the negation of the negative has to be simultaneously an affirmation and development of the positive, but Moltmann rarely acknowledges this. Instead he emphasises the way in which the promise evokes the possibility of the qualitatively new and therefore promotes radical change (e.g. FC 10–11). Eschatologically inspired hope therefore promotes revolutionary rather than evolutionary change, in the sense that it envisages a new state of affairs radically different from the present and only from that perspective identifies aspects of the present with which it can establish continuity (RRF 30–32). This emphasis on the qualitatively new shows how the eschatological hope can function to liberate people's thinking from the constraints of existing conditions, but it might also encourage quite unrealistic expectations of revolutionary change. As a generalised rhetoric, it also tends to level the differences between situations of glaring injustice which cry out for revolutionary change and situations in which, though the promise will always show them to be not yet what they might be, steady progress is possible and more appropriate than revolution. The dialectic of cross and resurrection is in danger, especially in Moltmann's work soon after *Theology of Hope*, of promoting a revolutionary political attitude in too simplistic a way.[23]

However, in this same period of the late 1960s, Moltmann did attempt some conceptual clarification of the relationship between eschatological hope and present possibilities of social and political change. He distinguishes two concepts of the future, which he calls *futurum* and *adventus* (DTH 210–12; FH 11–16; FC 29–30, 55; EH 52–53), meaning respectively the future which 'will be' and the future which 'comes'. *Futurum* is what develops out of the tendencies of the present, and can therefore be calculated by *extrapolation* from the past and the present. Adventus, on the other hand, can bring something radically new, which is not already contained in the present in potential, and as such it can only be known in *anticipation* (whether real or verbal) of the future. In dialogue with theologians who hold that the eschatological future is known to Christians by extrapolation (see DTH 210; FC 41–45), Moltmann argues that this is true only in the sense that when the Christ-event and Christian experience of the Spirit are understood as real anticipations of the eschatological future, then they can be the basis for extrapolation (DTH 213). 'Our statements spoken *out* of our present *into* the divine future are possible on the basis of the divine word spoken *into* our present *out* of God's future' (FC 45).

In a number of places Moltmann argues that *planning*, which corresponds to a concept of the ˇfuture as calculable *futurum*, and hope, which corresponds to *adventus*, must be combined in practice (DTH 212; FC 55–56; cf. HP VII). Hope gives direction to planning, by projecting a desirable future and then seeking the real possibilities of the present which correspond to this future (cf. FTO 106). Planning which limits itself to the calculable and hope which reaches out to the not yet possible must interact if the not yet possible is to become possible (cf. HP 181–82; M 42–44). Without hope, planning loses impetus and vision, but without planning, hope becomes unrealistic. The dialectical element is introduced into this picture by the observation that when planning takes place by extrapolation, it is in the interests of those who benefit from the present distribution of power in society, which mere planning perpetuates. But Christian hope, based on the anticipation of God's future in the crucified Christ, identified with the victims of society, will envisage the future in solidarity with the oppressed and neglected (FC 56–57; HFM 56–57). It is they who desire a different future, which arises not from the extension but from the critical negation of the present (FC 43; HFM 91).

The important concept of anticipation, not much used in *Theology of Hope*, plays an increasing role in Moltmann's writing in the following years, as he becomes more inclined to emphasise the positive effect of the eschatological future in the present (e.g. RRF 212–15; DTH 232–37; FH 37–38; FTO 112–13; FC 45–48; M 115–16; MSM 220–23). The frequently made criticism of *Theology of Hope*, that it stresses future at the expense of realised eschatology,[24] is met by Moltmann's use of the idea of anticipation, which not only gives a place to realised eschatology but also makes clear what the *connexion* is between realised and future eschatology, viz. that the future creates the present, and not *vice versa* (cf. DTH 209; FC 20). The following account of the 'waves of anticipation' in which the new future enters transitory history sums up Moltmann's use of the concept of anticipation:

It appears first in the mission of the Christ of God, who personally incarnates the future of freedom among the unfree and in his resurrection opens up the future to everything which is dying. Then in the mission of the gospel's words of the future the sinner is forgiven, the Godless justified, and the humiliated given hope. Then the new future comes in the mission of the community of Christ, which, as 'the new people of God' drawn from all nations and tongues, is the vanguard of the new humanity and the representative embodiment of freedom from the coercive powers of this world. Then it arrives in the new obedience of the believers, who in ordinary life refuse to conform to the scheme of this world, but anticipate the coming freedom. Finally, it comes in the 'new heaven and the new earth' where justice dwells, where Christ's presence purges heaven of religious myths and powers and frees the earth from pain, sorrow, and meaningless death (RRF 137–38).


The concept of anticipation makes Moltmann sometimes seem to be equivocal about whether Christian activity in the world actually contributes to the coming of God's Kingdom. On the one hand, 'the Christian is a fellow worker participating in the building of the kingdom' (FTO 112; cf. FH 45–46). On the other hand, Christian social and political action is not 'ultimately . . . in any direct sense labor for God's Kingdom. But it is obedience that seeks in the inadequate materials of transitory history that which bears correspondence to God's future' (RRF 122; cf. HP 129 n. 44). However, the point of such language is not, as Liberation theologians complain,[25] to sever all causal connexion between the eschatological Kingdom and present anticipations of it, or to deny that the Kingdom is in some sense really present in its anticipations (cf. CPS 193). The point is to deny that the anticipations create the Kingdom. The causal connexion is the reverse: the eschatological Kingdom by arousing hope and obedience produces anticipations of itself in history. This notion of anticipation therefore protects at the same time the initiative of God, in the present as well as in the *eschaton*, and the transcendence of the eschatological future beyond all the relative correspondences to it in history. The latter must be preserved if the future is not to lose the 'magic' of transcendence which stimulates the process of continual transcending in history towards a new future (DTH 217; FC 15–16).

**Political theology**  Although *Theology of Hope* pointed clearly in the direction of a Chrisitan *political* theory-praxis (TH 329), it scarcely provided one. In Moltmann's increasing attention to what was called in Germany in the late 1960s 'political theology', a number of influences converged. In the first place, the logic of the theology of hope inevitably led in that direction. A theology which 'wants to change the world rather than explain it' (RRF 5) must in the modern world, where the concrete possibilities for changing the world seem to be, in the broadest sense, political, interest itself in the goals and process of political change.[26] In treating politics, even in the broadest sense, as 'the inclusive horizon of the life of mankind', Moltmann's notion of political theology perhaps underplayed his own recognition of the importance of dimensions of life which are not politically determined (e.g. RRF 78), but in this he was in good company. He acknowledged that it was his Tübingen colleague J. B. Metz who led the way in developing eschatological theology into political theology (UZ 13). More broadly, Moltmann could scarcely have been unaffected by the mood of the times which became apparent in the enthusiastic reception of his *Theology of Hope* in so many parts of the world. To his surprise (UZ 11) his work encountered a widespread turning to the future (DTH 201–2), in which, among other concerns, the need for cooperative political action to realise the hopeful possibilities of and to avert the threats to the common future of humanity featured. A sense of the all-or-nothing urgency of the common human task in 'one world' faced with possible atomic self-destruction runs through Moltmann's lectures of the late 1960s (RRF 19, 27, 30–31, 60, 201; FTO 103–4, 115), though it appears surprisingly rarely thereafter (cf. MSM 206–7). Moltmann's participation in the Christian-Marxist dialogues, which culminated in the Marienbad meeting of 1967, he later looked back on as 'one of the happiest intellectual experiences of those years' (EG 13). In the Western humanistic Marxism of that period, inspired by the writings of the young Marx, Moltmann recognised the 'messianic hopes' which had, sadly, 'emigrated from the church' (RRF 201), and the challenge to concrete political realisation of Christian hope which Marxism therefore represents. During the year he spent in the United States (1967–68), as well as in Tübungen, Moltmann encountered the student protest movement, but whereas in American universities he warmed to the Christian radicalism of the movement, in Germany he was saddened by the fact that students who took to political action tended to abandon their Christian faith. Like his dialogue with Ernst Bloch, both the Christian-Marxist dialogues and his encounters with student political activists strengthened Moltmann's theological resolve to overcome 'this false alternative between an unreal God and a godless reality, between a faith without hope and a hope without faith' (UZ 13). But this required him to show that Christian faith need not be support for the status quo in society, but could be a powerful source of initiatives for political change.

In this period, following up the strikingly brief reference to non-Christian movements of human hope in *Theology of Hope* (34), Moltmann's work gains a new sense of critical solidarity with such movements, in principle with 'Liberals, Democrats, and Marxists' (RRF 70), but especially with Marxists. His most theologically affirmative verdict on such movements of social and political change is that Christians should recognise in them 'a spirit which is of the Spirit of Christ', since what is active in them is 'the latent Kingdom' (RRF 104). Though undeveloped, this is a significant step beyond the thesis of *Theology of Hope* that only God's word of promise creates hope, history and the missionary impetus to world-transformation. Without downplaying the significance of the proclamation of the Gospel, Moltmann moved, after *Theology of Hope*, to a view of the Spirit as mediating between the messianic impact of the Gospel and the possibilities of the world, creating a solidarity of believers with the felt misery of all creation (DTH 236–37), and inspiring cooperation between Christians and all who work to free the world from misery (CPS 192). Significantly, it was through pneumatology that Moltmann softened the Barthian exclusiveness of the Word, from which he began, so that the unique promise of the Gospel enters a world which, for all its god-forsakenness, is not devoid of God's presence in hope. This incipient theological development explains how Moltmann, in the context of a discussion of the common struggle of all humanity for a common future, can outline a phenomenology of hope and its dialectical process of negating the negative in purely immanent terms, without reference to the promise of God (RRF 27–32).[27] But such a recognition that not only Christians have a hope which enables them to break with the *status quo* raises the question of the distinctive identity of Christianity, which concerned Moltmann simultaneously with the development of political theology. Why, after all, should the student political activist remain a Christian? What difference would it make? What is the Christian's distinctively Christian contribution to the Christian-Marxist dialogue?

The dialogue and cooperation of Christianity with modern Western atheistic movements of hope had, for Moltmann, a special significance as raising the possibility of overcoming what he saw as the great schism of modern Western history: 'in the past two centuries, a Christian faith in God without hope for the future of the world has called forth a secular hope for the future of the world without faith in God' (RRF 200, cf. 20; DTH 208; FTO 115). Thus the biblical Christian tradition divided into two equally 'heretical' half-truths. One of Moltmann's responses to this situation was to go back to the young Marx's view of religion. In doing this he was examining, in effect, that point of origin of this schism by which he was divided from his Marxist dialogue-partners, in the hope of finding a way of transcending the schism. Moltmann points out that Marx recognised in religion an expression of and protest against the real misery of humanity. His criticism was not of this aspect of religion, but of the otherworldly eschatology which provided a merely illusory compensation for human misery and thereby helped to perpetuate the conditions which caused it. Marx's project was to inherit the religious protest against human misery in the form of political action to change society. In this sense, Marx's criticism of religion could be seen as a 'political hermeneutic' of religion, 'an interpretation of religion through the realization of what was merely conceptualized by religion' (RRF 95). Moltmann then sees his own 'political hermeneutic' of the Gospel as a parallel to Marx's: it finds in messianic Christian faith a protest against real misery and simultaneously (what was lacking in the Christianity Marx knew) the categorical imperative for revolutionary realisation of religious concepts in political and economic liberation (RRF 95). Consequently, 'the new criterion of theology and of faith is to be found in praxis.' After Marx there is no evading the insight that theory must be practicable: 'unless it contains initiative for the transformation of the world, it becomes a myth of the existing world' (RRF 138).

Thus Christian political theology as a theory-praxis parallel to Marxism must prove itself in its power to overcome the real misery of humanity. Yet Moltmann also maintained that the parallel with

Marxism was 'merely formal' (FH 43). In the *content* of its understanding of human misery and of its initiative for overcoming it Christianity differs from Marxism. The main point here is the familiar one of the transcendence of Christian hope. The Christian analysis of the misery of humanity certainly does not exclude the political and economic slavery which Marxists identify, and the Marxist possibilities for liberation in these dimensions are possibilities also for Christians' struggle for freedom. But Christians see human misery also in profounder terms of slavery to sin and death, and look to God for liberation from sin by grace and from death by resurrection (RRF 78). This transcendent hope is not simply something other than the immanent hopes which Christians share with Marxists. Rather, as Moltmann always insists, transcendent and immanent hopes interact. All the struggles of history are ambivalent and every revolution brings its disappointments. The Christian hope which transcends every relative anticipation in history makes possible frank recognition of the shortcomings of the revolutionary achievement, against the tendency to absolutise it, keeps alive the will to transcend every achievement, against the tendency to resignation through disappointment, and frees the revolutionary from legalistic compulsion and guilt in its awareness that God's future comes to meet us in grace and forgiveness (see FTO 115–17; RRF 79–81, 105–6, 145–47, 220; FH 48–50; M 56–58).

**Theology as the game of freedom** By the end of the 1960s Moltmann's thinking was already moving very much in the direction of a theology of the cross, which would complement the emphasis on the resurrection in *Theology of Hope*, but the path to *The Crucified God* was temporarily interrupted by the essay *The First Liberated Men in Creation*, published in 1971.[28] To some extent this was a response to the wish expressed by Harvey Cox in 1968, when, acknowledging the value of Moltmann's recovery of the theological significance of the future, he added that he would also 'like to see a theology which is a rediscovery of the celebrative aspects of life' (FH 80).[29]

In this work, Moltmann set himself against both the utilitarian moralism of revolutionary movements and the achievement-centred values of contemporary society. He countered these by an emphasis, relatively new in his theology, on play and celebration, beauty and enjoyment. He qualified the strongly ethical emphasis of the theology of hope and political theology by means of a kind of theological aesthetics. A definition of theology as theory-praxis therefore proved suddenly inadequate:

> On first glance *Christian theology* is indeed the *theory of a practice* which alleviates human need: the theory of preaching, of ministries and services. But on second glance Christian theology is also an abundant rejoicing in God and the *free play* of thoughts, words, images and songs with the grace of God. In its one aspect it is the theory of a practice, in the other it is pure theory, i.e. a point of view which transforms the viewer into that which he views, hence *doxology*. . . . Being aware of God is an art and – if the term may be permitted – a noble game (TJ 49).

But this rather uncharacteristic idea of theology as pure theory does not, as will become clear, reduce its relevance to human liberation.

The idea of life as, ideally, purposeless game, rather than as goal-orientated struggle and achievement, has theological value because it is rooted in God's free love in creation and redemption, and corresponds to justification by faith. God created out of sheer good pleasure, in order to enjoy his creation, and his free love in Jesus sets people free to enjoy God and each other and the world in God. Hence the end of history will not be the achievement of the purpose of history, but liberation from the compulsion to achieve purposes (TJ 56). It has to be understood in aesthetic categories, 'totally without purpose as a hymn of praise for unending joy, as an ever-varying round dance of the redeemed in the trinitarian fullness of God' (TJ 55). Such eschatological festivity in the presence of God's beauty and love is anticipated now and gives religion its intrinsic value, which is not dependent on its *usefulness* for meeting human needs or promoting morality (TJ 78–82). Religion is meaningful in itself, because God is to be enjoyed for himself and his free creative and redemptive love gives human beings value in themselves, not for their usefulness or achievements. Hence justification by faith sets one free from the compulsion to make oneself by doing good works. Whereas in contemporary society one's being is achieved by doing and having, justification by faith restores the priority of being to doing. Then good works are no longer under the necessity of legalism, but are free works, 'as if playing' (TJ 67), done for the delight of pleasing God and out of uncoerced love of neighbour.

All this might represent an irresponsible religious escapism if Moltmann did not relate it to his fundamental dialectic of cross and resurrection (TJ 49–54). It is the resurrection of Jesus which 'opens up the boundary-crossing freedom to play the game of the new creation' (TJ 53). In a sense this work completed Moltmann's exploration of the significance of the resurrection, before he was able to give his more sustained attention to the cross. However, as always, he refuses to forget that the *crucified* Jesus rose, and in order to preserve the real godforsakenness of the cross as the very opposite of the freedom and joy of the resurrection, he refuses to subsume the cross itself under the metaphor of 'game' (TJ 50–51). Easter does not abolish the cross but establishes it as the saving event by which freedom and joy can reach the guilty and the suffering. Consequently, the dialectic of the cross and resurrection creates a characteristic interrelation of joy and pain in the life of believers. Their 'game', with its memory of the crucified one, cannot be – what games and leisure in repressive societies so often are (TJ 31–34) – a mere compensation for the unfree conditions of the rest of life. By practising an alternative to oppression, it protests against and criticises oppression (TJ 53), and it leads into suffering solidarity with the oppressed (TJ 52). '*Life* as *rejoicing* in liberation, as *solidarity* with those in bondage, as *play* with reconciled existence, and as *pain* at unreconciled existence demonstrates the Easter event in the world' (TJ 52). Thus the idea characteristic of *Theology of Hope*, that the power of the resurrection in Christian life now takes the form of suffering in fellowship with the crucified Christ, is not abandoned but combined with the relatively new note of celebration and joy.

If the Christian religion is a liberating 'game' in which people discover the freedom of 'being-there-with-others' (TJ 86), then a further element in a Christian critique of Marxism emerges. In seeking to replace the alienating work of the capitalist system with freedom for self-determination, Marx failed to reverse the capitalist priority of doing to being. 'The achievement of self-determination itself may turn into pressure to achieve.' The insight of the doctrine of justification by faith is that a deeper liberation 'from the compulsive notion that [man] is what he produces' is needed (TJ 74). Religion can promote this because it is not just, as Marx thought, the sigh of the oppressed creature for liberty, but the actual, anticipatory practice and celebration of 'that creative play which heavy-laden and labouring mankind longingly desires when it desires liberty' (TJ 75).

# 3
## THE CRUCIFIED GOD AND AUSCHWITZ

**Towards the theology of the cross**  Moltmann's second major work, *The Crucified God*, was published in 1972. Its theme, as the subtitle puts it, is 'the Cross of Christ as the Foundation and Criticism of Christian Theology.' Just as in *Theology of Hope* Moltmann treated eschatology not as one theological topic but as an essential perspective on the whole of Christian theology, so in *The Crucified God* he treats the cross not as one distinct theme in theology but as the basis and the criterion of Christian theology as such. In *Theology of Hope* he claimed that 'the eschatological is not one element *of* Christianity, but it is the medium of Christian faith as such, the key in which everything in it is set' (TH 16). In *The Crucified God* he claims that 'the cross is the test of everything which deserves to be called Christian' (CG 7), with the consequence that '*theologia crucis* is not a single chapter in theology, but the key signature for all Christian theology' (CG 72).[1] Superficially, therefore, it might seem that *The Crucified God* is a fresh start in Moltmann's theology, substituting the cross for eschatology as the unifying theme in theology. But in reality this is not the case. Moltmann's theology in *The Crucified God* remains eschatologically structured, while already in *Theology of Hope* he maintained that Christian theology must be an *eschatologia crucis* (TH 83, 160), founded on the resurrection of the *crucified* Christ.[2] The dialectic of cross and resurrection in an eschatological perspective remains the determining centre of Moltmann's theology in both books, and once this is understood, the shift from a focus on the resurrection of the crucified Christ to a focus on the cross of the risen Christ (CG 5) is not only intelligible, but evidently an inner necessity of Moltmann's theological development. These two different approaches to the whole of Christian theology are not in competition, but complementary aspects of Moltmann's theological enterprise. Hence 'theology of hope is at its hard core theology of the cross' (EH 57), while conversely the theology of the cross is the 'reverse side' of the theology of hope, giving it 'a more profound dimension' (CG 5). *The Crucified God* therefore presupposes and takes up the argument of *Theology of Hope*, not infrequently developing themes which can already be recognised in embryo in *Theology of Hope*.

The extent to which *Theology of Hope* already implies a theology of the cross corresponds to the way Moltmann sees his theological development as deriving, in experimental terms, from his first experience of the reality of God and of Christian faith, in the period 1945–48 when he was a prisoner of war. This was an experience which united hope and pain, God's presence in abandonment and God as the power of hope (EG 7–9). But if Moltmann's theology of the cross represents both a drawing out of the darker side of this experience and a logical development of what was implicit in his theology of hope, nevertheless it took both the experiences of the late 1960s and the movement of Moltmann's thinking in the same period actually to produce *The Crucified God*.[3] Several lectures and articles from that period already contain the most important themes and arguments which the book develops at greater length: in particular, an important section of his answer to the criticisms of *Theology of Hope* (1967: DTH 222–29; cf. FH 23–34), his inaugural lecture at Tübingen on 'God and Resurrection' (1968: HP II), a lecture given in Basel on 'God in the Cross of Jesus' (1969: UZ 133–47), and an essay published in 1970 on 'The Cross and Civil Religion' (CCR). In these preliminary pieces, some of the important new sources of inspiration which contributed to Moltmann's theology of the cross are prominent: the critical theory of the Frankfurt school, Luther's theology of the cross, Camus' philosophy – as are the major theological concerns of *The Crucified God:* the cross as the mediation of salvation to the godless and the godforsaken, the theodicy question as the horizon for understanding the cross and the resurrection, the debate with protest atheism, the opposition between the crucified God and the idols of natural theology and political religion, and the attempt to understand the doctrine of God consistently in the light of Jesus' abandonment by God on the cross.

In the previous chapter we have noticed how the Christian involvement with non-Christian movements of hope, into which Moltmann's political theology led, raised the question of the distinctive identity of Christian faith. In conversation with Bloch and with Marxism, Moltmann tended to stress the Christian hope of resurrection, which gives power to hope in the face of meaningless suffering and death, as the Christian distinctive vis-à-vis Marxist hope. But this hope was founded on the resurrection of the *crucified* Jesus, who in his death was identified with the world in its abandonment by God. Thus it can also be said that the cross is the criticism and criterion of genuinely Christian resurrection faith and hence the criterion of Christian identity. If it is in the crucified Jesus that God has anticipated his kingdom under the conditions of this age, then Christian hope cannot endorse the progressivist optimism or the revolutionary realism which leaves behind the victims of the system or the victims of progress, but must anticipate the kingdom in solidarity precisely with those with whom Jesus was identified in his death – the oppressed, the hopeless, the dying, the utterly abandoned (cf. FC 17, 57; MSM 221–23). Moltmann's political theology in the 1960s increasingly turned in this way to the cross as the criterion of Christian praxis, and derives from it a new element of Christian distinctiveness vis-à-vis Marxist revolution (as well as other forms of political activity), since the poor with whom the crucified Jesus identified 'are not simply oppressed slaves and the exploited proletariat, but are in fact those "accursed of this earth," out of whom no state can be made, nor any revolution produced' (M 19; cf. MSM 218).

Moltmann's attempt to root his theology of hope more deeply in the cross became the more appropriate in the disappointments of hope of the late 1960s,[4] when the optimistic movements of the 1960s ran into contradiction (cf. HFM 90) – the Russian invasion of Czechoslovakia, the murders of John F. Kennedy and Martin Luther King, 'the crass absurdity of the Vietnam war', and setbacks for the reform movements in the churches (EG 13; CG 2) – and the hopes of the radicals all too often collapsed into disappointment and resignation. Western society as a whole, on the other hand, maintained a bland optimism oblivious to the plight of the suffering: 'a society whose official creed is optimism, and which is knee-deep in blood' (CG 4). A purely eschatological theology ran the risk of sanctioning such an attitude (CG 256). In such circumstances, Moltmann's turn to the theology of the cross represented a return to the root from which Christian hope and love can be sustained in the face of failure and contradiction and in solidarity with the suffering, as well as a critique of the false optimism which holds aloof from suffering (see EG 13–14; UZ 14; EH 189; CG 2).

Also by the end of the 1960s, German theologians were at last facing the issue of 'theology after Auschwitz', partly in response to the Jewish theological confrontation with the Holocaust. There was perhaps a psychologically necessary time-lapse before either Jewish or German theologians could come to terms with Auschwitz, and the mood of the 1960s, determined to put the evils of the past in the past, had been no encouragement to do so. But a political theology, especially one which ran into the political disappointments of the late 1960s, had to confront the problem of suffering in the overwhelmingly political form in which the twentieth-century raises it: the horrors of Auschwitz, Hiroshima, Stalinism, Vietnam. Increasingly in Moltmann's work the broad context for theological questions became the theodicy question: world history as the history of suffering and the question of God as the question of God's righteousness in the world. Accordingly, his dialogue with Ernst Bloch now became less important than the contribution of thinkers more preoccupied with the evils of modern history: the 'negative dialectics' of the Frankfurt school and the 'metaphysical rebellion' of Albert Camus. While scarcely really taking up the more radical forms of Jewish 'theology after Auschwitz',[5] Moltmann not only continued his sympathetic approach to Jewish messianism (cf. EH V; CG 98–102), but also deepened it by means of Abraham Heschel's theology of the *pathos* of God (CG 270–72; EH 75–77; FC 69–70; JM 47–49; TKG 25–27).

Moltmann's approach to the theodicy issue again developed consistently out of the central argument of his early theology. The key is still the identity-in-contradiction of the crucified and risen Jesus, whose resurrection is the promise of a new future for all reality because his godforsakenness on the cross matches the godforsakenness of all reality. This correspondence between the historical Good Friday and Hegel's universal Good Friday (taken up again in HP 41; CG 217), which makes the latter a provisional reality open to the future in which God's presence will overcome his 'death' and God's righteousness will overcome present unrighteousness, is extended and deepened as Moltmann focusses on the problem of suffering. The major development in his thought which enabled him to develop this concept further was his progress beyond the largely functional and representative Christology of *Theology of Hope* to an explicitly incarnational Christology (see especially DTH 222–29, in connexion with Hegel's speculative Good Friday and the theodicy issue). The cross is then not simply a representative experience of God's absence, contradicted by his promised presence in resurrection, but is God's own suffering of godforsakenness in the person of the Son of God. Then God not only reveals himself and the world's future in the contradiction of cross and resurrection (TH 171), but himself suffers that contradiction in solidarity with the world. The identity of Jesus in the total contradiction of cross and resurrection now establishes the presence of the coming God already within the world's history of suffering. Thus Moltmann can approach the theodicy question no longer only in terms of the hope of God's future righteousness, but also in terms of God's loving solidarity with the world in its suffering.

This development is accompanied by a comparable shift in Moltmann's argument with natural theology and atheism.[6] In *Theology of Hope* he rejected the kind of natural theology which finds God evident in or deducible from the world, on the grounds that the world does not yet correspond to the coming God. The same argument served to refute the atheism which concludes God's non-existence from the fact that the present state of the world does not manifest or require him. By *The Crucified God* this argument has been sharpened: the present state of the world not only fails to prove God, but provides serious grounds for rejecting him. The kind of atheism Moltmann now takes seriously is the 'protest atheism' that arises from the injustice of the world. But correspondingly, both the theism of natural theology and the atheism of protest are judged inadequate, in the light not only of God's future as the coming God but also of his suffering as the crucified God.

Thus Moltmann's movement, in the late 1960s, back from God's presence in the resurrection as the event of his promise to God's presence in the cross as the event of his solidarity with the world in its godforsakenness accounts for a major shift of emphasis in his theology, a shift from the God who has 'future as his essential nature' (Bloch, quoted TH 16) and moves history forward by his promise, to the God who enters history and suffers it, makes godless and god-forsaken humanity the sphere of his presence, and moves history forward by the power of suffering love. This shift of emphasis was designed to meet the growing pressure of the theodicy question on Moltmann's thinking, but it also brought with it, unexpectedly (EG 15), another development, which really constitutes a new departure in Moltmann's theology: a fundamental rethinking of the doctrine of God. If the godforsakenness of the world, 'an absolute *nihil* embracing also God' (TH 198), is *suffered by God himself* on the cross, if the total contradiction of cross and resurrection takes place in God, then the cross is an event of 'God against God' (CG 152) and God is there revealed as capable of suffering and as a trinitarian God who experiences and overcomes the contradiction of human history within his own history of trinitarian relationships. This development of the doctrine of God will engage our attention more fully in the next chapter.

**The structure and method of *The Crucified God*** If the heart of the argument of *Theology of Hope* is Moltmann's eschatological interpretation of the resurrection of Jesus, the heart of the argument of *The Crucified God* is an interpretation of the cross of Jesus as the abandonment of the Son of God by his Father, set within the horizon of the question of theodicy. Moltmann attempts to construct a theology of the cross on the basis of an open-eyed confrontation with 'the profane horror and godlessness' of the cross (CG 33), which is to be seen not only in Jesus' rejection as a blasphemer by the religious authorities and as a political rebel by the political authorities of his day, but also, and in its deepest dimension, in his rejection by his God and Father, expressed in the cry of desolation, 'My God, why hast thou forsaken me?' Only this stark negativity of the cross makes it, what the book's subtitle calls it, 'the Foundation and Criticism of Christian Theology.' It is the foundation of Christian theology because the death-cry of Jesus in his abandonment by God either makes all theology impossible, or else it must itself be the foundation for a specifically Christian theology which has only this foundation (CG 4, cf. 153). It is the criticism of Christian theology because in its stark contradiction of values and concepts of humanity and deity derived from elsewhere the cross of Christ is a permanent critique of all ideology and wish-projection in Christian theology. It exposes the difference btween the God of Jesus Christ and all the idols which both the non-Christian world and also empirical Christianity set up. The exclusiveness and radical implications of the theology of the cross as Moltmann expounds it follow from his attempt to do justice to Jesus' dying question to God, which sets at the heart of Christianity the seemingly impossible concept of a revelation of God in his opposite: in godlessness and godforsakenness.

It is worth noticing at once how the theological method of moving from the particular (the history of Jesus) to the universal, which Moltmann employed in *Theology of Hope*, is continued and radicalised in *The Crucified God*. There is the same rejection of theological approaches which start with universal concepts of God or humanity and allow these to govern the interpretation of the Christ-event, and the same method of criticising these approaches in the light of the history of Jesus itself and then taking up their questions, in corrected form, into a more adequate hermeneutical framework (especially in CG III and VI). The method is radicalised by its new focus on the cross. Of course, when Moltmann claims that 'all Christian statements stem from the crucified Christ' (CG 204) and that the God of Jesus Christ must be understood 'completely in the light of what happened on the cross' (CG 190), he does not mean that the cross can be isolated from the rest of the history of Jesus (CCR 19). On the contrary, it is still the cross of the *risen* Christ, and must be understood in the light of the resurrection, with its openness to the eschatological future of Christ (CG V). Furthermore, it must also be understood in the light of the preceding life and ministry of Jesus (CG IV), to which Moltmann paid scant attention in *Theology of Hope* but which becomes in *The Crucified God* a constitutive part of the history of Jesus in its theological significance. So not the cross as an isolated event or a doctrine, but *the crucified Christ*, who *is* the historical and the risen Jesus, is really, for Moltmann, 'the Foundation and Criticism of Christian Theology.' But whereas in *Theology of Hope* it is by raising the crucified Jesus from the dead that God defines himself, in *The Crucified God* it is his self-abandonment on the cross which contitutes the heart of his self-definition. The cross *contradicts* all other concepts of God, and so this theological starting-point obliges the theologian to distinguish sharply between the crucified God and all other gods (CG 196). Thus Moltmann's polemical distinguishing of biblical Christianity from 'theism' (natural theology) and bourgeois religion is sharpened as its basis moves from the resurrection of the crucified Christ to the cross of the risen Christ (cf. UZ 146).

*The Crucified God* is a complex work, in which a number of major themes are intertwined and not easy to unravel. A useful over-simplification might be to think of the argument as having three interconnected levels: Christian praxis in the world, soteriology, and the doctrine of God. Each level is rooted in the next, with the doctrine of God forming the deepest level of the argument, and very roughly the book moves from praxis through soteriology to the doctrine of God and then back from the doctrine of God through soteriology to praxis. One of the difficulties of the book is that it is so structured that Moltmann's understanding of soteriology is nowhere presented in a comprehensive statement. It develops throughout the book, and has to be assembled from its component parts which are scattered in various sections of the book.[7]

What I have called soteriology is much more broadly defined by Moltmann than in traditional dogmatics. At least since 1967 (DTH 229) he had been attempting to extend the soteriological significance of the cross to embrace 'both the question of human guilt and man's liberation from it, and also the question of human suffering and man's redemption from it' (CG 134). The two issues of justification and theodicy can be subsumed under the question of God's righteousness, which, in a juridical metaphor which Moltmann adopts also in the titles of chapters IV and V, makes the issue of a theology of the cross 'the universal trial concerning the righteousness of God, a trial which is the ultimate motive force of human history' (CG 134, cf. 174). Already in *Theology of Hope* (207) Moltmann had understood justification to involve not only the question of the sinner's righteousness before God, but also the question of God's righteousness, and to be an anticipatory fragment of the coming universal righteousness of God's kingdom. It was therefore not difficult for him to unite the existential dimension of salvation as justification and the universal historical dimension of salvation as theodicy (CG 178) in the question of God's righteousness in the world. Consequently, throughout *The*

*Crucified God*, Moltmann uses the double expression 'godlessness and godforsakenness' to refer to the plight of the world without divine righteousness and to the human situation with which the crucified Christ was identified. The divine righteousness which is at issue here is then shown, in the ministry and fate of Jesus, to be the righteousness of grace, i.e. unconditional love which at the cost of divine suffering accepts the unrighteous and identifies with the forsaken. Moltmann's attempt to keep both aspects – justification and theodicy – in view is reasonably successful in chapters IV and V, but in chapter VI the theodicy issue occupies the centre of the stage, primarily because it is with this issue that the modern problematic of the doctrine of God – the main theme of chapter VI – is closely involved.

Chapter I of *The Crucified God* presents an interesting contrast with chapter I of *Theology of Hope*, in which Moltmann found the point of entry to his theme in the purely theological debate about eschatology and revelation. In *The Crucified God* he starts instead with the double-sided crisis in which he sees Christian existence in the world involved. This is the crisis of identity and involvement:

> The more theology and the church attempt to become relevant to the problems of the present day, the more deeply they are drawn into the crisis of their own Christian identity. The more they attempt to assert their identity in traditional dogmas, rights and moral notions, the more irrelevant and unbelievable they become (CG 7).

One could have thought of more direct ways into the central issues of the book, for example by raising at once the problem of suffering posed by the horrors of modern history. But Moltmann's way-in not only reflects one of the ways by which he himself had been led through the issues raised by his own political theology in the 1960s into a theology of the cross; it also allows him to move from the actual issues posed by contemporary Christian praxis into the central theological discussion of the book and then back into issues of praxis in the final chapter. On the one hand, this represents the problem of suffering not as a theoretical issue for armchair theology, but as directly concerning Christian praxis in solidarity with the suffering. On the other hand, it shows how the kind of Christian involvement with the world which Moltmann's theology advocates cannot cut loose from its specifically Christian allegiance and dissolve theology into politics or sociology. Moltmann has never seen the question of the relevance of theology or the Church to the modern world as a matter of adapting or assimilating the Gospel or the Church to the world, but rather as a matter of that critical openness to the world that faithfulness to the Gospel itself demands. Christian theology does not become relevant by allowing itself to be determined by its contemporary context, but by being faithful to its own determining centre and criterion, which is the crucified Christ (cf. CG 2–3). In this way it finds its relevance in having something *different* to say to the world in *solidarity with* the world. The following quotation encapsulates much of the way in which Moltmann's method in *The Crucified God* aims to find the contemporary relevance of the Christian faith in doing justice to the theological heart of the Christian faith:

> Sharing in the sufferings of this time, Christian theology is truly contemporary theology. Whether or not it can be so depends less upon the openness of theologians and their theories to the world and more upon whether they have honestly and without reserve come to terms with the death-cry of Jesus for God (CG 153).

Hence in chapter I the double-sided dilemma of identity and involvements leads, in Moltmann's argument, to its resolution in the theology of the cross. Christian involvement in the world seems to lead to mere assimilation to the world and, conversely, the attempt to preserve Christian identity leads to sectarian withdrawal from the world, until Christian faith in the crucified Christ is seen to be the source both of Christian identity and of Christian solidarity with others. Christian identity lies in identification with the Crucified, which entails identification with those with whom the Crucified was identified in his death. But this is only understandable if identification or solidarity represents a way beyond either assimilation or withdrawal, as it does in Moltmann's exposition of the dialectical principle of identification with those who are unlike oneself. This is the principle of God's loving identification with the godless and the godforsaken in the crucified Christ. Thus the contemporary crisis of Christian praxis – the crisis, in a sense, of Moltmann's political theology – in fact leads him directly to a fundamental aspect of his understanding of the cross: that God reveals himself in his opposite (in the godlessness and godforsakenness of the cross) in order to be known by those who are unlike himself, the godless and the godforsaken. Thus the stark negativity of the cross is precisely the way in which God's love embraces the negative, reaching sinners and those who suffer.

After this introduction, chapter II begins the book's main sequence of argument. Its aim is to allow 'the unique, the particular and the scandalous' in the cross (CG 41) to reemerge from behind the religious interpretations of it. The method is a favourite one (cf. TH I; CPS II.1, III.1) in which Moltmann discusses critically a series of theological interpretations, arranged in an order of progressively greater adequacy, before concluding with a preliminary account of the theology of the cross, as put forward by Paul and Luther, which it is the aim of the book to take further. The enquiry has to be pursued beyond 'the word of the cross' as it is found in Paul and Luther, because this has the crucified Christ himself as its inner criterion by which it must be tested (CG 75). After chapter II, therefore, Moltmann moves to the foundation of a theology of the cross in the crucified Christ himself, thereby both verifying and extending the Pauline and Lutheran insights. This involves him, first of all, in chapter III, in the question of the proper approach to Christology, which combines the particular history of Jesus ('the Jesus of history') with his universal significance expressed in the Christological titles ('the Christ of faith'). The twofold task of Christology is the critical verification of its historical origin – in the person and history of Jesus – and the critical verification of its universal significance – in its consequences for present and future. This sets the agenda for much of the rest of the book, given that the really critical point at which the *combination* of the two aspects must be tested is Jesus' death on the cross. Christologies stand or fall by their ability to give universal significance to the Jesus who died on the cross in the way that, historically, he did. By this criterion Moltmann finds the major forms of patristic and modern German Christology wanting. This is the cross functioning as the 'criticism of Christian theology', 'the source of a permanent iconoclasm of the christological icons of the Church and the portraits of Jesus in Christianity' (CG 87), which, because they are constructed to suit people's own desires (83), cannot accommodate the real scandal of Jesus' death.

This clears the ground for chapters IV and V, which are the biblical-theological centre of the book. Here Moltmann pursues, in his own way and with a focus on the cross, the 'new quest' of the historical Jesus in which many of his colleagues in New Testament studies were engaged, and also continues (as in *Theology of Hope*) his concentration on Pauline theology, with attention now also to Markan theology.[8] In these chapters Moltmann is attempting to understand the death of Jesus in the light both of his ministry and of his resurrection. The need for both these perspectives arises from Moltmann's fundamental principle of the identity of the crucified and risen Jesus (CG 112), which here gives rise to a double reading of history 'forwards', in the manner of historical narration, and 'backwards', from the perspective of its eschatological significance (see DTH 215–29; HP 42; CG 113,184). An historical reading of history 'forwards' needs to be supplemented by the 'reversed sense of time' which reads history 'backwards' from the eschatological future.[9]

In terms of history and its sense of time, Jesus first died and was then raised. In eschatological terms the last becomes the first: he died as the risen Christ and was made flesh as the one who was to come. In historical terms Christ can be called the *anticipation* of the coming God on the basis of his resurrection from the dead. In eschatological terms, however, he must be called the *incarnation* of the coming God in our flesh and in his death on the cross (CG 184).

This is why, in the thinking of the early church, the resurrection of Jesus did not simply cancel out the cross and the message of the resurrection did not leave the cross behind. If God had acted in raising Jesus from the dead, the perplexing question of his activity in the cross of Jesus necessarily arose. The same logic as led Paul and Mark to their theologies of the cross leads Moltmann to his.

Chapters IV and V establish, historically and eschatologically, Moltmann's radical interpretation of the cross as an abandonment of God by God. This leads beyond soteriology into the doctrine of God in chapter VI. But then in the light of the 'revolution' in the concept of God argued in chapter VI, the working out of salvation becomes a matter of human life in the new situation of the crucified God and of

world history in the process of God's trinitarian life. The argument
must therefore be completed by a move towards praxis in both the
psychological (chapter VII) and the political (chapter VIII) spheres.
Moltmann's political theology now becomes a theology of *liberation*
(the term which had been popularised in black and Latin American
theology) rooted in the theology of the cross.[10]

**Luther and critical theory**   Moltmann understands the cross as the
criterion of Christianity, in the sense of Luther's epigram, *Crux probat
omnia* ('The cross is the criterion of all things': CG 7), and as the
criticism of Christianity (CG 2) and society (CG 317), in the sense of
the critical theory of the Frankfurt school.[11] His turning to Luther's
theology of the cross is not surprising. His earlier theology was
indebted not so much to Luther as to the Reformed theology of his
own denominational allegiance and his historical-theological study,
while his approach to political and social reality belongs more obviously in the Reformed than in the Lutheran tradition. But Luther's
dialectical mode of theological thinking, combined with his radical
theology of the cross,[12] proved highly congenial to Moltmann, who in
*The Crucified God* takes over and extends Luther's central theses on the
theology of the cross.

In the *Heidelberg Disputation* (1518) Luther contrasted his *theologia
crucis* with the theology of glory (*theologia gloriae*), a term which sums
up his objections to late medieval Scholastic theology. The two terms
represent two approaches to the knowledge of God: the theologian of
glory perceives the glory of God, his power, wisdom and goodness,
manifest in the works of creation, while the theologian of the cross
perceives God hidden in the suffering and humiliation of the cross.
Luther does not deny that, in theory, there is a natural knowledge of
God to be had from the created world, but he insists that in the
soteriological context in which we, as sinners, must know God, it is in
practice useless. Indeed, it is worse than useless, because the sinner
distorts it to create an idol who supports his own attempts at self-
justification and self-deification by moral and intellectual achievement.
But God's revelation of himself in the *cross* provides a quite different
way of knowing God, which cannot be misused in the interests of
human self-exaltation. The cross shatters all human presuppositions
about divinity and human illusions about how God may be known.

In the cross God is not revealed in the power and glory which natural reason recognises as divine, as the kind of God the sinner would like to be like. Rather he is revealed in the very opposite of divinity, in human disgrace, poverty, suffering and death, in what seems to us weakness and foolishness. To recognise God in the crucified Christ is therefore to realise that God is not truly knowable to those who pride themselves on their progress towards divine wisdom and goodness, but can only be known at the point where human wisdom is silenced and human ethical achievements are worthless. 'To know God in the cross of Christ is a crucifying form of knowledge, because it shatters everything to which a man can hold and on which he can build, both his works and his knowledge of reality, and precisely in so doing sets us free' (CG 212). It sets us free from the dehumanising compulsion to set ourselves up as gods, and makes us truly human again, able to acknowledge our weakness and our need of justification, since we see that it is in the crucified humanity of Jesus that God meets us and accepts us in his love. The human God makes sinners intent on self-deification human again: 'he makes us of the same form as himself and crucifies us by making us true men instead of unhappy and proud gods' (Luther, quoted CG 212–13).

Moltmann observes that Luther's concern with the interest that guides knowledge of God marks a transition from a 'pure theory' to a 'critical theory' of God (UZ 135; CG 69, 208), which uncovers the use to which knowledge of God is put and its practical effects in human life. The terminology, of course, Moltmann borrows from the critical theory of the Frankfurt school, of whose members Theodor Adorno, Max Horkheimer and Herbert Marcuse are the writers to whom Moltmann pays most attention. From them he learned to ask of all theory, 'Whose interests does it serve?' (cf. TJ 31), and to distinguish a positivistic 'theory of what is' (cf. CG 67) which justifies the *status quo* and benefits the ruling class, from a 'critical theory' which destroys illusions and exposes the falsity of existing society and its values. These concerns are essentially continuous with the orientation of the theology of hope towards criticism and transformation of the status quo, but the Frankfurt school's emphasis on the 'negative dialectics' of criticism fits the attention Moltmann came to give to the cross as the iconoclastic element in Christian faith, smashing the idols and contradicting accepted values. Just as Moltmann's theology of hope had aimed to be a Christian *parallel* to Bloch's Marxist theory-praxis, so Moltmann's theology of the cross aims to be a Christian *parallel* to the critical theory of the Frankfurt school. It is the crucified Christ who unmasks ideology in church, theology and society, and who constitutes the 'scandal of the qualitative difference' (Marcuse) between the unfree and the free world, between false and true life (CG 173, cf. 68; CCR 20–21). 'Because of its subject, the theology of the cross, right down to its method and practice, can only be polemical, dialectical, antithetical and critical theory' (CG 69). (For Moltmann's use of the terminology of critical theory with reference to the cross, see also HP 37, 40–41; UZ 143: HFM 59; CCR 38; CG 2–3, 24, 67–68, 72, 283–4.)

Luther made the theology of the cross a critical theory in relation to the teaching and the power structure of the late medieval church, but failed to formulate it as a social and political criticism against the oppressive society of his day (CG 72). In fact, he abused the theology of the cross in the interests of the oppressors, when he called on the peasants to accept their suffering as their cross.

> Instead, a sermon on the cross would have done the princes and the bourgeoisie who ruled them a great deal of good, if it was aimed at setting them free from their pride and moving them to an attitude of solidarity with their victims (CG 49).

It is Moltmann's alliance between Luther's theology of the cross and critical theory which enables him to turn Luther's critical theology against himself in this way and to insist on the inescapable political dimension of the theology of the cross (CG 72–73).

**The dialectic of the cross** The critical theology of the cross which Moltmann derives from Luther and critical theory involves what he calls the 'dialectical principle of knowledge.' Ostensibly he takes this from Hippocrates, Anaxagoras, Schelling[13] and Bloch (CG 27, 31 n. 22; DGG 188: FC 78), but he finds it exemplified in Luther's theology of the cross (cf. CG 212–3), and the latter has more to do with the way he actually uses it. He contrasts this epistemological principle ('like is known by unlike') with the analogical principle of knowledge ('like is known by like') and sees them as the principles respectively of the theology of the cross and natural theology (Luther's 'theology of glory'). Strictly applied, the analogical principle would mean that God is known only by God. But the analogical method of theology proceeds by seeking to know God from the analogies to him in the world, his nature reflected in his works: God is revealed in what is like him (CG 26–27, 68). By contrast the dialectical method finds God in his opposite: God is revealed in Christ's abandonment by God on the cross. The motive behind the analogical method is self-deification: man seeks to know God in order to become like God. By contrast, the dialectical knowledge of God in the cross is possible only for those who abandon every kind of self-deification and find God where he had made himself like them: godless and godforsaken (CG 27).

The precise meaning of this concept of 'revelation in the opposite' is not immediately clear, and it has therefore caused some puzzlement and confusion (cf. DGG 47–48, 143–4, 152, 158, 188–9). If it means literally that God is revealed by what is opposite to him then it is hard to see either how a revelation of God could be recognised or how anything of God would be revealed. To take one of Schelling's examples quoted by Moltmann (CG 27), how is love revealed only in hatred? The example is appropriate because Moltmann believes that God 'himself is love with all his being' (CG 205). The statement 'love is revealed only in hatred' – or, as Moltmann corrects it, 'love is in actual fact revealed in hatred' (FC 78)[14] – cannot mean that hatred is a revelation of the love of God. It must mean that love is revealed *in the context* of hatred. This is certainly its meaning when Moltmann adopts it to characterise Christian love (CG 18): love comes into its own when it is tested in the encounter with hatred. Applied to the cross this would mean that the full extent of God's love is revealed only in Christ's suffering at the hands of men who hate him. Certainly this is part of Moltmann's meaning, for he says of the unconditional love which is God:

> As its purpose is freedom, it is directed towards freedom. So it cannot prohibit slavery and enmity, but must suffer this contradiction, and can only take upon itself grief at this contradiction and the grief of protest against it. . . . That is what happened on the cross of Christ. God is unconditional love, because he takes on himself grief at the contradiction in men and does not angrily suppress this contradiction. . . . God suffers, God allows

himself to be crucified and is crucified, and in this consummates his unconditional love. . . . The fact of this love can be contradicted. It can be crucified, but in crucifixion it finds its fulfilment and becomes love of the enemy. Thus its suffering proves to be stronger than hate (CG 248–9).

In that case 'revelation in the opposite' means that God is revealed where he is seen to be contradicted by his opposite, where his love suffers the contradiction of hatred.

However, the form in which Moltmann most frequently applies the principle is this: God is revealed in the godforsakenness of Christ's dying on the cross, or in the godlessness of the cross (CG 27). This paradox is understood primarily in terms of the incarnate God's solidarity with sinners: God 'enters into the situation of man's godforsakenness' (CG 276); 'God is on the cross of Jesus "for us", and through that becomes the God and Father of the godless and the godforsaken' (CG 192). Here we are closer to what the dialectical principle means for Moltmann: it is the epistemological corollary of the nature of God's love. God loves what is unlike himself; he loves the godless and the godforsaken. And the love of God reaches godless people when the Son of God empties himself and identifies with them, becoming 'the brother of the despised, abandoned and oppressed' (CG 24). The cross therefore reveals God in his loving identification with godforsaken men and women. God is revealed in his opposite because he is love which identifies with what is alien to him and finds his identity in self-emptying solidarity with others (cf. CG 17–18, 213–4). Similarly, the analogical principle is the epistemological principle corresponding to the social principle of friendship with those who are like oneself (CG 26). It was probably a mistake for Moltmann to try to put the cross under some *general* dialectical principle of knowledge. The principle he is concerned with is one which corresponds to the nature of God's love and makes sense as applicable to this love and to the same kind of love in human relationships. The other paradoxes of the cross – the almighty God in a helpless man, the righteous God in a man condemned by the law (CG 190) – are not additional illustrations of a general principle, but also derive from the nature of God's love. The love of God is most powerful in the helplessness of the cross; the righeousness of God is the righteousness of his unconditional love in justifying those whom the law condemns (FC 78).

We have not yet, however, entirely clarified the dialectical principle in its application to the cross. How is the death of Jesus seen to be not merely the death of a godless man but the form of God's love for godless men and women? Moltmann distinguishes identification with what is alien from assimilation to what is alien (CG 25–26, 28). In self-emptying love the Son of God abandoned his divine identity and entered the situation of godless men and women, adopting both the weight of their godforsakenness and the cry of the godforsaken to God. He did this for the sake of the godless, out of the creative love which makes righteous the unrighteous and brings new life to the dying and liberation to the oppressed. Thus he died not as another godless man, but as one who took the side of the godless. So the godless do not recognise him as one of themselves, just another condemned criminal or another innocent victim. Rather, they recognise him as one who in love became their brother (CG 50–51). His godforsakenness is his loving solidarity with them.

But how can he be recognised as such? Not from the cross in isolation, but from the cross understood in its context both of Jesus' earthly life and of his resurrection. Here the argument of chapters IV and V comes into play. 'Jesus did not suffer passively from the world in which he lived, but incited it against himself by his message and the life he lived' (CG 51), i.e. his message of God's justifying grace for the godless and his life of fellowship with sinners. His death was the result of a life of proclaiming God to be on the side of the godless and so making their enemies his enemies. Here we approach the notion of representative death 'for' sinners, but Moltmann does not allow this to be concluded from the life of the pre-Easter Jesus alone. The life and death of Jesus must be illuminated by his resurrection. 'Only in the light of his resurrection from the dead does his death gain that special, unique saving significance which it cannot achieve otherwise, even in the light of the life he lived' (CG 182). The death of Jesus is understood to be the death of the Christ, the Son of God, only in the light of his resurrection. It therefore becomes evident that God is seen to be revealed in the abandonment of Jesus on the cross only when in the light of both his earthly life and his resurrection Jesus is seen to be the incarnation of the coming God. The theology of the cross must read the history of Jesus 'forwards' and 'backwards' before it may begin to comprehend the God who 'reveals himself in his opposite' on the cross.

Although Moltmann contrasts the dialectical principle with the analogical principle, he does not intend the former simply to replace the latter. Rather the dialectical principle makes the analogical principle possible (CG 27; FC 79; DGG 189). Only through God's revelation of himself in his opposite, in the cross, can he be known to the godless and the godforsaken. But this knowledge of God brings them into correspondence with God and gives them, in contrast to the false ambition of idolatrous self-deification, the hope of true likeness to God (CG 27). Although Moltmann does not quite do so (cf. CG 231), one might radicalise the old soteriological epigram of the Fathers ('he became man so that we might become God') in terms of the theology of the cross: he became like us, in godlessness and godforsakenness, so that we might become like him in his eschatological glory (cf. TJ 61–62).

This makes it, finally, clear how closely related the dialectical principle of knowledge is to Moltmann's fundamental dialectic of cross and resurrection (cf. already TH 57). In the cross, which corresponds to the godforsaken reality of the world as it is, God is necessarily revealed in his opposite. But the resurrection, which contradicts the world as it is because it contradicts the cross, is the promise of the world's transformation into *correspondence with* God in the new creation, when 'natural theology', with its analogical principle, will at last be valid. The identity of the crucified and risen Jesus, an identity in total contradiction, is already in *Theology of Hope* the promise of the world's transformation from godforsakenness to the glory of God. *The Crucified God* deepens this notion. Jesus who was raised into the glory of the coming God is in his cross the incarnate God who identifies with godless and godforsaken people so as to bring the new life of the resurrection to them in their situation. 'Through his suffering and death, the risen Christ brings righteousness and life to the unrighteous and the dying' (CG 185). The promise of God reaches the godless and the godforsaken through the incarnate God's solidarity with them in his identifying and suffering love. Thus Moltmann's supplementing of the dialectic of the cross and the resurrection in *Theology of Hope* with the dialectic of revelation in the opposite or love for the alien in *The*

*Crucified God* is a way of supplementing the promise of God, the salvific theme of *Theology of Hope*, with the salvific theme of *The Crucified God:* God's solidarity, in suffering love, with sinners and those who suffer.

This also implies directly the starkest scandal of the cross and the strictly theological consequence which Moltmann develops in chapter VI. God in the crucified Jesus identifies with those who are abandoned by God and thus reveals himself in the abandonment of God by God. Only so can he be known to and his love reach the godforsaken (DGG 178). But then the absolute contradiction of abandonment by God and nearness to God, which the crucified and risen Jesus sustains in the identity given him by his Father who abandons him and raises him, is taken into the being of God himself (cf. CG 246). The dialectic of cross and resurrection thus gives rise to a trinitarian dialectic of 'God against God', the Father abandoning the Son, on the cross. The soteriological dialectic is at the same time a dialectic of the divine being which requires the 'revolution in the concept of God' which Moltmann attempts in chapter VI of *The Crucified God* and which we shall examine more closely in the next chapter.

**The iconoclasm of the cross** There is yet another aspect of the dialectical nature of the revelation of God in the cross: in the cross God is revealed as contrary to the false gods of the law, political religion, and natural theology (CG 68–69). Moltmann works throughout the book with this trio of idols whom the crucified God contradicts, thereby liberating humanity from enslavement to them.[15] This is the dialectic of the cross as 'negative dialectic', destroying the religious illusions by which the world is sanctioned and maintained in its present state of untruth. It is also the theology of the cross as the radical Christian realisation of the Old Testament prohibition of images (CCR 35–36, 40; EH 112; CG 284), and therefore it can take up the modern critique of idolatry, in the interests of human liberation, by Feuerbach, Marx, Freud and the Frankfurt school (cf. CG 38, 224, 283–4, 296–7; CCR 38–39; EH 113). Not least in the Church and theology the permanent criticism of idolatry by the cross of Christ is needed, against the constant Christian tendency to substitute a false god for the crucified God. Moltmann characteristically stresses the absolute distinction between the crucified God and every version of the 'counter-God' whom he contradicts: there can be no gradation but only contradiction between the two (CG 196, 201).

Since Jesus was crucified as a blasphemer against the law by the guardians of the law and vindicated by his Father in his resurrection, the God of Jesus Christ must be distinguished from the god of the law – or, more correctly, the god of a false interpretation of the law (CG 133, 135), the god who sanctions self-justification by works-righteousness. (Whether Moltmann's strongly Lutheran interpretation of Jesus' relationship to the Judaism of his day is historically justified cannot be discussed here, but it cannot fairly be labelled potentially anti-Semitic,[16] as Moltmann's discussion in CG 134–5 makes quite clear.) Moltmann follows Luther very closely in treating legalism as idolatry: the person who wants to justify himself by works idolises his own achievements and becomes a slave to this idol, to the compulsion to justify himself by his works. His anxiety leads him to project his desire for self-confirmation and security in the form of a god who sanctions his self-justification and holds him under his law by fear (cf. EH 112; CCR 36–37). Going beyond Luther in a psychological analysis of idolatry, Moltmann connects it also with inability to accept the 'other', those who are different from oneself. The idol is the projection of the person's anxiety to confirm his own existence. Enslaved to this idol he can only accept people who are like himself, who worship his idol and help to confirm him. Those who live very differently threaten his idolised self. The 'inner compulsion to idolise the self is a cramping self-justification that invariably leads to the oppression of those who are "other" ' (CCR 37; cf. CG 302).

The crucified God liberates people from the idols of legalism. In him people find the gracious love of God who accepts those who are alien. Through the painful contradiction of their idolatrous self-image people are set free from the anxiety that underlies it, learn to accept themselves and to accept the 'others'.

Moltmann extends Luther's analysis of the idolatry of legalistic religion to a critique of the idolatry of *political* religion (see especially UZ 143–44; PR; CCR; EH VIII; CG 195–96, 325–29).[17] Jesus was crucified 'in the name of the state gods of Rome who assured the Pax Romana' (CG 136), and behind the misunderstanding involved in his condemnation as a political rebel lay a deeper recognition of the threat which his message of God's unconditional grace posed to all political religion – to the politics of the Zealot rebels as well as to those of Rome (CG 136–45). Political religion occurs wherever religion serves to integrate society and to sanctify the existing political and social system. It is religion as self-confirmation on a social or national scale, in which the society absolutises itself and excludes or oppresses the 'others'. Although early Christianity opposed all political religion, in subsequent history Christianity has often fulfilled the functions of political religion, and can do so even today as the supposedly nonpolitical religion of bourgeois society, which in fact provides 'for the symbolic integration of society and its homogenization and self-confirmation' (EH 103). There is also a kind of political idolatry (whether explicitly religious or not) in the absolutising of rulers, in which an alienating desire for security leads to a pattern of domination and enslavement like that of legalistic religion. This can happen even in democracies when 'the representatives go over the heads of those whom they are meant to represent' (CG 328; cf. EH 114). The idolatrous absolutising of political realities takes many forms, explicitly religious and overtly secular, conservative and also radical, as when progressive political movements absolutise the future society which is their aim (cf. CG 17, 38, 252, 323).

The crucified God who died in powerlessness at the hands of the political powers can never serve as a religious sanction for political power:

> Glory no longer rests upon the heads of the mighty. For believers, Christ crucified was made the righteousness of God, and for them political authority was deprived of its religious sanctions. Christ, crucified in powerlessness and shame, has become their highest authority. Consequently, they no longer believe in religiopolitical authority, for the anxiety and fear that demanded it has been eliminated (CCR 35; cf. CG 195).

The cross destroys any justification of political authority 'from above' and the monarchical or hierarchical structures which result, and permits only political authority 'from below' and the radical democratisation of political life (CG 328: EH 112; CCR 40). The 'stateless and classless God' (CG 329) of the cross requires of Christians 'a witnessing non-identification with the demands and interests of society' (CG 17) and, as its corollary, political solidarity with the 'others', those who are the victims of the dominant political religion and its compulsive need for self-confirmation (EH 116–17). 'With the cross, the future of God allies itself with those whom a self-satisfied and conformist society has reduced to nothing' (CCR 43; cf. FC 102; M 117).

Political religion is 'the practical side of natural theology' (UZ 143; cf. CG 196, 215), since the God of natural theology or 'theism' is the God of the existing state of the world, who sanctions the status quo in nature and society. Moltmann's critique of natural theology, in terms of its contradiction by the cross, has several facets, of which we have already noticed some in Luther's attack on 'the theology of glory.' But the issue comes down especially to the question of the concept of divine nature which was part of patristic and traditional theology's inheritance from Platonic philosophy. Theism – as Moltmann uses this term in the sense of the traditional metaphysical concept of God – defines God's infinity over against humanity's finiteness: the indivisible, immutable, impassible, immortal, omnipotent God is contrasted with finite, mortal, weak, suffering, threatened humanity. Moltmann interprets this concept of God as a projection of 'the religious need of finite, threatened and mortal man for security in a higher omnipotence and authority' (CG 214). In particular, suffering and death must be excluded from the divine being so that humanity, in its helplessness before the threat of chaos and nothingness, can find support and security in God. But the cross cannot be reconciled with this concept of a God who cannot suffer or die (CG 214), and the early Church's attempt to effect such a reconciliation in the two-natures Christology Moltmann judges a failure (CG 227–31). In fact, the cross exposes this concept of God as 'tantamount to idolatry' (CG 250), and brings liberation from its projection of childish needs for authoritarian protection (CG 216).

Thus the God who suffers and dies on the cross contradicts the impassible God of metaphysical theism. Similarly, and in close connexion with this, as we shall see in the next chapter, the God who in the event of the cross is trinitarian contradicts the God of philosophical and general religious monotheism (CG 235–36, 247). On this contradiction of all other concepts of God Moltmann bases his attempt to understand God's being from the death of Jesus on the cross. But this demands also a corresponding concept of salvation, just as every form of idolatry involves a correlative understanding of humanity and human salvation. Against the idolatry of self-justification by works, the crucified God represents liberation through his unconditional grace to the godless. Against the idolatry of political religion, the crucified God represents liberation through loving solidarity with the victims of society. Against the idolatry of theistic religion, which seeks freedom from suffering and death through participation in a god who cannot suffer and die, the crucified God represents liberation from suffering and death through loving solidarity with those who suffer. The last point will be further explained in the final section of this chapter.

**Camus and protest atheism**  The fundamental problem of theism, for Moltmann, is the problem of theodicy:[18] how can an all-powerful and invulnerable creator and ruler of the world be justified in the face of suffering? If such a god is not to function as a justification for suffering, silencing all protest against suffering and inculcating meek submission to suffering, then there must be rebellion against him in the name of goodness and righteousness. So theism has as its counterpart 'the only serious atheism' (CG 252; cf. EH 50), the atheism of protest. Thus Moltmann takes up, in chapter VI of *The Crucified God*, not only theism but also the atheism which rejects theism, in order to find in the crucified God a way beyond both theism and atheism and an understanding of God that neither suppresses nor evades the problem of suffering.

For his understanding of protest atheism, Moltmann turns especially to Albert Camus' analysis of it. Just as the influence of Bloch in *Theology of Hope* is greater than a reader unacquainted with Bloch's work would suspect from the few explicit references to him, so Camus's great work *L'homme révolté*[19] has influenced *The Crucified God* more than might appear on the surface.[20] To some extent Camus here replaces Bloch as Moltmann's atheistic dialogue-partner, and the reason for this is that Moltmann is now able to place Bloch in a tradition of thinkers whom, following Camus, he reproaches for having 'overlooked the dark side of evil in man and the problem of suffering in the world' (CG 252).[21]

Two aspects of Camus' work especially interested Moltmann: his analysis of the 'metaphysical rebellion' which lies at the root of all the revolutionary history of the modern age, and his attempt to explain how this rebellion so betrayed itself as to issue in the horrors of modern history, both in Nazism and in Stalinism. As Camus sees it, the original rebellion of modern thought against the injustice and absurdity of the human condition contained not only the negative element of a rejection of the world as it is, but also a positive affirmation of value, a sense of human dignity and human solidarity from which the desire for justice in the face of the world's injustice arose. But in the philosophical and political developments, from Hegel and Nietzsche to Stalinism and Nazism, which created political revolution out of metaphysical rebellion, the original positive element in rebellion succumbed to the triumph of nihilism. As a result, the rebel has become as oppressive and murderous a tyrant as the tyrants against whom he originally rebelled. Camus (like many modern writers) uses the figure of Ivan Karamazov, in Dostoevsky's novel, as the archetype of metaphysical rebellion, and finds the later historical developments foreshadowed in the fact that Ivan, whose rebellion begins in a principled refusal to accept that the suffering of an innocent child could ever be justified, himself betrays the generous origins of rebellion by embracing nihilism (HR 76–83). In tracing the logic of this betrayal, Camus is posing the problem: How can the positive element in which metaphysical rebellion originates be maintained? How can one stay faithful to the spirit of revolt without lapsing into nihilism? In more concrete political terms, how can one resist the inhuman conditions in which human beings suffer and die without producing a regime which itself imposes such conditions?

Moltmann too is concerned with these questions in chapter VI of *The Crucified God*,[22] and although he takes a different route from Camus' in attempting to answer them, he is much indebted to Camus' analysis of the problem. It is important to see that Moltmann is therefore wrestling with the problem of suffering in a form which has both metaphysical and political dimensions. The atheism which stems from metaphysical rebellion rejected God as a response to the classic problem of theodicy, as a protest against suffering, but went on to inspire revolutionary movements which pose a new problem of suffering: the problem of how the revolt against suffering can be maintained and take political form in the face of political nihilism. The problem as Camus poses it therefore engages equally Moltmann the theologian concerned with the classic issue of theodicy, which the suffering of the modern age makes no less urgent, and Moltmann the political theologian, for whom theology must entail political praxis for overcoming the misery of the world. But whereas in the political theology which developed out of the theology of hope in the 1960s Moltmann was largely content to develop a Christian theological parallel to Marxism, an initiative for revolutionary political change to overcome suffering, he is now more aware of the problem of the suffering which even 'the societies which call themselves Marxist' (CG 223) impose. It is not enough to see the modern revolutionary movements of hope as forms of biblical messianism which have emigrated from the Church. The tendency of modern messianism to betray its own hopeful origins – which Camus exposes and which came home to Moltmann especially sharply when Russian troops suppressed the Czech experiment in 'socialism with a human face' – suggested to Moltmann that neither Marx nor Bloch (CG 252), nor even his own political theology in its claim to be 'the practical answering of the theodicy problem' (FH 47–48), had yet probed the problem of evil and suffering deeply enough. Though Moltmann, whose theology has retained a greater affinity with Marxism than Camus' philosophy ever had, is not as severe as Camus in his condemnation even of Soviet communism (cf. EH 87, 98–99), there runs through chapter VI of *The Crucified God* a milder version of Camus' sense that the modern age's revolt against injustice has betrayed itself (cf. especially CG 251–52). Previously, Moltmann had spoken of a 'history of revolutions for freedom', in which the shortcomings and failures of each provide the starting-point for the next, in a continual struggle for ever greater freedom (RRF 70–77). In *The Crucified God* the modern age appears in a rather darker light, as the age of 'the hells of Auschwitz, Hiroshima and Vietnam' (220). Consequently, political theology must now have its roots in a deeper theological treatment of the problem of suffering. It is with this that Moltmann is primarily concerned in chapter VI of *The Crucified God*, but it would be a mistake to miss the political dimension which Moltmann deliberately takes over from Camus.

For Camus, metaphysical rebellion has two enemies: Christianity and nihilism. Christianity both prevented the emergence of metaphysical rebellion until modern times and, at the beginning of the modern age, provoked its emergence as rebellion against the God of Christianity. In *L'homme révolté* Camus discusses Christianity only in this way, as the historical background from which metaphysical rebellion emerged. Most of his attention is given to the way in which atheistic rebellion succumbs to atheistic nihilism. However, for Moltmann's reading of Camus in *The Crucified God*, the relationships of metaphysical rebellion both to Christianity and to nihilism are equally important and, as in Camus, they are interrelated. The two fundamental and connected arguments which Moltmann adopts from Camus are as follows. First, metaphysical rebellion came about as protest against the God who, as all-powerful ruler of the world, can be held responsible for its condition. (For Camus, this is the biblical God, but for Moltmann, he is the god of 'theism'.) In a sense, metaphysical rebellion presupposes such a god: 'For its protest against injustice and death, does it not need an authority to accuse, because it makes this authority responsible for the state of affairs?' (CG 221; cf. HP 34; HR 46). Hence the atheism which flows from metaphysical rebellion and which is seen in exemplary form in Ivan Karamazov does not, in the first place, deny the existence of God so much as assert that the world for which he can be held responsible is unacceptable (cf. HR 40). The innocent suffering of even a single child is too high a price to pay for the achievement of any purpose God might be supposed to have for the world, as Ivan asserts in the famous argument quoted by Moltmann (CG 220). For the God who presides over such a world as this no theodicy is possible. But since this God, in traditional religion, is the divine sanction for the injustices of the *ancien régime*, the rebel who wishes to overthrow unjust conditions must destroy the God who is held responsible for them. The regicides of the French Enlightenment are succeeded by the deicides of German philosophy and the Russian Revolution. Hence there follows the second basic argument which Moltmann takes over from Camus: that metaphysical rebellion against God leads to metaphysical revolution in which humanity replaces God (HR 41–42). Humanity must take control of its own destiny in order to replace the unjust world of the dead God with its own new world of human justice. But in order to subject history to this purpose, the revolutionary group or the party in fact steps into the divine role and makes use of any means to this all-justifying end. The terrible paradox which results is that the innocent suffering which, in Ivan's argument, no divine purpose could justify, is now justified by the revolutionary purpose of finally establishing justice. The appeal to justice which first functioned, in metaphysical rebellion, to render innocent suffering unjustifiable, now functions, in metaphysical revolution, to justify the infliction of innocent suffering. In the revolutionary regime the party silences revolt quite as effectively as God did in the *ancien régime*. The divinisation of humanity in place of God makes politics religion and the state a divine absolute, whose tyranny is even more oppressive than the old divine right monarchy. All this Moltmann takes from Camus (see CG 223, 251–52; cf. M 56–57, 106; EH 117–18).

He interprets it in his own way. The god against whom metaphysical rebellion is directed is, of course, the god of political religion, and, more fundamentally, the god of theism, the apathetic, omnipotent god of the cosmological argument. Both theism and protest atheism depend on a logical inference from the world to God, but whereas theism finds the world to be a mirror of the power and wisdom of its creator, protest atheism finds it impossible to believe that such a world as this could be grounded in a good and righteous god: 'in the broken mirror of an unjust and absurd world of triumphant evil and suffering without reason and without end it does not see the countenance of a God, but only the grimace of absurdity and nothingness' (CG 219). Thus theism and atheism are 'brothers' (CG 221). Theism, by claiming that this world demonstrates the existence of a good and omnipotent god as its ground, provokes the atheism which questions the righteousness of a god who presides over the sufferings of the world. However, this atheism's own contrary inference from the world – that its ground and meaning are nothingness and absurdity – leads to the nihilism which betrays its protest. Nihilism removes the hope or longing for divine righteousness without which atheism cannot sustain its protest against the unrighteousness of the world. Thus in the end neither theism nor atheism can keep the protest against suffering alive. It is silenced by traditional theism, which justifies suffering and accepts the world as God has ordained it, and it is dropped by traditional atheism, which accepts the world with nihilistic realism and justifies suffering with political realism (CG 221, 225).

The 'brotherhood' of theism and atheism appears again in the metaphysical revolution which divinises humanity or the revolutionary vanguard of humanity. The attributes which humanity thus takes upon itself are those of the apathetic, omnipotent ruler, the theistic god, and the inhumanity of this god becomes the inhumanity of those who rule their fellow men and women in the name of divinised humanity (CG 251–52). Thus both for the sake of keeping the question of suffering and divine righteousness alive and for the sake of keeping humanity human, Moltmann seeks a way 'beyond theism and atheism'.

In this he appeals first to Horkheimer, who in his later thinking[23] developed a kind of negative theology of 'longing for the wholly other,' epitomised in the 'longing that the murderer should not triumph over his innocent victim' (quoted CG 223, cf. 175, 178, 253).[24] Horkheimer's point is that only the thought of the 'wholly other', an absolute truth or divine righteousness, can prevent the absolutising of the empirical world of the present and bring to light its real finitude and abandonment. Consciousness of present abandonment and hope, not certainty, of a positive absolute, the wholly other which cannot be represented or defined, are dialectically related. Although the horrors of modern history make theistic belief impossible, it is equally impossible to abandon the hope for divine truth and righteousness without lapsing into a positivistic atheism which can only accept – and justify – the world as it is. Horkheimer therefore affirms the need to go beyond both theism and protest atheism in a 'longing for the wholly other' which can keep the consciousness of evil and the protest against suffering alive.

However, Horkheimer's 'longing for the wholly other' takes Moltmann no further than the God of his theology of hope, who in promising a 'wholly other' future does not, like the god of theism, justify the present but contradicts it and thus maintains 'the protest of the divine promise against suffering' (TH 21). In *The Crucified God* Moltmann goes further than this. The crucified God is not simply the God of hope who contradicts suffering, but the God who enters the sufferings of the present and takes them upon himself. But at this point Moltmann is again interacting with Camus, who 'comes nearer to the mystery' than Horkheimer (CG 226), because he partly understood that the God of Christianity was not simply the god of theism but the crucified God. According to Camus, Christianity managed to forestall metaphysical rebellion against the God of the Old Testament by means of its theology of the cross.[25] This claimed that on the cross God himself, apparently laying aside his divine prerogatives, suffered the evils of the human condition to the limit, as the cry of desolation shows (HR 50–51). Since he himself suffered them, they cannot be the ground for revolt against him, and so the spirit of revolt is quelled by the cross. By accepting on the cross the punishment of a slave, Christ bridged the gulf between the Lord God and his human slaves, made the slaves' sufferings a route to heaven, and therefore inculcated acceptance of suffering (HR 141–42). In this way Christianity identified itself with the perpetuation of injustice and averted metaphysical rebellion until the period of the Enlightenment, when the divinity of Christ was thrown into doubt. The crucified Jesus then no longer mediates between divine master and human slaves, but is just 'one more innocent man whom the representatives of the God of Abraham tortured in a spectacular manner' (HR 53). Robbed of its crucified God, theism now provoked the modern metaphysical rebellion (HR 53, cf. 142).

The line between this understanding of the crucified God and Moltmann's is a narrow but important one. It is the line between what Moltmann calls 'the traditional passion mysticism' (CG 226; cf. 45–49), which Camus here reflects reasonably accurately, and Moltmann's own theology of the cross. Both speak of God's utter involvement in human misery, evidenced in Jesus' cry of godforsakenness, but whereas for Camus this sets an example of submission to suffering, for Moltmann it is God's protest against suffering in loving solidarity with those who suffer (cf. CG 48–52 for the difference). Understood in this way, the theology of the crucified God does not quell the 'metaphysical rebellion' but takes it up into itself, since in the crucified God's protesting cry of desolation it sees a 'rebellion in God himself' (CG 227). Here Moltmann finds the ground for maintaining the protest against suffering.

Thus Moltmann turns the theology of the cross, which Camus saw as the enemy of metaphysical rebellion, into its ground, and he does so by interpreting Jesus' dying cry as a protest against suffering. Even here, however, he has taken the hint from Camus, who gave the cry of desolation the same kind of prominence in his interpretation of the cross as Moltmann does. When Camus goes back behind the Christian theology of the cross and interprets Jesus as the mere man he took him to be, he takes his dying cry as the complaint of an innocent man against the injustice done to him (HR 83).[26] Camus (or rather his character Clamence in *La Chute*) even suggests that the third evangelist attempted to censor this 'seditious cry',[27] a notion which Moltmann translates into the terminology of New Testament criticism (UZ 137; HP 35; CG 147). It is doubtless to the cry of desolation that Camus refers in a footnote in *L'homme révolté:* 'Of course, there is a metaphysical revolt at the beginning of Christianity' (HR 34n). But in his view this rebellion of the crucified Christ was immediately neutralised by the doctrine of the resurrection and the promise of eternal life, which made the cross the model of the way through suffering to heaven.[28] Moltmann's final response to Camus is to take utterly seriously this 'act of metaphysical rebellion at the beginning of Christianity,'[29] allowing it neither to be neutralised by the resurrection[30] nor suppressed in a theology of the crucified God, but interpreting it as 'rebellion in God'. Restoring the deity of Jesus to the cross without suppressing the rebelliousness of his death-cry makes the cross an event in which 'God is against God' (UZ 145). This in the end is his answer to Camus' problem of how the positive element in metaphysical rebellion can be maintained. It takes him not only 'beyond theism and atheism', but also 'beyond obedience and rebellion', since the crucified God not only suffers and protests but does so in loving solidarity with protesting humanity. Beyond mere submissiveness and mere protest, there is the active suffering of love (CG 252–56).

For Moltmann, the protest atheism which Camus describes had its origins in a rebellion against God 'for God's sake' (cf. HP 33), in the sense that only a longing for divine righteousness provokes and sustains its rebellion against divine authority. Thus Bloch's notion of 'atheism for God's sake' takes, within the horizon of theodicy, the form of protest atheism (cf. CG 252). The formula 'God against God' can be applied to the dialectical thinking of the man who, between theism and atheism, protests for the sake of God's righteousness against the unrighteousness of God's world (HP 34). Indeed, it is the reality of his situation: 'God is hidden and unrecognisably present in those who quarrel with God, destroy all images of God, and are never satisfied' (HP 34). Whether Moltmann first grasped the notion of God's conflict with God here in the dialectic of the theodicy question or in the theology of the cross it is impossible to tell, but it was the applicability of the formula 'God against God' to both that enabled him to correlate the two. If God is implicitly taking the side of the protester against himself in those who argue with God for God's sake, he does so openly and definitively in the death-cry of the crucified Jesus (cf. HP 43). But

that means that in the light of the cross the suffering protester against
God can find in God no longer simply a heavenly authority to accuse,
but also the transforming power of loving solidarity in suffering:

> Anyone who cries out to God in [undeserved] suffering echoes the
> death-cry of the dying Christ, the Son of God. In that case God
> is not just a hidden someone set over against him, to whom he
> cries, but in a profound sense the human God, who cries with
> him and intercedes for him with his cross where man in his torment
> is dumb (CG 252).

**The problem of suffering and the suffering of love**   Moltmann
follows the Frankfurt school, especially Walter Benjamin, in rejecting
any possible justification for suffering (cf. TJ 56; CG 165, 278). Any
claim that, for example, historical progress justifies the sufferings of
humanity for the sake of a greater good that results in the end can be
used to justify the infliction of suffering. Many of the horrors of modern
history which raise the theodicy question today result from just such
justifications of suffering. To any claim that innocent suffering is the
price of progress, Moltmann's response is Ivan Karamazov's: 'I refuse
to pay the price' (HFM 58; cf CG 220). Thus Moltmann's is not an
eschatological theodicy in the sense that in the end suffering will be
seen to have been worthwhile for the sake of its eschatological result
or compensation, but only in the sense that in the end God will *overcome*
suffering (cf HFM 49–50; TJ 56; CG 278). The problem of suffering
cannot be met by explanation, but only by redemption and liberation
(TJ 56–57; FC 77). One should not therefore be misled by the echoes
of Hegel in chapter VI of *The Crucified God* (see 246, 253–254) into
thinking that Moltmann justifies the negative as a necessary element
in the dialectic of the history of God,[31] a misunderstanding of his
work which Moltmann has explicitly repudiated (FC 76–77). On the
contrary, evil has no meaning and suffering cannot be justified. While
there is still evil and suffering, there can be no theoretical theodicy.
The question of God's righteousness in history must remain an open
question which can be neither answered nor abandoned (CG 178; T
565). The proper approach to theodicy must be one which maintains
the protest against suffering and the hope for the overcoming of

suffering without which protest lapses into resignation. As such it will also be one which issues in concrete praxis in the struggles for liberation and justice in the world: 'The question of theodicy leads us into these struggles. Only the future of the coming God leads us out of them' (HP 51).

However, if suffering cannot be justified, it can be embraced in loving solidarity with those who suffer. Moltmann's attempt to go beyond theism and protest atheism takes the form of transcending the opposition which both presuppose between God and suffering (CG 226–27). In the cross we see that God should not simply be set over against suffering. Rather suffering is in God because he is love. God does not offer hope for the world simply by contradicting its negativity. Rather his love embraces the world in all its negativity, suffers the contradiction and overcomes it.

A brief summary of Moltmann's understanding of the cross as a trinitarian event of divine suffering must suffice at this point. In his suffering and dying, in which his Father left him to die, Jesus experienced rejection by the very God of whose gracious nearness he had been uniquely aware:

> Just as there was a unique fellowship with God in his life and preaching, so in his death there was a unique abandonment by God. . . . The torment in his torment was this abandonment by God (CG 149).

Thus Jesus' abandonment in his death was an event between Jesus and his Father, between God and God. But in the light of Easter, in which the nearness of God vindicated Jesus' preaching of God's gracious love, it is possible to understand the cross only as an event of divine love for the world. Jesus' abandonment is the divine act of solidarity with all who cry out to God in their abandonment. However, it is not only Jesus, the Son of God, who suffers. While the Son suffers abandonment by the Father in his dying, the Father suffers in grief the death of the Son. The divine suffering in solidarity with the world involves both the Father's grief in surrendering the Son to death and the Son's agony in surrendering himself to the cross. Thus at the point at which Father and Son are most deeply separated, they are also united in a deep community of will. Hence Moltmann's language about 'God against God' is not to be understood in terms of those caricatures of traditional atonement doctrine in which the loving Christ appeases the angry Father. It is precisely because the Father and the Son are united in their love for the world that the event which separates them overcomes the godforsakenness of the world. The cross is the salvific event of God's love because in it the love between the Father and Son spans the gulf which separates the godless and the godforsaken from God. The trinitarian being of God includes this gulf within itself and overcomes it.

By this act of divine solidarity with all who suffer, God identifies with all suffering, makes it his own and takes it within his trinitarian history in hope for participation in the joy of his future. 'To recognise God in the cross of Christ . . . means to recognise the cross, inextricable suffering, death and hopeless rejection in God' (CG 277, cf. 246). This is the only possible 'Christian answer' to the horror of Auschwitz: that, as the famous passage from Elie Wiesel's *Night* put it (CG 273–74; EH 73),[32] God himself was hanging there on the gallows. This is true in 'a real, transferred sense' (CG 278) because of God's act of identification with all abandonment when he hung on the cross of Christ. 'Even Auschwitz is taken up into the grief of the Father, the surrender of the Son and the power of the Spirit' (CG 278). It would be a mistake to take Moltmann to mean that the formula 'God in Auschwitz and Auschwitz in God' is a 'solution' to the 'problem' of Auschwitz. It is rather more like saying that God accepts the problem as his own, suffers its pain, and thereby sustains hope for the over-coming of Auschwitz in 'the resurrection of the dead, the murdered and the gassed' (CG 278).

At this point it is worth taking up two problems which have been seen in Moltmann's view of the cross, because they will help to clarify the concept. Dorothee Soelle complains, in effect, that Moltmann's God the Father is still the god of theism, 'the ruling, omnipotent Father' who deliberately causes the suffering and death of Christ. He is therefore identified, not with the victims, but with their executioners.[33] In reply, it must be said that this is plainly not Moltmann's intention. The Father's surrender of the Son to death is an act of suffering love for the world: 'the Father suffers the death of his Son in his love for forsaken man' (CG 192). The cross is not just the Son's but *God's* act of loving solidarity with the godless and the godforsaken, in which the Son suffers the pain of identification with the godforsaken and the Father suffers his Son's identification with their fate. The cross shows not just the crucified Son, but the trinitarian God not to be the god of theism who presides invulnerably over a suffering world.

However, two further points need to be made. In the first place, this understanding of the matter is only credible to the extent that the Father's surrender of the Son to death is seen as simultaneously the Son's own self-surrender to death (CG 191–92, 243; FC 73).[34] Only the latter establishes that 'the loving Father has a parallel [not a contrast] in the loving Son' (CG 248), i.e. the 'deep community of will' (CG 243) between the Father and the Son in their common love for the godforsaken. Indeed, only if the Son willingly surrenders himself to a godforsaken death can it be an act of loving solidarity with the godforsaken. Moltmann, in fact, anchors this Christological notion of the Son's self-surrender in the history of Jesus by arguing that Jesus in a sense knowingly brought suffering on himself by his friendship with the outcasts (CG 51). But there does seem to be some tension, at least in psychological terms, between the idea that Jesus willingly went to his death as the final consequence of his embodiment of the Father's love for the abandoned and Moltmann's forceful claim that Jesus experienced his being left to die as rejection by God (CG 145–52).

This tension only makes sense if we allow a second observation: that for Moltmann the feeling of being abandoned by God which those who suffer pointlessly have (CG 46, 252) is not a sheer misconception, but corresponds to the fact that God allows evil to take its course and does not intervene to prevent suffering. God does not cause suffering, but in this sense he is responsible for it (cf. T 565). He does not, like the god of theism, justify suffering, but he does bear a responsibility for it. There is therefore some real point in the 'metaphysical rebellion' against God which the dying Jesus takes up. The cross does not absolve God of responsibility for suffering. Rather it shows that the one who bears overall responsibility for this suffering world is on the side of those who suffer to the extent of sharing their pain and adopting their cause. If he were not in some sense an authority responsible for the world (cf. CG 252), it is hard to see how his fellow-suffering with those who suffer would be any ground for hope for the cessation of suffering.

Although Moltmann does not make any of this very clear, it seems to me the only way to understand his argument consistently.

However, this raises a further problem about Moltmann's view of the cross in relation to theodicy. Grace Jantzen objects that Moltmann has not answered the real problem of suffering, which is: Why does God allow suffering if he is able to prevent it? Is it really good enough for God to suffer with us and to be involved with us in the struggle against suffering, unless we know that he is doing all he can to overcome suffering? If he is omnipotent, it is hard to believe he is doing all he can, and we are therefore left with at least an important residuum of the protest atheist's case against the god of theism.[35]

It seems to me that Moltmann thinks we really are and must be left with a residuum of the protest atheist's case – until the *eschaton*. Jesus' death-cry remains an 'open question', which is greater than all the answers Christian theology can give to it, and can be finally answered only by God at the end (UZ 137–38). But we need to take account also of what Moltmann says about the power of God's suffering love to overcome suffering. The cross does not mean simply that God sympathises, in the weak sense of that word. Much of Moltmann's point in *The Crucified God* is to argue that in a world of pointless suffering which cannot be justified, the power of liberation from suffering belongs to the suffering of love. The love which God enacts in the event of the cross and which the Spirit reproduces in the world is the love whose 'suffering proves to be stronger than hate' and whose 'might is powerful in weakness and gains power over its enemies in grief'. The cross means that instead of overcoming evil by suppressing evildoers, God overcomes evil by embracing evildoers in his love and bearing the pain (CG 248–49).

Solidarity in suffering – in the first place, the crucified God's solidarity with all who suffer – does not abolish suffering, but it does overcome 'the suffering in suffering'.

For the suffering in suffering is the lack of love, and the wounds in wounds are the abandonment, and the powerlessness in pain is unbelief. And therefore the suffering of abandonment is overcome by the suffering of love, which is not afraid of what is sick and ugly, but accepts it and takes it to itself in order to heal it (CG 46).

But lest this kind of 'passion mysticism' suggest a mere submission to fate, it is important to add that solidarity, the active suffering of love, is necessarily combined with love's protest against the infliction of suffering on those it loves (cf. CG 51–52). It helps transform 'dumb suffering' into 'conscious pain', and 'quiet apathy' into 'noisy protest' (FC 97). In this exposition of the liberating power of suffering love, Moltmann is not offering a speculative theodicy, which could only justify suffering. But instead, he points to the divine source of a process of overcoming suffering, in which men and women participate when they follow the crucified Christ in his solidarity with the suffering.

Essential to Moltmann's argument is the intrinsic connexion, in this world, between suffering and love. The god of theism who cannot suffer cannot love, and so is poorer than men and women who suffer because they love (CG 222–23, 253). But – because theology and anthropology are reciprocally related (CG 267) – he has his human counterpart in an apathetic humanity. Moltmann sees apathy as the spiritual sickness of contemporary society. In an 'officially optimistic society' which worships 'the idols of action and success', people become orientated to achievement and success, suppress their own vulnerability to others, become oblivious to the suffering of others – in short, no longer love or suffer out of love (cf. EH 70–71, 83; CG 9, 256; HP 47–48; OC 19–22).

> Life becomes inhuman; it becomes superficial. Work and
> consumption have the effect of repressing suffering, one's own as
> well as the other's. And when suffering is repressed, so is love.
> Finally, with the loss of love, comes the demise of interest in life.
> One walks over dead bodies and one becomes a living corpse (EH
> 96).

'Resurrection' from this 'death' comes through the cross of Christ which mediates his resurrection life to the dead. In the situation of the crucified God are found the conditions for a life of unconditional love which is vulnerable and open to the other. It does not seek freedom from suffering in ceasing to love, but in God's love finds the freedom to love and to continue to love despite suffering, disappointment and death (cf. CG 253–54). In the end *The Crucified God* is about love: the love which empties itself in solidarity with others and identifies with what is alien, which embraces the negative and bears the pain of the negative and overcomes it, which undertakes suffering and protests against suffering and liberates from suffering. God is this suffering love. The cross is the event of his suffering love by which it embraces the world, so that human life can be truly lived in love and suffering and the struggle against suffering. It does not solve the problem of suffering, but it meets it with the suffering of love.

# 4

# THE TRINITARIAN
# HISTORY OF GOD

This chapter runs chronologically parallel to the other four chapters and traces the development of Moltmann's doctrine of God up to, but not including, *The Trinity and the Kingdom of God*. It will be seen that the decisive breakthrough to Moltmann's particular form of trinitarianism occurred in the late 1960s, and that the position then set out in *The Crucified God* was further thought through and, to some extent, adjusted in order to become the mature doctrine which is most fully expounded in *The Trinity and the Kingdom of God*.[1]

**God in Moltmann's early theology**  Moltmann's doctrine of God in *Theology of Hope* is not explicitly trinitarian. The main reason for this is that the doctrine of God is discussed primarily in the context of the modern problematic of divine revelation (TH I), where Moltmann's concern is to establish a concept of revelation as promise in contrast to the prevailing tendency to conceive revelation as the epiphany of eternal truth. God does not make himself known in a moment of non-temporal present, without history or future. For Moltmann such a notion of revelation always derives ultimately from a Greek understanding of temporality, according to which truth cannot be found in the movement of history but only in an absolute present which has no extension in time. The biblical God, by contrast, makes himself known in his promises for the temporal future, whereby history acquires direction and meaning. What is promised is no mere unveiling of what is already true, but rather a new, not yet existing reality.

In this context Moltmann criticises Barth's understanding of the self-revelation of God in relation to the immanent Trinity. In so far as Barth's concept means that God reveals himself by taking humanity within the circle of his own eternal self-knowledge, it is a version of the epiphany of the eternal present. Here Barth is still affected by the Platonic thinking of his dialectical phase. It is true, of course, that Barth's concept of the self-revelation of God is intended to refer to the history of Jesus Christ, but Moltmann finds it inappropriate for that purpose. The event of the resurrection of Christ cannot be understood as 'the pure presence of God,' 'a present without any future'; it must on the contrary be understood as an event of promise which points beyond itself to the not yet existing reality of the future (TH 50–58). 'Then the word of God – *Deus dixit* – would not be the naked self-proof of the eternal present, but a promise which as such discloses and guarantees an outstanding future' (TH 58). Moltmann here sees his work as continuing the direction of the greater emphasis on the temporal future in Barth's own later work (TH 87).

Moltmann's fundamental criticism of Barth's doctrine of the immanent Trinity, then, is that it makes the history of Jesus Christ a revelation of eternity instead of a revelation of the future. This is not a rejection of the doctrine of the Trinity as such, but an argument for a version of that doctrine which takes more seriously the historical and eschatological character of the economic Trinity. Moltmann's theology cannot do without a doctrine of the Trinity, since the eschatology which controls it is founded on the cross and resurrection of Christ and is in process through the work of the Spirit. But the trinitarian truth of God is not given as the disclosure of supra-temporal truth; it is the truth of Jesus Christ who still awaits his future, of the Spirit which is the power of the resurrection of the dead, and of God who still waits to be 'all in all'. *Theology of Hope* points in the direction of a concept of the Trinity as process open to the future of God, but such a concept is not yet developed. Instead, Moltmann is content to replace the theological primacy which Barth gave to the doctrine of the Trinity as the analysis of the concept of revelation with the primacy of eschatology. God is not in an equally immediate relation to all time (TH 58) but has 'future as his essential nature' (Bloch, quoted TH 16). No attempt is yet made to put the latter in trinitarian terms.

However, it can already be seen that for Moltmann the traditional doctrine of God as immanent Trinity in himself is going to be problematic. Although such a doctrine seems necessary, as Barth saw, in order to guarantee that the economic Trinity is God as he really is (TH 56), its danger will be its tendency to obscure the eschatological direction of God's trinitarian activity in history, reducing the latter to a mere temporal reflection of God's eternal being (cf. TH 57). Moltmann's thought seems to demand the recognition of an element of genuine temporality in God, since only this will guarantee the biblical perception that truth is to be found in event, in history and eschatology, rather than in the eternal being of the Greeks. This seems to suggest that instead of simply an immanent Trinity non-temporally 'behind' the economic Trinity, we shall need to think of both a trinitarian origin and a trinitarian goal of God's economic activity.

Just such a concept we shall see that Moltmann develops in his later work. That he was already thinking along these lines soon after writing *Theology of Hope* is clear from a letter he wrote to Karl Barth in April 1965. Barth had written to him about *Theology of Hope*, criticising its one-sided emphasis on the futurity of God and suggesting that if Moltmann had retained Barth's doctrine of the immanent Trinity his concept of God would have been richer.[2] Moltmann's reply confessed that this point in Barth's criticism caused him 'the most cogitation'. It is New Testament exegesis which obliges him to think of the lordship of Christ first of all in eschatological terms. 'In so doing I thought I could so expound the economic Trinity that in the foreground, and then again in the background, it would be open to an immanent Trinity.'[3] The issue of what it means for the concept of God to acknowledge a history and a future of God will remain a key question in Moltmann's subsequent work.

In the period after *Theology of Hope*, Moltmann attempted, in the first place, to develop a new understanding of God's relation to time which closely parallels Pannenberg's more detailed attempt in the same period.[4] In criticisms of the 'one-sidedly' future orientation of *Theology of Hope* on the grounds of Barth's trinitarian concept of God as equally past, present and future (DTH 215, 221), Moltmann recognises again the Greek view of God's timeless eternity indifferently related to all time. The God who simply 'was, is and will be' is not the biblical God who 'was, is and *is to come*' (Rev. 1:4, 8), a definition which gives priority to the future, and suggests a concept of God as 'the power of the future' who as such is sovereign over past and present. The differ-

ence of emphasis from Pannenberg at this point is Moltmann's characteristic stress on the *transforming* future which divides time into what
passes away and the new future which comes. This concept of God's
future as a differentiating power of historical change distinguishes the
God of dialectical eschatology from the final cause of Aristotelian
metaphysics and the Omega point of Teilhardian world process (DTH
215–221). But it requires, Moltmann now recognises, an eschatological
doctrine of the Trinity in which the future is given its temporal priority
(DTH 221).

Had he continued this line of thinking, Moltmann's resulting
doctrine of the Trinity would have resembled Pannenberg's[5] more than
it does. In fact, after 1967, Moltmann dropped the attempt to define
God purely as future in relation to history. However, the priority of
the future does remain essential to his thinking. In God's history with
the world he acts throughout in the direction of the eschatological
future (see most recently VZ; GC 118–124).

What took Moltmann's thought about God in a new direction was
his shift of emphasis, in the period after *Theology of Hope*, from concentration on the resurrection to concentration on the cross. The question
of the trinitarian nature of God arose more explicitly and radically
from reflection on the cross than it had from reflection on the resurrection, and in a way which shifted attention from the need for an
eschatological doctrine of the Trinity to the need to understand the
Trinity as God's involvement in the suffering history of the world.

This already becomes clear in writings from 1967 and 1968 (RRF
200–220; FH; DTH 215–229), where he raises the Christological question of Jesus' identity with God. This will be differently understood
according as it is approached from the perspective of the resurrection
or from the perspective of the cross. From the perspective of Jesus'
resurrection as the prolepsis of the eschatological future results a functional, adoptionist Christology. In the resurrection God 'identifies
himself with Jesus by receiving the crucified one into his future as
mode of his being. If we start with the resurrection, we must say that
God in his being does not become identical with Jesus, but identifies
with Jesus through an act of his will' (FH 24; cf DTH 225). Jesus thus
becomes God's deputy or 'stand-in', who in the period between his
resurrection and ours, reigns over the world to subject it to God. He
serves the limited function of preparing the way for God's kingdom.

Moltmann calls this type of Christology 'eschatological subordi-
nationism' (DTH 226).

However, such functional Christology is no longer adequate when
one moves from the *eschaton* and the resurrection to the cross. The
future of God's kingdom is not only anticipated in Jesus' resurrection;
it is mediated to sinners by his cross. But the cross is not only, like
the resurrection, God's act on Jesus. Not only did God offer up Jesus,
'but Jesus also offered up himself and is one with the Father in his
self-giving.' The Father's love takes the form of the obedience of the
Son. 'In the obedience of the Son, therefore, we find the true image
of God and not only a mediation which would become superfluous.
The trinitarian relationship of the Father to the Son becomes the
permanent characteristic of God. It is the inner rationale of God's
reign' (FH 27). Thus God's future is not only anticipated in Christ;
as the Son of the Father he is already the incarnation of the coming
God (RRF 214; cf FH 27) who mediates God's future to sinners as
the fatherly love of God. The final handing over of the kingdom to the
Father will be the consummation of the Son's obedience, not the end
of his sonship (FH 28; DTH 226–227; cf CG 262–265). Moltmann
here seems to be arguing that the relation of Jesus to God must be
understood as a relationship within the being of God because this
relationship is the form which God's love for sinners takes. Jesus is no
mere dispensable deputy for God because his very being as the Son of
his Father is the form of God's love for sinners. This way of thinking
of the incarnation enables Moltmann to conceive the unity of Father
and Son in terms of will rather than substance: Jesus 'is one with the
Father in his self-giving' (FH 27).

Finally, at this stage Moltmann finds that the significance of the
cross of Christ requires not only trinitarian language of the relationship
of Father and Son, but also patripassian language: 'In Jesus' cross
and resurrection God not only acts as Lord, but also suffers as Father
in offering up his Son' (FH 28). After this tentative approach to
a trinitarian theology of the cross, the real breakthrough came in
Moltmann's 1969 lecture, 'God in the cross of Jesus' (UZ 133–147),
which anticipates the central argument of *The Crucified God*, to which
we turn in the next section. The extent to which this is a breakthrough
in Moltmann's theological development he himself indicates:

the work on this theology of the cross meant a surprising turning-point. Having asked in many different ways what the cross of Christ means for the Church, for theology, for discipleship, for culture and society, I now found myself faced with the reverse question: what does Christ's cross really mean for God himself? (EG 15).

Although Moltmann's trinitarian theology of the cross resulted from the development of his own thought, it also, like his theology of hope and his political theology, coincided with wider developments in German theology, both Protestant and Catholic. In the background lie Karl Barth's insistence on the identification of the Christian God from the history of Jesus Christ, with an emphasis on the cross as the revelation of God's true deity,[6] and Karl Rahner's attempt to relocate the doctrine of the Trinity in its essential connection with the history of salvation by identifying the immanent and the economic Trinities.[7] In the foreground are Hans Urs von Balthasar's and Eberhard Jüngel's trinitarian theologies of the cross,[8] both of which, in somewhat different ways, stress the radically godforsaken character of the death of Jesus, which can only be adequately understood in a trinitarian context and as the event in which God is love. Moltmann has much in common with both, and in particular shares with Jüngel the conviction that trinitarian theology of the cross constitutes the specifically Christian understanding of God which is equally distinguishable from metaphysical theism and from atheism as a denial of theism. But if the main themes of Moltmann's development of the doctrine of God in *The Crucified God* are thus held in common with others, their distinctiveness lies in their integration into Moltmann's dialectical eschatology of the cross. In this process Moltmann's earlier concern to reconceive God's relationship to history is continued but also transformed by the complex of interrelated new concerns in *The Crucified God:* the cross as the criterion of Christianity which therefore defines the Christian God, the critique of metaphysical theism especially in view of the problem of suffering and the challenge of protest atheism, and the understanding of divine love as suffering involvement in the history of the world. The result is Moltmann's dialectical trinitarianism.

**Trinitarian theology of the cross**   The significance of the cross for

the concept of God is such, according to Moltmann, as to call for a
'revolution in the concept of God' (CG 152). This radical significance
depends on recognising the cross as an event between God and God,
between the Father and the Son, in which Jesus suffered abandonment
by his Father: 'there God disputes with God; there God cries out to
God; there God dies in God' (FC 65). Moltmann considers the words,
'My God, why hast thou forsaken me?' to be an early interpretation,
but an accurate interpretation of Jesus' dying cry (CG 146–147).
Abandoned by the God whose closeness as his Father Jesus had known
and whose identification with him Jesus had claimed in his ministry,
Jesus on the cross sees his whole proclamation of God at stake. In his
rejection the deity and the faithfulness of the God he called Father are
at stake (CG 150–151), and while God vindicated Jesus and confirmed
his faithfulness in raising Jesus from the dead, it is still necessary – or
rather it is therefore necessary – to understand God's activity in Jesus'
passion. Here Moltmann's basic concept of the total contradiction of
cross and resurrection, the contradiction between the godforsakenness
of the crucified Jesus and the nearness of God in the raising of Jesus,
is restated in terms which demand the revolution in the concept of
God:

> The cross of the Son divides God from God to the utmost degree
> of enmity and distinction. The resurrection of the Son abandoned
> by God unites God with God in the most intimate fellowship. How
> is this Easter day fellowship of God with God to be conceived in
> the Good Friday cross? (CG 152).

'The death of Jesus is a statement about God himself' (CG 202):
Moltmann attempts to work out consistently this observation of Karl
Rahner. If God reveals himself in the godforsakenness of Jesus on the
cross, then all other concepts of God must be given up and the attempt
be made to understand the Christian God completely from the cross
(CG 190). Once the total contradiction of Moltmann's dialectic is seen
in the cross as a conflict of God with God, then the only way to think
of God is in 'dialectically trinitarian terms' (FC 66). The cross then
'stands at the heart of the trinitarian being of God; it divides and
conjoins the persons in their relationships to each other and portrays
them in a specific way' (CG 207). The death of Jesus is then to be

understood not simply as the 'death of God', a simplification with which Moltmann reproaches Barth and his successors in German theology (CG 201–204), but as 'death *in* God', an event within the relationship of the three persons, from which the meaning of Godhead emerges (CG 207).

If it is the event of the cross which requires trinitarian language, then the doctrine of the Trinity is no mere theological speculation remote from salvation-history, 'a kind of theological higher mathematics for the initiated' (FC 80). 'Anyone who really talks of the Trinity talks of the cross of Jesus, and does not speculate in heavenly riddles' (CG 207). If the relationships within the being of God are found in the event of the cross, then they are found within our human reality. The trinitarian nature of God is not a divine nature remote from humanity, but the human history of Jesus (CG 239). Moltmann's formula for the relation between the theology of the cross and the doctrine of the Trinity therefore makes each necessary for the other: 'The material principle of the doctrine of the Trinity is the cross of Christ. The formal principle of knowledge of the cross is the doctrine of the Trinity' (CG 241). In this way Moltmann brings the doctrine of God and soteriology into the closest possible relationship. Since the doctrine of the Trinity results from asking what *the cross* means for God himself, it is also a statement about who God is for us. In the trinitarian event of the cross God is in himself what he is for us. Hence Moltmann agrees with Rahner in rejecting the distinction between the immanent and the economic Trinities (CG 239–240).

What then is the cross as an event between the persons of the Trinity? It is the event of God's love in which the Father forsakes the Son and delivers him to death so that the godless may not be god-forsaken. The surrender of the Son to death is the action of both the Father and the Son and in the suffering of the Son both Father and Son suffer, though in different ways. The Son suffers abandonment by the Father as he dies; the Father suffers in grief the death of the Son. 'The grief of the Father here is just as important as the death of the Son' (CG 243).

Thus, in the cross, the Father and the Son are united in separation.[9] Their unity is their 'deep community of will', in that the Son willingly surrenders himself to death, but this community of will 'is now expressed precisely at the point of their deepest separation, in the godforsaken and accursed death of Jesus on the cross' (CG 243–244). The cross is the salvific event of God's love because in it the love between the Father and the Son spans the gulf which separates godforsaken sinners from God. The trinitarian being of God includes this gulf within itself and thereby reaches sinners. The powerful love which proceeds from this event between the Father and the Son is the Holy Spirit: the Spirit which 'justifies the godless, fills the forsaken with love and even brings the dead alive' (CG 244). The Spirit is 'the creative love proceeding out of the Father's pain and the Son's self-surrender and coming to forsaken human beings in order to open to them a future for life' (TTC 294–295).

Thus the cross is a *dialectical* trinitarian event in which God identifies with what contradicts him – in the Son's alienation from the Father – so that the divine love – the Spirit of mutual surrender in which Father and Son are united – may suffer the contradiction and overcome it. The Spirit resolves the dialectic, reconciling the godforsaken to God. The Trinity is therefore a dialectical historical process which, by means of the Son's identification with all godlessness, godforsakenness and the nothingness in which transitory being ends, takes up into itself all human history in its negativity: 'this history of God [the trinitarian event of the cross] contains within itself the whole abyss of god-forsakenness, absolute death and the non-God' (CG 246). But this also means that, through the Spirit of the resurrection and the new creation, all nothingness is done away with in this history of God and history opened to its new, eschatological future (CG 218). In this sense, the 'history of God', which is the event of the cross, is not an event within the history of the world but contains all the history of the world (CG 246). And since this 'history of God' *is* the inner trinitarian life of God, this means that the salvation of the world consists in its being taken into the divine life within which it is reconciled and transformed:

A trinitarian theology of the cross perceives God in the negative element and therefore the negative element in God, and in this dialectical way is panentheistic. For in the hidden mode of humiliation to the point of the cross, all being and all that annihilates has already been taken up in God and God begins to become 'all in all'.

If Moltmann's language sometimes suggests that the event of the cross itself is the history of God which contains all history, he elsewhere makes it clear that it is so only as the event which initiates the reconciling work of the Spirit, which opens up history to its eschatological consummation. 'One should think of the Trinity as a dialectical event, indeed as the event of the cross and then as eschatologically open history' (CG 255). Hence, in the present, in love, suffering and hope, human beings 'participate in the trinitarian process of God's history' (CG 255), and at the *eschaton*, when God becomes 'all in all' (1 Cor. 15:24: Moltmann's favourite eschatological text), the inner-trinitarian relationships will be consummated (not abolished) in the Son's handing over his rule to the Father (CG 265–266).

It is in the context of this eschatological openness of the event of the cross that one must understand Moltmann's attempt to say that God *is* the event of the cross. He means that God is this trinitarian relationship which *happens* in God's history with the world:

> God's being is historical and . . . God exists in this specific history of Jesus Christ. . . . The word 'God' means an event, precisely this event. . . . Anyone who intends to speak in a Christian way about God must recount and proclaim this story of Christ as the story of God, that is, as something which occurred between Father, Son, and Spirit, and out of which the concept 'God' is constituted, not only for men but also for God himself (TTC 294–296; cf CG 247; GTT 35).

This is what it means for Moltmann to identify the immanent and the economic Trinities: God's trinitarian history for us makes him what he is for himself. There is no immanent Trinity supra-temporally 'behind' God's temporal, worldly history, so that he would be who he essentially is independently of this history. This history is who he is. The problems of this radical view of God's historicality will be raised after we have discussed the closely connected theme of divine passibility.

**The *pathos* of God**  It is *essential* to Moltmann's trinitarian theology of the cross to be able to say that God *suffers:* not simply, as Chalcedonian Christology always maintained, that he suffers in the humanity of Jesus which is his own human nature, but that he suffers *in himself*.[10] This is so because 'God exists as love in the event of the cross' (CG 244): what there takes place between the persons of the Trinity is God's essence as love. But, as we have seen in the previous chapter, God's love in the event of the cross is *dialectical*, i.e. love which identifies with what is alien to God, embraces the godlessness and godforsakenness of the world, suffers and overcomes the contradiction. Dialectical love is necessarily suffering love, and as a trinitarian event, in which the Son identifies with the godless while the love between the Father and the Son embraces and overcomes the contradiction, it must involve both Father and Son in suffering, though in a differentiated way: the Son as the one who, identified with the godforsaken, suffers god-forsakenness, and the Father as the one who in compassion suffers his Son's participation in the fate of the godless. This trinitarian dimension means that Moltmann rejects the label 'theopaschitism' in favour of the term 'patricompassionism' (FC 73), which differentiates the Father's suffering from the Son's.[11] Unlike the modalistic patripassianism condemned by the early Church – the doctrine that the Father suffered crucifixion – Moltmann sees the differentiated suffering of Father and Son as constituting their trinitarian distinction, while at the same time they are united in community of loving will (CG 244; FC 73). Divine suffering is therefore no mere *opus ad extra;* it takes place within the inner trinitarian life of God (cf. CG 249; FC 67).

Consequently, Moltmann's critique of metaphysical theism in *The Crucified God* is based not merely on an assertion of God's historicality – at this level, the critique is to some extent anticipated in *Theology of Hope* – but, more pointedly, on an assertion of God's passibility. Insofar as, in *The Crucified God*, it is also a trinitarian critique of 'monotheism', this is because the divine suffering is trinitarian.[12] On the other hand, in criticising the Platonic axiom of divine *apatheia*, which made it impossible for the Fathers and traditional theology to attribute suffering to the divine nature, Moltmann is engaged in no narrow modification of the doctrine of God, but is distinguishing the Christian from the theistic God at the key point:

Within the Christian message of the cross of Christ, something new and strange has entered the metaphysical world. For this faith must understand the deity of God from the event of the suffering and death of the Son of God and thus bring about a fundamental change in the orders of being of metaphysical thought and the value tables of religious feeling (CG 215).

The criticism of the old philosophical concept of God, which the Fathers began by developing the doctrine of the Trinity (CG 215) and by associating the divine *apatheia* with the freedom of God's agapic love (CG 269–270; EH 74), stopped short (with rare exceptions[13]) of asserting divine passibility, but this can now be seen as the critical point at which the theology of the cross must differentiate the crucified God from 'the gods of religion, race and class' (CG 201), i.e. the idols of psychological and political monotheism which Moltmann connects with philosophical theism (cf. CG 214–216).

For the Greeks the divine *apatheia* meant, most fundamentally, that God cannot be *affected* by anything else, because he is absolutely self-sufficient, self-determining and independent. *Pathos*, which the divine *apatheia* excludes, means both 'suffering', in our sense of pain or calamity, and also 'passion', in the sense of emotion, whether painful or pleasurable. The connecting thought is passivity. Suffering is what comes upon one, against one's will. It is something of which one is a passive victim. Thus suffering is a mark of weakness and God is necessarily above suffering. But, for the Greeks, one is also passive when one is moved by passions or emotions. To be moved by desire or fear or anger is to be affected by something outside the self, instead of being self-determining. Again this is weakness and so God must be devoid of emotion. To suffer or to feel is to be *subject* to pain or emotion and the things which cause them. God cannot be subject to anything.

The divine impassibility is also closely linked with other aspects of the Greek understanding of God. Suffering is connected with time, change and matter, which are features of this material world of becoming. But God is eternal in the sense of atemporal. He is also, of course, incorporeal. He is absolute, fully actualised perfection, and therefore simply is eternally what he is. He cannot change because any change (even change which he wills rather than change imposed on him from outside) could only be change for the worse. Since he is self-sufficient, he cannot be changed. Since he is perfect, he cannot change himself. Thus suffering and emotion are both incompatible with the God of the eternal present.

On such a view God's love can only be his benevolent will and activity towards the world; it cannot involve a two-way relationship in which God can be *affected* by the objects of his love. In his criticism of the tradition Moltmann is arguing for the latter understanding of God's love, because he understands love as *passion* in the double sense of *pathos* (cf. TKG 22–23; OC 25); passionate concern (*Leidenschaft*) which involves vulnerability to suffering (*Leiden*). Love requires the ability to be moved and affected through involvement with others. The clash with the Greek concept is most apparent when Moltmann represents the apathetic God's inability to suffer as a *deficiency* rather than a perfection:

> A God who cannot suffer is poorer than any man. For a God who is incapable of suffering is a being who cannot be involved. Suffering and injustice do not affect him. And because he is so completely insensitive, he cannot be affected or shaken by anything. He cannot weep, for he has no tears. But the one who cannot suffer cannot love either. So he is also a loveless being (CG 222)

But even Moltmann sees that it would be mistaken to set the apathetic God and the crucified God in absolute contrast. He does recognise that the patristic doctrine contained important elements of truth: that God is not changeable *as creatures are*, and not passible *as creatures are* (CG 229–230). In other words, he cannot be *subjected* to change or suffering against his will, because of a deficiency of his being. In that sense the doctrine protected the *freedom* of God's love, which is 'apathetic' in the sense that it is free, generous and self-giving, not a 'need-love' dominated by self-seeking desires and anxieties (CG 269–270; FC 68). But the Fathers made the mistake of recognising only two alternatives: 'either essential incapacity for suffering, or a fateful subjection to suffering. But there is a third form of suffering – the voluntary laying oneself open to another and allowing oneself to be intimately affected by him, that is to say, the suffering of passionate love' (TKG 23; cf. CG 230). Precisely the freedom of God's love, which in the light of the cross does not correspond to the ancient world's idea of freedom, makes it necessary to go beyond the concept of divine *apatheia* to a concept of divine *pathos*.

It is significant that Moltmann uses the Barthian definition 'the freedom of God's love', with which Barth had already countered a metaphysical concept of God which made God 'his own prisoner':[14]

We must drop the philosophical axioms about the nature of God. God is *not unchangeable*, if to be unchangeable means that he could not in the freedom of his love open himself to the changeable history of his creation. God is *not incapable of suffering* if this means that in the freedom of his love he would not be receptive to suffering over the contradiction of man and the self-destruction of his creation. God is *not invulnerable* if this means that he could not open himself to the pain of the cross. God is *not perfect* if this means that he did not in the craving of his love want his creation to be necessary to his perfection (CPS 62).

But a good deal is at stake in this appeal to 'the freedom of God's love.' Divine freedom no longer means that God is pure causality or absolutely self-sufficient. Indeed, in the last sentence of the quotation Moltmann steps beyond even Barth's concept that God could have been self-sufficient without creation, but in his eternal self-determination has chosen not to be. Rather, *because* God is love, he desires and enters a reciprocal relationship with his creation which both involves him in pain and augments his joy. In *The Crucified God* it is not yet clear how far this reciprocity goes, but it already produces a notion of God's 'history' in which God's relationship with the world changes not only the world but also God.

When he wrote *The Crucified God* Moltmann was apparently unaware of much Christian precedent for a doctrine of divine passibility, such as the strong nineteenth- and twentieth-century tradition in English theology, which he later discovered (TKG 30–36).[15] He did know the Japanese Lutheran theologian Kazoh Kitamori's pioneering *Theology of the Pain of God* (1946), with its trinitarian interpretation of the Father's pain in allowing the Son to die (EH 80; CG 47; GTT 7), and of course he cites Bonhoeffer's famous remarks (CG 47, 290 n. 170; cf. UZ 147). But more important to his argument is the Jewish theologian Abraham Heschel's theology of the *pathos* of God.[16] This was in the first place an exposition of the theology of the Old Testament prophets, in which, with the help of his own background in kabbalistic and

hasidic Judaism, Heschel was able to recognise a quite different understanding of God from the Greek philosophical theism which informs
scholastic Jewish theology as much as Christian. In deliberate opposition to the doctrine of divine *apatheia* Heschel used the word *pathos*
to describe God's concern for and involvement in the world. 'Not self-
sufficiency, but concern and involvement characterise His relation to
the world.'[17] Through his passionate concern for his people God is
affected by them and suffers over them and with them. Moltmann
finds in Heschel a 'bipolar theology of the covenant' (JM 48–49), in
which 'God is free in himself and at the same time interested in his
covenant relationship and affected by human history' (CG 272), and
further thinking along the same lines in the rabbinic doctrine of the
divine self-abasement, in which God is both in heaven and present
with his people sharing their suferings (CG 272–273). The link between
ideas of God's suffering involvement in history and at least incipient
concepts of self-distinction in God (more or less strongly stated: cf.
EH 76–78; JM 49–52; AH 200–201; IU 52–53) is important to
Moltmann. It not only brings modern Jews and Christians closer
together (JM 46), not least in the attempt to speak of God in relation
to Auschwitz (CG 273–274). It also means that Moltmann need not
oppose Christian trinitarianism to Old Testament monotheism, and
so go back on the principle of *Theology of Hope*, that the Old Testament
sets the context for the correct understanding of the Christ-event. *Pace*
Harnack, the doctrine of the Trinity has fundamentally Jewish rather
than hellenistic roots (DGG 176–177). The God of Israel is as different
from the God of Greek philosophical monotheism as the crucified God
is (JM 46), and 'the *pathos* of God perceived and proclaimed by the
prophets is the presupposition for the Christian understanding of the
living God from the passion of Christ' (CG 275). In relation to the
Old Testament, 'Christian faith does not have a new idea of God, but
rather finds itself in a different God-situation' (EH 78) – that of the
cross.[18]

Thus Moltmann's criticism of the concept of divine *apatheia* is not
concerned narrowly with God's ability to suffer, but more widely
with God's *pathos*. It rejects the unmoved, self-sufficient God of the
philosophers in favour of the living God of the whole Bible, whose
'anthropopathisms' in the Old Testament and incarnate *pathos* in the
New Testament are to be taken quite seriously as revealing God's

*Leidenschaft* and his *Leiden:* his passionate interest in the world, which becomes most apparent in 'Jesus' passion for life' (OC 24), and his readiness to suffer in his involvement with the world, which becomes most apparent at the cross. The dialectical love which embraces its own contradiction remains the cruciform centre of this divine *pathos*, but the latter provides a more comprehensive account of the love which God is in relation to the world. And as, for Moltmann, it is the cross as the event of dialectical love which requires trinitarian doctrine, so it is the divine *pathos* which provides the context, in *The Trinity and the Kingdom of God*, for his fuller development of trinitarian doctrine in relation to the whole history of God with the world (TKG II). The further issues of divine freedom and divine becoming must be discussed within this framework of divine *pathos*.

**Problems and clarifications**  The most serious criticisms of *The Crucified God* revolve around the charge of Hegelianism, summed up in Hill's description of the way Hegel's trinitarianism differs from that of the Christian tradition:

> Hegel's God is not the free creator of a world distinct from himself, a Divinity who is triune in his own inner being apart from that world. Rather, the world is a necessary stage in the dialectical becoming of the Absolute, explaining the sense in which the Absolute is triune. God is a Trinity in the necessary unfolding of history and does not transcend that process, because it *is* that process in its universality.[19]

Without entering the discussion of whether Hegel's thought is correctly described as pantheistic, panentheistic or atheistic, we can take this quotation as indicating the dangerous direction in which many critics saw Moltmann's trinitarianism moving in *The Crucified God*.[20] By eliminating any distinction between the immanent and the economic Trinities *and* by interpreting the cross as a dialectical trinitarian event, Moltmann identifies world history 'in the history of God' with the process of God's own self-realisation. At worst this means that 'the dialectic collapses into identity',[21] i.e. God empties himself into what is alien to him in order to resolve identity and non-identity into a higher kind of identity. God is dissolved into history. At best Moltmann seems to make world history the process by which God realises himself. This has two consequences. First, it compromises the freedom of God in relation to the world: the world is necessary to God's becoming himself.[22] This charge is also connected with the discussion of divine passibility, which necessarily makes the relationship between God and the world a reciprocal one in which God is affected by the world. But secondly, and perhaps most seriously, if the world is the process of God's self-realisation, then evil, the negative which is taken up and overcome in the trinitarian dialectic, becomes a necessary moment in the divine process.[23] The cross, it could be said, becomes a rational necessity and is robbed of its scandal.[24]

Moltmann is undoubtedly indebted to Hegel, whom he calls 'the philosopher of the Trinity' (FC 82) and to whom he thinks theology owes the idea of a doctrine of the Trinity which includes the contradiction of the cross (DGG 175). His trinitarian dialectic is certainly Hegelian in structure (explicitly at CG 246, 253–254; GTT 37; FC 74), but not necessarily therefore entirely Hegelian in content.[25] It was in response to the kinds of criticisms mentioned above that Moltmann seems to have become aware of problems which, in the period after *The Crucified God*, he attempted to resolve both by clarification and by further developments of his thought. This becomes clear not only in explicit answers to the critics (DGG 149–156, 168–187), but also in the 1973 essay, 'The Theology of the Cross Today' (FC V),[26] which contains some careful restatements designed to avoid misunderstandings.

The charge which Moltmann is perhaps most anxious to deflect is that of making evil necessary for the sake of good (DGG 151; FC 76–77), since it is essential to his approach to theodicy that evil must not be explained and thereby justified. But Moltmann's most extreme statements about the meaning of the cross – as the self-constitution of the Trinity (DGG 178; TTC 296) – make this difficult, whether these statements are understood, in the most Hegelian and perhaps the most obvious reading of *The Crucified God*, as meaning that in the event of the cross God *becomes* Trinity,[27] or in a less intelligible way as suggesting that the temporal event of the cross constitutes God's trinitarian being from eternity. In either case, godlessness, godforsakenness and death are necessary to the dialectic which constitutes God's trinitarian being, so that either evil is necessary or God's trinitarian being is contingent on unnecessary evil.

Moltmann avoids this dilemma only by retreating from the position, if he ever really intended it, that God is Trinity only through the cross. Instead, he gives the cross a central but not uniquely determinative place in God's trinitarian history. Already in 1973, he raises the possibility that 'the eternal *generatio filii*' could be the prior condition in God for the *derelictio Jesu* on the cross, so that God's history has a trinitarian origin before the cross, just as it has a trinitarian goal at the *eschaton* (FC 74–75). Moltmann is here reverting to the suggestion of his 1965 letter to Barth that the economic Trinity could be seen as open both behind and in front to an immanent Trinity, and anticipating the concept which will be developed more fully in *The Church in the Power of the Spirit*. However, it is important to notice that Moltmann is not repudiating the main intention of his identification of the immanent and the economic Trinities in *The Crucified God*. This was to deny that God is self-sufficient in his immanent trinitarian being – as a 'closed circle' (CG 255; FC 78) – while the economic Trinity is an external activity which does not affect God in himself. Instead, the doctrine of the Trinity means that God's inner life is open to human history and the future: God's human temporal history on the cross and in the Spirit is internal to his own trinitarian experience. For Moltmann to say that God is already trinitarian before the cross is not to deny this, but to claim that God's trinitarian being has from eternity been open to human history and open to the difference the cross makes to the trinitarian relationship (cf. FC 93). From eternity God's essence as love has been not only the love of like for like, which would make him self-sufficient in the immanent Trinity (FC 78; cf. TKG 58–59), but the dialectical love for his other which is open to the world.

Pursuing this thought enables Moltmann still to maintain a sense in which the cross is constitutive for the trinitarian relationships even, so to speak, retroactively in God's eternity (cf. TKG 161). If God as he has always been in eternity corresponds to God as he is in the event of the cross, then suffering love must characterise the eternal trinitarian relationships in the sense that 'God's essence is from eternity a love which is capable of suffering, ready to sacrifice and to give itself up' (JM 54; cf. DGG 179–180). In this sense, the Lamb was slain from the foundation of the world (DGG 179). So far, if Moltmann means that God is such that, if and when his love is contradicted, he will suffer, the contingency of evil is preserved. But when he later puts it more strongly – that 'the Son's sacrifice of boundless love on Golgotha is from eternity already included in the exchange of the essential, the consubstantial love which constitutes the divine life of the Trinity' (TKG 168), so that 'the pain of the cross determines the inner life of the triune God from eternity to eternity' (TKG 161) – we seem to be back with the original problem. If this does not make evil necessary, then contingent evil not only affects God in the course of his trinitarian history (cf. FC 77), but essentially determines his inner life from eternity. This conclusion results from the temptation, which Moltmann from *The Crucified God* onwards seems unable to resist, to see the cross as the key to the doctrine of God, not only in the sense that it reveals God as the kind of love which is willing to suffer, but in the sense that the actual sufferings of the cross are essential to who God is. This attempt to take God's temporal experience as seriously as possible oddly ends by eternalising it.[28]

The charge that Moltmann's thinking in *The Crucified God* compromises the freedom of God occasioned a good deal of reflection on his part. In the first place, he makes it clear that he did not intend to dissolve God into world history (DGG 155; FC 75), but to refer to a history of reciprocal relationship between God and the world. In this relationship God is really affected, but only because he has voluntarily opened himself in love to the world. This could have been enough to protect the divine freedom, but, dissatisfied with the Barthian view that God could have remained self-sufficient but from eternity chose not to be, Moltmann denies that the contrast between freedom of choice and necessity is real in God. God's freedom is not arbitrary choice but the inner necessity of his being, i.e. the God who is love cannot choose not to love (FC 77; DGG 155, 168, 174). 'Love is self-evident for God' (TKG 151).[29] Thus the distinction between the immanent and the economic Trinities is not needed to protect God's freedom. Because his freedom is his love, he is in himself related to the world as the Trinity from eternity open to world history.

Finally, two further criticisms of Moltmann's concept of God concern the trinitarian persons. One charges Moltmann with tritheism: the Trinity 'seems to be *three* Gods, separate in being yet united in intention. The unity of the Trinity seems to be volitional, but not ontological.'[30] Moltmann's response to this charge set him on the road to the fully social doctrine of the Trinity expounded in *The Trinity and the Kingdom of God*, where the unity of God is found neither in one substance nor in one subject, but in the perichoresis of three subjects united in their love (TKG 177–78). Moltmann's trinitarian critique of monotheism likewise develops into a full-scale attack on the 'modalism' he finds implicit in most modern doctrines of the Trinity along with the claim that monotheism promotes monarchical rule in church and state (cf. CG 325–326), whereas in the kingdom of the triune God there is freedom in friendly relationships (DGG 181–184; TKG *passim;* HG 90–106; FHS 293–294). These developments lie beyond the scope of this book.

The second criticism, acknowledged by Moltmann (DGG 184), finds his doctrine of the Holy Spirit in *The Crucified God* inadequate. The Spirit in *The Crucified God* is the divine love which overcomes the negative, resolves the dialectic, and opens the future (cf. especially CG 244, 254–255). In acknowledging his difficulty in speaking of the Spirit in fully personal terms, Moltmann attributes it to the traditional trinitarian 'order' in which all activity proceeds from the Father and then also from the Son. This gives the Spirit his own activity of which he is the subject in relation to the world, but in relation to the Father and the Son he is purely passive. The key to the personality of the Spirit – which for Moltmann means that he is a subject in the trinitarian life itself – is to recognise the Spirit's activity in relation to the Father and the Son: that of *glorification* (DGG 185–186). The importance of this step in Moltmann's trinitarian thinking is not only that it constitutes a fully social Trinity of three subjects (cf. TKG 125–126;. FHS 299), but also that it introduces Moltmann's mature understanding of the trinitarian history of God as a history of *changing trinitarian relationships*, in which the Trinity has no fixed order as an immanent Trinity must, but is a living history of changing trinitarian patterns (DGG 186–187; cf. TKG 94–96). This leads directly to the doctrine of the Trinity in *The Church in the Power of the Spirit*.

**The trinitarian history of God**   Douglas Meeks observes that the development of Moltmann's theology corresponds to the three trinitarian 'moments' of resurrection, cross and Pentecost (EH xi). The God of *Theology of Hope* is the God who raised Jesus from the dead, the God of hope who has future as his essential nature. The doctrine of the Trinity acquires much greater attention in *The Crucified God*, because here God is the incarnate God who takes all humanity within his suffering love. Humanity as much as future is the mode of his being. In his third major work, *The Church in the Power of the Spirit*, Moltmann takes up the third trinitarian moment, Pentecost, and sees the church within the trinitarian history of God initiated by the Christ event, and the Spirit as the power of God's trinitarian love moving history towards the eschatological kingdom. In this context, Moltmann is able to return to some of the themes of *Theology of Hope* – the mission of the church and the eschatological goal of history – but to see them in the newly gained perspective of God's trinitarian history. The future of God is at last redefined in truly trinitarian terms.

In the section, 'The Church in the Trinitarian History of God' (CPS 50–65) Moltmann sketches a doctrine of the Trinity in narrative form. The changing trinitarian relationships, as relationships open to the world and the future, effect God's history with the world, in which he is also affected by the world. Moltmann now allows, in a sense, the validity of the traditional and Barthian inference back from the economic Trinity to an immanent Trinity, but the latter is 'the Trinity in the origin' rather than the immanent Trinity in the traditional sense. The trinitarian history of God derives from the historical missions of the Son and the Spirit. But theological reflection must enquire about the origin of these missions, and following the principle that God corresponds to himself, must conclude that these economic relationships between the persons correspond to relations in eternity. The missions *ad extra* reveal missions *ad intra:* the eternal generation of the Son by the Father, and the eternal procession of the Spirit from the Father (or 'from the Father and the Son': Moltmann at this stage refuses to adjudicate the *filioque* issue). Only this inference from 'the Trinity in the sending' (as Moltmann now calls the economic Trinity) to 'the Trinity in the origin' can ensure that in the history of Jesus and the experience of the Spirit we have to do with God himself. The inference also has a second function: it shows the Trinity to have been from eternity

an open Trinity. It is open for its own sending. . . . It is open for men and for all creation. The life of God within the Trinity cannot be conceived of as a closed circle – the symbol of perfection and self-sufficiency . . . . The triune God is the God who is open to man, open to the world and open to time (CPS 55–56).

Thus the Trinity in the sending is not a mere manifestation of what God is already in himself in eternity. Moltmann still maintains an important element of historical becoming in God.

For this reason, the trinitarian history is not sufficiently described by the inference back to the Trinity in the origin. It must also be understood from a future perspective towards its goal, for if the experience of history is real for God the eschatological Trinity will not be the same as the Trinity in the origin. Moltmann holds that theological tradition has stressed too exclusively the backward perspective from the history of Jesus through the incarnation to his origin in the immanent Trinity. This perspective, though valid in itself, needs supplementing by the forward perspective through his resurrection to the eschatological goal of the Christ event (CPS 57).

This goal Moltmann calls 'the Trinity in the glorification'. 'Glory' is the biblical term for the divine splendour in which the whole creation will participate in the End. In eschatological perspective the history of Christ and the history of the Spirit are movements of the glorification of God: the glorification of the Father by the Son and the glorification of the Father and the Son by the Spirit – which is at the same time the glorification of humanity, since God is glorified only in the liberation of his creation.

This glorification of God in the liberation of his creation takes place by the inclusion of creation within the divine life. Moltmann pictures God opening himself in seeking love in the missions of the Son and the Spirit, and then in gathering love in the work of the Spirit gathering the whole creation into union with himself. The Spirit here plays his active trinitarian roles of glorification and unification.

It follows, claims Moltmann, that the *unity* must be differently conceived in the Trinity in the origin and the Trinity in the glorification. In the former case the divine unity is 'that which is ontologically the foundation of the sendings of Son and Spirit': Moltmann declines to specify how this unity is to be understood (CPS 61; see TKG 177 for his later account). But the unity of God in his eschatological goal 'contains within itself the whole union of creation with God and in

God' (CPS 62). In this Trinity in the glorification, then, the inner-trinitarian relations are fulfilled precisely in the inclusion of creation within their liberating life (CPS 63). The eschatological 'panentheism' of *The Crucified God* (CG 277) now achieves fully trinitarian form, and at last Moltmann's aim of producing an eschatological doctrine of the Trinity (cf. DTH 221) is achieved. The eschatological future retains its priority as the goal of God's own trinitarian being which is an openness in love for the union of his creation with himself. And in this synthesis of Moltmann's eschatological and his trinitarian thinking, he also achieves a doctrine of the Trinity which is both soteriological (as in *The Crucified God*) and doxological (cf. FC 95–96; FHS 300), thereby giving trinitarian form to that strand of his thought which began with *Theology and Joy*.

Finally, Moltmann comments further on the historical experience of God. 'By opening himself for this history and entering into it . . . God also experiences the history of this world in its breadth and depth' (CPS 62). This divine experience of history 'has two sides to it'. From the sending of the Son to the cross, he *experiences* history as suffering, death and hell. From the resurrection to the End, he experiences joy in the *creation* of history:

> God experiences history in order to create history. He goes out of himself in order to gather to himself. He becomes vulnerable, takes suffering and death on himself in order to heal, to liberate and to confer his eternal life. This means that there is a tendency for the resurrection to take supremacy over the cross, for the exaltation to acquire ascendancy over the humiliation, and for the joy of God to have more weight than his pain. Consequently the Trinity in the glorification also has the tendency to predominate over the Trinity in the sending. Formally it corresponds to the Trinity in the sending, but in content it goes beyond it, just as the gathering love corresponds to the seeking love of God yet goes far beyond it through the gathering and uniting of mankind and the world with God (FC 95).

This future-orientated narrative of the Trinity is then able to function as the context within which Moltmann understands the *Church* to participate in God's experiences of both suffering and joy.

# 5

## MESSIANIC ECCLESIOLOGY

**Towards a messianic ecclesiology** *The Church in the Power of the Spirit* seems to have attracted less interest and has certainly provoked far less theological discussion than Moltmann's other major works. This can hardly be because its proposals are less controversial, but it may be because, though rooted in theological argument, they are controversial in their practical thrust towards reforming the life and structure of the Church. As such they cross 'the growing gulf between systematic and practical theology' (HC 128) and fall outside the central interests of academic theology, which tends to keep its distance from the Church, especially from the Church as actual 'grassroots' communities of Christians, which for Moltmann are the real subject of ecclesiology. This latter emphasis on the Church 'from below' and the need for renewal and reform of the Church to proceed 'from below' (CPS 275, 317; HC 21, 55) also distances Moltmann's ecclesiology from the general run of ecclesiological discussions in the ecumenical movement.

For his part, Moltmann is clear that the professional theologian should feel himself in the first instance to be a member of the Christian community, which does not mean being identified with an ecclesiastical hierarchy but being identified with the local congregation of Christ's people, which, just as much as the university and the seminary, is where theology should be done (HC 41, 128–129; OC 9). This is not because theology is a matter of narrowly inner-ecclesiastical reflection, but because theology is in the service of the Church's mission to the world. Theology's own critical openness to the world would remain purely abstract if it were not devoted to the Church's mission and to the actual congregations of Christians as the bearers of that mission in the world.

Consequently, ecclesiology has always been integral to Moltmann's theological project and in fact as early as 1966 he was giving lectures on ecclesiology which were the forerunner of *The Church in the Power of the Spirit* (CPS xiv). His earlier works already have important ecclesiological implications which lay the foundations for *The Church in the Power of the Spirit*. In *Theology of Hope*, the eschatological promise given in the resurrection of the crucified Christ creates an *essentially missionary* church of *dialectical hope*. The Church exists in mission to the world in the service of the universal future of the kingdom of God, and in its hope for the world it suffers the contradiction between the promise and the reality of the present. It is characteristically the 'exodus church', always on the move towards the new future opened up by the promise and charged with keeping the world in historical movement towards the promised future. Thus the dialectical eschatology of *Theology of Hope* serves to open the Church to history, to the world and to the future, giving the Church both a dynamic existence in future-orientated mission and a critical openness to the world which is not yet but is to become the kingdom of God. In the political theology which developed out of *Theology of Hope* Moltmann then laid more emphasis on the liberating political praxis which is therefore incumbent on Christians. In recognising that 'a missionary church cannot be apolitical' (CPS 15), Moltmann broke decisively with the German Protestant Church's postwar commitment to political neutrality, just as in chapter V of *Theology of Hope* he set his face against contemporary German tendencies to integrate Church and society (cf. CR 109; TGT 189). Vis-à-vis the civil religion which sanctions the present structures of bourgeois society, eschatological hope creates an exodus Church committed to liberating and even revolutionary praxis in society.

In *Theology and Joy* the Church of missionary hope becomes also the Church which celebrates the *festival of freedom*, complementing its missionary ethic with the anticipated joy of the new creation. Then, with Moltmann's resolute turn to the cross in *The Crucified God*, the Church's dialectical hope for the world is deepened by the addition of *dialectical love*. The Church which finds its identity in identification with the crucified Christ can be involved in the world only by identification with those with whom Christ on the cross identified. The principle of its life cannot be the love of like for like, but openness to those who are different, the vulnerability of love which identifies with others, and solidarity especially with the victims of society, the most wretched and the most hopeless. The Church's critical openness to the world in hope gains new dimensions when combined with the openness of suffering love.

Finally, it was Moltmann's development of the concept of the trinitarian history of God as an overarching theological context for the doctrine of the Church which enabled him to integrate these earlier ecclesiological insights into a comprehensive ecclesiology in *The Church in the Power of the Spirit*. We shall see how this happens in the rest of the chapter, but first we should also notice that Moltmann's growing experience of the worldwide Church, through his extensive travels and his involvement in the World Council of Churches, also contributed to the making of his ecclesiology. If *Theology of Hope* was Moltmann's most Reformed book and *The Crucified God* his most Lutheran, *The Church in the Power of the Spirit* was, in its own way, his most ecumenical book so far. This is to be seen not so much in his attention to non-Protestant theology, though this has steadily increased throughout his career[1] and in *The Church in the Power of the Spirit* there are the beginnings of interest in Orthodox theology (CPS 36–37; cf. 256). The point is rather that Moltmann's ecclesiology in *The Church in the Power of the Spirit* is inspired by the actual churches he experienced in his travels outside Europe: by the commitment to political liberation in various churches of the Third World (CR 111; CPS xv), the charismatic worship of the Pentecostal and independent churches of Africa (CPS xv, 112; OC 65–66), the 'voluntary religion' of the Protestant free church tradition in the United States (TGT 190–191), the 'base communities' of Latin America (CPS 329–330), and the fellowship of persecuted Christians in many parts of the world (OC 89; EC 427). If *The Church in the Power of the Spirit* naturally speaks most often of conditions in the Protestant churches of West Germany and directs its reforming proposals to that situation, it is nevertheless ecumenically open in its inspiration. Moltmann believes that ecumenical solidarity with the churches of the Third World, in their sufferings and in their commitment to liberation, cannot leave the German churches unchanged (CR 111–112; CPS 343–344; OC 88–90; PPL 165–166; EC 427–428).

**The structure and method of** *The Church in the Power of the Spirit* Moltmann describes his ecclesiology alternatively as 'relational ecclesiology' (CPS 20) or as 'messianic ecclesiology' (CPS subtitle). The meanings of the two terms are closely connected and together point to the dominant theme which holds all the facets of Moltmann's ecclesiology together and determines their character. 'Messianic ecclesiology' is shorthand for 'a christologically founded and eschatologically directed doctrine of the church' (CPS 13), or, more precisely, for an ecclesiology rooted in Moltmann's eschatological Christology. The Church is the Church of Jesus Christ, subject to his lordship alone, and so 'ecclesiology can only be developed from christology' (CPS 66). 'Every statement about the church will be a statement about Christ. Every statement about Christ will be a statement about the church' (CPS 6). But statements about Christ always also point beyond the Church to the universal future of Christ, the messianic kingdom. The Christ (Messiah) who is the foundation of the Church is 'the eschatological person' (CPS 73) whose past history has yet to be fulfilled in his future. So his Church must be a 'messianic fellowship' (Moltmann's favourite description of the Church in *The Church in the Power of the Spirit*) orientated in mission towards the coming kingdom of God. It participates in Christ's own mission on the way to his future, and lives 'between remembrance of his history and hope of his kingdom' (CPS 75). This makes the Church a *provisional* reality, where eschatology and history are mediated in the category of *anticipation* (CPS 191–194). 'The church . . . is not yet the kingdom of God, but it is its anticipation in history. . . . Christianity is not yet the new mankind but it is its vanguard' (CPS 196). In an anticipatory and fragmentary – and, naturally, imperfect (CPS 167) – form, the Church represents the future of the whole of reality and so mediates this eschatological future to the world (CPS 194–195). Therefore the Church does not exist for itself but in the service of the kingdom of God in the world (CPS 68, 164). For the Church to be the messianic fellowship means to participate in Christ's mission in this sense.

It should be clear how much Moltmann's ecclesiology in *The Church in the Power of the Spirit* is determined by the eschatological Christology of his earlier work. However, his more recent development of this into the concept of the trinitarian history of God with the world enables him to set the Church's eschatological mission not only in Christological but also in *pneumatological* perspective, so that 'messianic ecclesiology' is at the same time and is intended by Moltmann to include 'charismatic ecclesiology' (CPS 36–37). It is this pneumatological dimension which permits a stronger emphasis on the Church's life and mission as anticipation of the kingdom than was possible in *Theology of Hope*. Pneumatology for Moltmann is the doctrine of the eschatological fulfilment of the history of Christ. The way from the history of Christ to his future is also the history of the Spirit in his work of unification and glorification through which the eschatological future enters history. It is therefore the Holy Spirit who mediates eschatology and history and the Church is this mediation only as it exists in the presence and power of the Holy Spirit (CPS 35, 197–198). 'Messianic ecclesiology' is a function of messianic pneumatology as well as of eschatological Christology.

Moltmann's pneumatology in *The Church in the Power of the Spirit* is Christological in the sense that the mission of the Spirit follows from that of the Son (CPS 54) and the history of the Spirit fulfils the eschatological purpose and direction of the history of Christ (CPS 34). But because both Christology and pneumatology are eschatologically understood, this does not make the latter mere 'application' of 'the finished work of Christ', as Protestant dogmatics up to Barth have tended to suggest. Rather than subordinating pneumatology to Christology or *vice versa*, Moltmann relates the mission of the Son and the mission of the Spirit, in their common direction towards the eschatological kingdom, within the broader concept of 'the trinitarian history of God's dealings with the world' (CPS 37). The Christological, pneumatological and eschatological perspectives in ecclesiology likewise all come together, as complementary rather than competing perspectives, when the Church understands itself in this broadest context of the trinitarian history of God. It is this context – of the missions of the Son and the Spirit from the Father on their way to the unification of all things in the triune God and the glorification of God in all things (CPS II.4) – which constitutes the Church, the messianic fellowship, which is equally 'the Church of Jesus Christ' (CPS III), 'the Church of the kingdom of God' (CPS IV) and 'the Church in the presence and power of the Holy Spirit' (CPS V and VI).

The same conclusion can be reached by considering the term 'relational ecclesiology'. Like everything else that exists in a living history – including the trinitarian God – the Church exists in *relationships* with others. Consequently, it cannot understand itself as an entity simply in itself: 'The Church cannot understand itself alone. It can only truly comprehend its mission and its meaning, its roles and its functions in relation to others' (CPS 19). Ecclesiology, therefore, cannot be a doctrine in itself, but must be developed in relation to Christology, pneumatology and eschatology. It must understand its particular subject, the Church, in relation to the total context in which the Church comes into being and lives. This is 'the trinitarian history of God's dealings with the world': the universal history within which alone the significance of the Church's particular existence can come to light (CPS 50). In this context, too, the Church is able to understand itself *in its particularity* and avoid falsely absolutising itself:

In the movements of the trinitarian history of God's dealings with the world the church finds and discovers itself, in all the relationships which comprehend its life. It finds itself on the path traced by this history of God's dealings with the world, and it discovers itself as one element in the movements of the divine sending, gathering together and experience. It is not the church that has a mission of salvation to fulfil to the world; it is the mission of the Son and the Spirit through the Father that includes the church, creating a church as it goes on its way. . . . If the church understands itself, with all its tasks and powers, in the Spirit and against the horizon of the Spirit's history, then it also understands its particularity as one element in the power of the Spirit and has no need to maintain its special power and its special charges with absolute and self-destructive claims. It then has no need to look sideways in suspicion or jealousy at the saving efficacies of the Spirit outside the church; instead it can recognize them thankfully as signs that the Spirit is greater than the church and that God's purpose of salvation reaches beyond the church (CPS 64–65).

The Church is *related* to the whole, through its participation in the universal mission of Christ and the Spirit on the way to the universal future of all reality in the messianic kingdom, but it *is not* the whole and will never itself become the whole (CPS 348–351). Consequently, ecclesiology can and must recognise the *relativity* of its subject and its own standpoint, without subsiding into mere *relativism* (cf. CG 11; CPS 155–157). As a particular related to the unique eschatological person, Jesus Christ, and his universal future, the Church fulfils its eschatological mission in open and critical relation to other particulars, its partners in history on the way to the kingdom of God (Israel, the world religions, the secular order). Because it is itself 'on the move' (CPS 1), as one element in the movement of God's trinitarian history, it can engage in real relationships with these partners, living relationships in which both participants are open to change, and direct these relationships in hope towards the common future of the kingdom of God (cf. CPS 133–135). In other words, although the Church (as 'the Church of Jesus Christ', the eschatological person) does have a *special* relationship to the universal (the kingdom of God), it has this special relationship *only in relation to other particulars*. It fulfils its messianic vocation not by absolutising itself but in open relationships of dialogue and cooperation.

This principle of relationality is a development of Moltmann's basic understanding, since *Theology of Hope*, of the Church's *openness* to the world and to the future. Appropriately taken up in the English title (*The Open Church*) of his popular version of the themes of *The Church in the Power of the Spirit*, the concept of the Church's openness runs through *The Church in the Power of the Spirit* as the corollary of its relationality. Because of the Church's relative place in the wider context of the trinitarian history of God, it is 'open for God, open for men and open for the future of both God and men. The church atrophies when it surrenders any one of these opennesses and closes itself up against God, men or the future' (CPS 2).[2] The principle should also be linked with the open relationality of the triune God, who is 'from eternity an open Trinity' (CPS 55) and in his trinitarian history opens himself in vulnerable love to the world. The Church participates in and testifies to this history of God when it opens itself in vulnerable love to dialogue and relationship with others (CPS 160–161).

'Relational ecclesiology', Moltmann claims, 'leads to an understanding of the living nature of the church' (CPS 20), i.e. the Church is understood as a *movement* within the living, moving relationships of the trinitarian history of God with the world, created by the missions of the Son and the Spirit (CPS 64). Moltmann therefore tries to avoid a definition of what the Church is, which could abstract it from this movement, and instead insists that the Church finds itself – through a participatory knowledge from within the divine movement in which it is caught up (CPS 52) – *where* it participates in the mission of Christ and the Spirit (CPS 65, 122). In other words, its characteristics, which make it the true Church, are not its own, but those of the presence and activity of Christ and the Spirit (CPS 338): 'the whole being of the church is marked by participation in the history of God's dealings with the world' (CPS 65). *The Church in the Power of the Spirit* attempts to work out this principle consistently by understanding every aspect of the Church's life and activity as a function of the mission of Christ and the Spirit, a participation in God's trinitarian history with the world. In doing so, it also performs a critical function with a view to the reform of the Church (CPS 2). By enabling the Church to recover its bearings within the trinitarian history of God – its Christological origin, its pneumatological commission and its eschatological goal – ecclesiology should not only serve 'the theological justification of the church's actions; it also serves the criticism of those actions' (CPS 5). In part this criticism consists in liberating the Church from its adaptations to and justifications of the *status quo* in society, in order for it to regain the freedom of its messianic vocation (CPS 225), and in this respect the criticism of the Church in *The Church in the Power of the Spirit* follows on from the critical role of eschatology in *Theology of Hope* and the iconoclasm of the cross in *The Crucified God*. 'The trinitarian history of God' includes both these critical perspectives and others. As we shall see, it is from the Church's messianic vocation within the mission of Christ and the Spirit that Moltmann argues the book's broadest reforming intention: 'to point away from the pastoral church, that looks after the people, to the people's own communal church among the people' (CPS xvi).

'Every doctrine of the church starts from experiences in the church and with the church in the world' (CPS 18): because knowledge of the Church in the trinitarian history of God with the world is necessarily participatory and engaged knowledge (CPS 52). Consequently, Moltmann begins with those dimensions of ecclesiology which have come to be seen as necessary as a result of the Church's experiences this century: that the Church is necessarily Christ's Church, the missionary Church, the ecumenical Church and the political Church (chapter I).

These four dimensions form a sort of *inclusio* with the four marks of the Church which are the subject of the last chapter of the book (VII): all four dimensions can easily be seen to characterise the discussion of the four marks.

However, Moltmann's project of 'relational ecclesiology' really begins in chapter II, whose first three sections lead up to the key section 4. This provides the only fully comprehensive context for the understanding of ecclesiology in its sketch of the trinitarian history of God, and so supplies the framework of understanding within which the rest of the book seeks to show how 'the whole being of the church is marked by participation in the history of God's dealings with the world' (CPS 65). The basic plan of the next four chapters is then relatively straightforward.

Chapter III deals with the church's participation in the messianic history of Christ. In section 1 Moltmann follows his favoured method of reviewing various ways of understanding the relationship between Christ and the Church before arriving at the most satisfactory: 'Christ as the eschatological person.' This preserves the kind of temporal structure which is basic to Moltmann's thought: that the Church's remembrance of the past history of Christ does not tie the Church to the past in a backward-looking relationship, as though it were a mere extension or repetition of a past event, but points it to the future, thus orientating its mission to something beyond itself: the coming kingdom of Christ (CPS 75). Moltmann then uses the structure of the traditional Protestant dogmatic scheme of the three offices of Christ as prophet, priest and king, correlating them with the ministry, death and resurrection of Christ and explaining the Church's participation in each. From Jesus' messianic mission of proclamation of the Gospel and liberating action follows the Church's universal mission of liberation (III.2); from Jesus' passion follows 'the church under the cross' which participates in his passion through suffering and solidarity with the godforsaken (III.3); and from Jesus' exaltation as the Lord of the coming kingdom, who changes the meaning of lordship into loving service and self-sacrifice, follows the Church as the fellowship of freedom and equality in the Spirit (III.4). If the first of these three aspects of the Church corresponds to the exodus Church of *Theology of Hope* (though here derived from the ministry rather than the resurrection of Jesus) and if the second corresponds to the Church of *The Crucified God*, identified with the crucified Jesus in his solidarity with the godforsaken, the third aspect is the one which is relatively new and most distinctive of *The Church in the Power of the Spirit*. Its Christological aspect here will be complemented by its pneumatological aspect in chapter VI.

To the traditional three offices of Christ Moltmann adds two more. One is Christ in his transfiguration, which brings out the 'aesthetic' rather than the ethical significance of his resurrection. The worship and life of the Church participate in the risen life of Christ as a festival of freedom (III.5). Here the ecclesiological aspect of *Theology and Joy* finds its place in Moltmann's comprehensive ecclesiology. Secondly, Moltmann restores to pride of place the neglected Christological 'title' of friend. The concept of the friendship of Jesus, in which friendship signifies fellowship in freedom, makes the Church's fellowship with God in Christ the source of its own fellowship as open friendship (III.6). In discussing all five of these forms of the Church's participation in the mission of Christ, Moltmann is careful to represent the Church's activity as having an outward and forward direction. In each case the Church follows the direction of Christ's own mission, serving not itself but the world and its future.

In the final section of this chapter (III.7) Moltmann completes the Christological aspect of the Church's participation in the trinitarian history of God by considering, not the activities but the *presence* of Christ, on the principle that 'the true church is to be found where Christ is present' (CPS 122). Here a neat scheme gives the Church its place in relation to the crucified, risen and coming Christ. According to his promises Christ is present now in two forms by identification, both of which anticipate his future presence in person at the parousia. As the exalted Christ he identifies with the Church in its apostolic mission of proclamation, and in this way is present in the Gospel, sacraments and fellowship of the Church, which anticipate his kingdom in the world. These are therefore signs of his presence and so of where the true Church is to be found. But also, as the crucified Christ, he identifies with the poor,[3] who anticipate the kingdom, not in active mission but in suffering expectation. The true Church is therefore to be found in fellowship with the poor. The Church exists in the presence of Christ only when it links the two forms of Christ's presence by missionary presence among the poor: 'the church with its mission would be present where Christ awaits it, amid the downtrodden, the sick and the captives' (CPS 129).[4]

Chapter III has therefore orientated the Church in the trinitarian history of God by reference to its Christological origin which points to its Christological future at the ˇparousia. Chapter IV reverses the direction and orientates the Church by reference to its eschatological goal as this already affects the present. The final section (IV.5) is a systematic account of how Moltmann understands the eschatological kingdom to be already present in anticipation and therefore of the Church's role as mediator of the eschatological future into the present, a role which is then more fully developed pneumatologically in chapter V. But the rest of chapter IV concerns the Church's relationships with those partners in history 'who are not the church and will never become the church' (CPS 134): Israel, the world religions, and the economic, political and cultural processes of the world. In this discussion the relationship to Israel, as 'Christianity's original, enduring and final partner in history' (CPS 135), has methodological priority, because it is in recalling its Israelite origins and in open relationship to contemporary Israel that the Church is kept aware of the still unredeemed state of the world and therefore of its direction towards the coming kingdom.[5] Thus giving priority to the relationship with Israel ensures that the Church gives messianic direction to the rest of its relationships (cf. CPS 150).

The Church's place within the trinitarian history of God is given its pneumatological dimension in chapters V and VI. Since it is the Spirit who, between the history of Jesus and the coming of the kingdom, is the divine presence and activity mediating the eschatological future to the world now, the pneumatological dimension to ecclesiology makes possible the fullest description of the life of the Church: 'It is the doctrine of the Holy Spirit in particular that depicts the processes and experiences in which and through which the church becomes comprehensible to itself as the messianic fellowship in the world and for the world' (CPS 198). These 'processes and experiences' are the 'means' or 'mediations of salvation' (preaching, baptism, the Lord's supper, worship and lifestyle) and the ministries or charismata, dealt with in chapter V and chapter VI respectively. Interpreted in the context of the mission of the Spirit, these characterise the Church as the messianic fellowship open to the world and its future, existing for the world and its future, and so they are *the way in which* the Church lives out its messianic vocation between the remembrance of Christ (chapter III) and the hope of the kingdom in relation to its partners in history (chapter IV). It is in these chapters V and VI in particular that the argument leads to criticism of the contemporary Protestant Church in Germany and proposals for reform of its life, worship and ministry. These proposals focus on the renewal of congregational life 'from below' to produce communities which are the subjects of their own history and can therefore assume the vocation of the messianic fellowship in the world. The proposed reforms of baptism, the Lord's supper, worship, ministry and structure all lead away from civil religion, clericalism and the pastoral church 'for the people', towards the local church as free fellowship of committed disciples, responsible for its own life and mission, a real community which is at the same time open to the world, 'the people's own communal church among the people' (CPS xvi). Only this kind of Church corresponds to the mission of the Spirit within which the Church exists. The Spirit creates fellowship in freedom and equality, and, just as importantly, fellowship which is orientated outwards and forwards, to the world and its eschatological future. By keeping in the forefront of the discussion the nature of the Spirit's activity as eschatological anticipation for the sake of the future of the whole of creation, Moltmann throughout these two chapters keeps the renewal of the Church's communal life and worship in unbroken connexion with its messianic mission. In the presence and power of the Holy Spirit, the Church is the 'messianic fellowship' with equal stress on both words.

Since considerations of praxis run right through *The Church in the Power of the Spirit*, Moltmann does not need to end this book with a turn towards praxis, as he did *Theology of Hope* and *The Crucified God*. Instead, the final chapter (VII) is a masterly exposition of the four traditional, credal marks of the Church interpreted in terms of messianic and relational ecclesiology, i.e. in terms of the Church's participation in the trinitarian history of God's dealings with the world. The marks are all understood Christologically, as characteristics of Christ's activity before they are characteristics of the Church's participation in his mission; eschatologically, as 'messianic predicates' which point to the coming kingdom for which the Church exists; and as the Church's task in the world, with an outward as well as an inward direction. Finally, in order to make the marks more precisely character-istic of the Church's mission in relation to the contemporary world situation ('our divided, fought over, unjust, inhuman world'), each is given an additional qualification: unity in freedom, holiness in poverty, apostolicity in suffering, catholicity in partisanship for the oppressed (CPS 341–342).

In the rest of this chapter we shall discuss some of the main themes which recur throughout *The Church in the Power of the Spirit* and Moltmann's minor ecclesiological writings.

**Suffering and joy**  Moltmann's attempt to understand the Church within the trinitarian history of God explains the *dialectic of suffering and joy* in the Church's experience, which colours much of his account of the Church's life and especially his view of the centrality of worship in the Church's life and mission. In the concept of the trinitarian history of God, Moltmann's fundamental dialectic of the cross and the resurrection leads to a dialectic of pain and joy in the divine experience with history. One side of God's history is the suffering he experiences as he opens himself in vulnerable love to the world: his suffering in the passion of Christ continues in the 'sighings of the Spirit' until he finally turns his and the world's suffering into joy at the end. But, on the other hand, in the movement of unification and glorification which leads from the resurrection of Christ to the new creation, God antici-pates his eschatological joy. Since he is glorified in the liberation of his creation, he experiences joy in the Spirit's work of glorifying the Father and the Son by liberating humanity (CPS 63–64). In this movement, of course, suffering is for the sake of joy: God suffers in love for his creation in order to liberate it: 'God's pain in the world is the way to God's happiness with the world' (OC 93).

As the Church participates in God's history with the world it shares this dialectic of the divine experience. As it lives in the presence of the Spirit it suffers with God's suffering with the world and experiences his anticipated joy (CPS 65). This makes the dialectic of suffering and joy in the Church's life not merely the Church's experience but the Church's experience *of God*, and accounts for Moltmann's growing sympathy for mysticism in the period after *The Church in the Power of the Spirit* (cf. EG 55–80; TA). However, in this sympathy Moltmann will not allow the contemplative mysticism of the cross (cf. CG 45–53; CPS 93) to be a substitute for what we might call the active mysticism of discipleship (EG 71–76) and the latter is the focus in *The Church in the Power of the Spirit*. 'The church shares in Christ's sufferings only when it takes part in Christ's mission. Its Christian suffering is apostolic suffering' (OC 91). Conversely, 'the church is apostolic when it takes up its cross' (CPS 361). It is as it takes part in the *mission* of Christ and the Spirit that it participates in the passion of Christ and the sighings of the Spirit. Its sufferings are therefore, like God's, messianic sufferings *with and for the world*.

The Church 'is fundamentally born out of the cross of Christ' (CPS 97, cf. 86; OC 85), because it is the fellowship of those who have been liberated by Christ's self-giving. As such, it must be *both* the 'Church under the cross,' which, remembering the crucified Christ, is led into solidarity with the godforsaken with whom he identified (CPS 97–98), *and* the Church which celebrates the festival of freedom, glorifying God in the joy of the new exodus to eschatological freedom (cf. CPS 76–78). Consequently, it participates in Christ's mission not only in the obedience of discipleship but also in *doxology*. These two aspects influence and reinforce each other (CPS 190). On the one hand, without the 'aesthetic categories' of freedom and joy, which are the Church's participation in the glorified life of the risen Christ, 'the imitation of Christ and the new obedience would become a joyless legalistic task' (CPS 109). On the other hand, doxology which did not lead into discipleship of the crucified Christ would be an irresponsible escape from the world. It is saved from this by its character precisely as *anticipation* of the new creation in the midst of this still godless and godforsaken world. As such it creates resistance to the godlessness of the world and solidarity with the godforsaken of the world (cf. CPS 97–98; OC 88). Joy in liberation won through Christ's suffering leads into suffering for the liberation of others. As always in Moltmann's thought, the dialectical identity of the crucified and risen Christ is operative. Fellowship with the risen Christ in his eschatological glory is possible only in fellowship with the crucified Christ in his suffering, but conversely the crucified Christ mediates the joy of the new creation to those who must still suffer with him in the unredeemed world (cf. CPS 59, 273–274). So, while the Church must suffer until the end of all suffering, 'there are encouraging signs of joy and even more joyful songs of liberation to be heard within and under the passion of God and the world' (OC 93–94). Even if suffering predominates, it is joy which in the cross and resurrection of Christ has gained the eschatological ascendancy which transforms the character of suffering even now.

A central role in the Church's dialectical experience of suffering and joy is played by worship, because it is this which sets the Christian community, with all the pains and joys of its everyday life, within the trinitarian history of God, and enables it to understand itself as the messianic fellowship in the presence of the Spirit and to live out this vocation in the rest of its life (CPS 261–262). Worship is – or should be! – the festival of freedom, in which the new freedom of those liberated by Christ is celebrated in spontaneity and exuberant ecstasy (CPS 111–112), and the eschatological glorification of God in all things is anticipated in joyful thanksgiving (CPS 256). 'Before the liberation experienced in faith is translated into new obedience, it is celebrated in festal ecstasy' (CPS 112). This ensures that the new obedience stems from the experience of liberation in Christ. Moltmann's emphasis on worship as festival is intended to protect Christianity from the excessive moralisation and rationalisation which see no point in such 'play' except for the sake of work (cf. OC 64–65; LF 74, 83). 'Worship has priority over ethics' (CPS 271), because only so can Christian life be a matter of liberated love rather than compulsive legalism.

There is the danger that festivals can function as mere safety-valves which, by compensating for the unfree conditions of everyday life, leave them unchanged and even reinforce them. Christian worship can all too easily fulfil this function in rationalised industrial society (CPS 111–112, 265–267). But, celebrated in the Spirit as eschatological anticipation, the Christian feast of freedom can have a quite different significance. As a *real* anticipation of the future it *demonstrates* the alternatives offered by the creative Spirit to the lack of freedom in everyday life and so encourages the search for ways of mediating this liberation into the individual lives of Christians and the public life of society (CPS 111–112, 261–262, 274). Because of its character as anticipation of the new creation, the feast will always contain an excess of freedom which cannot be translated into liberation in the rest of life yet, but this provides the transcendent eschatological stimulus which leads beyond every provisional realisation of freedom: 'it points enduringly to the resurrection as the great alternative to this world of death, stimulating the limited alternatives to death's dominion, keeping us alive and making us take our bearings from the victory of life' (CPS 113, cf. 274; LF 84).

The feast not only leads into the suffering of resistance and solidarity. As celebration of the resurrection of the crucified Christ, suffering is never far from it. In the presence of the crucified Christ, it can make room for the free expression of pain and grief and protest (CPS 112, 273–274; OC 79–80; cf. LF 79). In its experience of fellowship it will give expression to its solidarity with persecuted Christians (cf. OC 89–90). Moltmann has increasingly come to see real ecumenical unity as realised 'under the cross' in shared suffering (CPS 97; OC VI: EC).

**The mature and responsible congregation**    Moltmann sees himself as 'a "free-church" person in the midst of a *Volkskirche*' (CR 110). In other words, the kind of Church to which he is committed in principle is the voluntary fellowship of committed disciples, a Church *of* the people, while the German Protestant Church to which he belongs is a pastoral Church *for* the people, 'a public institution to administer the religion of society' (TGT 189). The latter still belongs to the heritage of the Constantinian adoption of Christianity as the state religion. No longer a state Church, it is still civil religion, since it sees itself as the people's Church for all the people and must therefore maintain a neutral stance towards all social and political divisions in society. In fact this supposedly nonpolitical stance is in the interests of the groups that control the status quo in society (CR 111). Restricting itself to the narrowly religious needs of the people, it is the clerical institution looking after the people – like the social services – and administering their religious affairs – like a government bureaucracy. Consequently, it is a Church without any critical effect on society. It is a Church of non-committal religion, 'an institutionalized absence of commitment' (PPL 159), since membership of the Church is involuntary and the clerical institution takes care of the people's religious needs for them. 'This is the explanation of the curious situation in Germany, where 95 per cent of the people "belong" to a church, only 10–15 per cent participate actively' (CR 109). Finally, it is a 'church without community' (TGT 191). Where everyone 'belongs' but has no responsibility for the life of the Church, real fellowship is impossible. (For this account of the *Volkskirche* in Moltmann's view, see CPS 224, 318–319, 326–328, 334; CR 109–110; TGT 189–192; OC 96, 98–99, 120–123; PPL 100, 158–160.)

In his criticism of this kind of Church, in which Christianity has lost its character as messianic fellowship, Moltmann is not only identifying, broadly, with the 'free church' (or Congregationalist) tradition in Anglo-Saxon ecclesiology, which stems from the left wing of the Reformation (OC 117),[6] though he has some criticisms of this tradition (PPL 160–161, 162). He is also impressed by the evidence that it is through the development of 'the mature and responsible congregation' that the contemporary Church in many parts of the world is finding its identity as messianic fellowship and fulfilling its messianic vocation, in persecution, in experienced fellowship, in missionary service to the world, in social and political criticism and involvement (cf. CPS 329–330; CR 111).[7] Even in Europe the growth of 'grassroots communities' is a sign of the weakness of the pastoral Church and a sign of hope: these 'are changing the church from the inside out and making it into the congregation' (OC 117; cf. CPS 328; PPL 104; CR 109–110). This, for Moltmann, is the great hope for the Church, whose renewal must come 'from below' (HC 21).

The 'mature and responsible congregation' (HC 41; OC 117) towards which renewal must be directed is characterised by the committed discipleship of all members, in the service of the kingdom, by fellowship in freedom and equality, by mutual acceptance and care, and by openness to the world, especially in solidarity with the poor and the oppressed. This vision of the Church is rooted theologically in its relationship to the trinitarian history of God. The hierarchical, authoritarian and clerically managed Church depends, according to Moltmann, on a monarchical image of God as power and rule: fundamentally a monotheistic doctrine of God. Clerical rule in the Church is then legitimated by a descending authority structure in which 'the people' are subjects to be ruled and administered. But this thinking is non-trinitarian. It neglects Jesus' transformation of the notion of rule into liberating service, his open friendship and identification with 'the people', and his cross, which smashes all idols of religious power. Equally it neglects the Holy Spirit, who is not a divine or clerical instrument, but the one who liberates for free fellowship, calls and empowers all Christians for messianic service, and unites, not by subjection to a single ruler, but in loving community. As he unites the persons of the Trinity in their loving fellowship, so in his eschatological mission of liberation and unification he unites the Trinity with humanity in free fellowship. God in his trinitarian history is not a justification for clerical rule, but is the vulnerable and liberating love which makes possible open fellowship in freedom and responsibility (see CPS 225, 293–294, 305–306; HC 40; OC 115; cf. TKG 200–202; FHS 293–294). In this trinitarian context ecclesiology cannot be reduced to 'hierarchology', preoccupied with the authority of the ministry, but must begin with the fact that every believer is a responsible member of the messianic fellowship (CPS 289).

Every believer is called to *committed discipleship* in the service of the kingdom in the world and thereby participates actively in the messianic vocation of the Church. Against the non-committal Christianity of the pastoral Church, Moltmann stresses that justification leads to liberated life (CPS 36) and that faith is inseparable from discipleship of Christ (PPL 86). As disciples called to responsible participation in Christ's mission (HC 132), the Christian community becomes 'the conscious agent of its own history with God in the Holy Spirit' (HC 41; cf. OC 108–112; PPL 163–164). To this concern for a fellowship of committed disciples belongs Moltmann's interest in the description of a 'messianic lifestyle' which will witness to the coming kingdom which it reflects (CPS 275–288; OC III), and also his criticism of current baptismal theory and practice (CPS 226–242; OC 124–125; HC 46–51). Moltmann sees the practice of infant baptism as the cornerstone of civil religion, since it perpetuates *involuntary* membership of the Church: 'There is no possibility of creating a voluntary, independent, and mature community out of the institutional churches to which people belong simply on the basis of being baptised as children' (HC 47). But, in line with his messianic ecclesiology, Moltmann substitutes for infant baptism not 'believer's baptism', in which the believer confesses his faith (although of course this is presupposed), so much as 'baptism into Christian calling' (*Berufungstaufe*), i.e. baptism 'as incorporation into the Christian calling to *discipleship and service*' (HC 50–51). Baptism is each Christian's call to a task in the messianic vocation of the whole Church. Obviously, the restoration of such a significance to baptism depends on and must go along with the renewal of mature and responsible congregational life (CPS 242).

As a fellowship of committed disciples, the Church is also a *free* society of *equals*. Its common calling to share in Christ's messianic mission as prophet, priest and king *precedes* the particular assignments which the Spirit gives to particular members, and so the latter can never set certain 'office-bearers' who share in the offices of Christ over their fellows who do not (CPS 300–301). The Spirit in fact assigns his gifts to all members of the community, who are all 'office-bearers' in this sense. Differences are of function, not rank, consequently, not hierarchy but 'freedom, diversity and brotherliness' characterise the community, whose principle Moltmann formulates as: 'to each his own: all for each other; testifying together to the world the saving life of Christ' (CPS 298).[8]

Finally, the messianic fellowship is an *open* fellowship of *friends*. Moltmann's preference for the term 'friendship' to characterise both the fellowship of Christians with God in Christ and the fellowship among Christians in the Church – the latter deriving from the former – is based on the nature of friendship as a *free* relationship which combines affection with respect and loyalty (CPS 115, 316). It is not, like social and familial relationships, a necessary relationship but a freely chosen one, a 'simple liking-to-be-with-others' (OC 53) in total acceptance. It 'arises out of freedom, consists in mutual freedom, and preserves this freedom. . . . We are not by nature free, but become so only when someone likes us. Friends open up to one another free space for free life' (OC 52).

However, friendship as characteristic of the Church needs to be to some extent redefined by the friendship of Jesus which is its source. Jesus' friendship was not the closed circle of fellowship of like with like, nor was it the privatised friendship of modern society. It was open and public friendship for the unrighteous and the despised (CPS 119–121). 'Through Jesus, friendship has become an open term of proffer. It is forthcoming solidarity' (OC 61).[9] We recognise here the dialectical love of God for his other which already in *The Crucified God* made identification with those who are different the social principle of Christianity (CG 28; cf. FC 79). Moltmann has now made this the principle for the renewal of the Church as congregation, in the form of friendship and of the closely related principle of the acceptance of those who are different (OC II; PPL XII).

Not only God's dialectical love but also its soteriological consequence, justification by faith, lies at the theological basis of this principle of open fellowship with those who are different. Only because we have been accepted by God, in his dialectical love for us, is it possible for us to imitate his dialectical love in the acceptance of others. Only through justification by faith are we freed from the compulsion to confirm ourselves by associating only with those who are like ourselves. Accepting only those like ourselves and disparaging or fearing others is the social form of self-justification. Liberated from self-justification by God's accepting love, the Church can practise 'the social form of justification by faith', which is 'recognition of the other in his otherness, the recognition of the person who is different as a person' (CPS 189). The Church is then a society in which all kinds of people accept each other 'in a new kind of living together' (OC 33) and in which the *pathos* of God's dialectical love is lived out as mutual involvement in each other's joy and pain. Such a fellowship is necessarily open to others in an unqualified way. The themes of friendship and acceptance are ecclesiological themes to which Moltmann seems especially to warm in treating both their theological depth and their practical outworkings in the life of the Church (CPS 114–121, 182–189, 314–316; OC II, IV; PPL XII, XIII).

As a society of open friendship the Church is set in the history of the Spirit, as the Spirit of God's dialectical love flowing from the event of the cross and anticipating the kingdom: 'Open and total friendship that goes out to meet the other is the spirit of the kingdom in which God comes to man and man to man. . . . Open friendship prepares the ground for a friendlier world' (CPS 121). The fundamental openness of the Church in friendship for the unlike is the essential openness of its messianic mission. Hence Moltmann is careful to protect his vision of the Church from the sectarian tendencies of those free churches and fellowship groups which lack openness to others (CPS 224–225, 242, 321, 325; PPL 160–161). The 'open identity' of the friendship of Jesus makes possible a community which does not lose but finds its identity in being turned outwards to the world in evangelism, practical acts of liberation and solidarity with the poor. But its openness to the world is quite different from that of the pastoral Church. Since it is not the religion of society, its own life can break free of conformity with society and offer a radical alternative: the free fellowship created by the Spirit in anticipation of the kingdom (CPS 316). This life of freedom in mutual acceptance can be the source for influencing society in the same direction: revitalising democratic freedom and participation, promoting reconciliation in the face of racialism, sexism, prejudice against the handicapped, and other types of inability to accept those who are different, overcoming the apathy of modern society by spreading the passion for life which is open to suffering (cf. HC 41; CPS 292). The whole of Moltmann's section on 'Christianity in the processes of the world's life' (CPS IV.4) uses the principles of the Church's own life as those by which it seeks to promote liberation in the various spheres of secular life. Furthermore, the messianic fellowship is freed from the need for the neutral stance which ties civil religion to the prevailing interests in society (TGT 111): it is free to identify with the victims of society (CPS 225). Its open friendship especially takes the form of Jesus' solidarity with the poor: not simply charitable activity for them, but fellowship with them (HC 25). Unlike the pastoral church which is for everyone in an undifferentiated way, 'the Christian community is present for everyone only when it is first present for the poor, the sick, the sinners' (HC 46; cf. CPS 334–335). It can be seen how closely Moltmann's ecclesiology of the voluntary fellowship is linked to his concern for a socially critical Church which identifies with the most marginalised in society.

Moltmann's concept of the Church as a society of open friendship strongly influences his proposals on the meaning and practice of the Lord's supper (CPS V.4; HC 52–56; cf. already CG 44). It confers the fellowship which derives from Christ's self-giving on the cross and so 'creates solidarity among people who are in themselves different' (CPS 252). But this fellowship round the Lord's table must be in principle *open* to the whole world, since it is based on Jesus' table-fellowship not only with his disciples but also with the poor and the unrighteous, since it derives from the crucified Christ's open identification with all the godless and the godforsaken, and since it points in anticipation to the eschatological banquet of the nations. The supper represents and actualises the open fellowship of the Church's messianic mission as it is created by the universal tendency of the mission of Christ and the Spirit. Thus 'it is the Lord's supper above all that ought to show in its eschatological openness the openness to the world of the Christian mission' (CPS 247). This means that the only condition which can be set for participation in the supper is 'that we be clear that in this meal we have to do with the Jesus who is crucified for us and that in this meal the kingdom of God stands open to us' (HC 55).

Perhaps the most cogent criticism[10] of Moltmann's concept of the Church as free fellowship is that in simply opposing power and authority, on the one hand, and love and freedom, on the other, Moltmann too easily equates the former with domination. He neglects the inevitability of some kind of power and authority in human society and therefore misses the opportunity to explore the way in which power and authority can be based on consent, exercised in love, and directed to fostering, rather than suppressing, freedom and responsibility. However, his brief discussion of *leadership* in the congregation (CPS 309–310) and the more general discussion of the relationship between the community and the particular assignments of its members (CPS 302–306) have potential in this direction and show that he is not wholly unaware of the issues.

**The Church for the world**   It has always been a basic principle of Moltmann's theology that the Church exists as a provisional reality to serve the coming universal kingdom of God in the world, or, to put in another way, that the Church exists in mission. This principle is fundamental to the way Moltmann develops various aspects of the Church-world relationship in *The Church in the Power of the Spirit.*[11] One formal way in which he refines its meaning is in the categories of anticipation and representation. The Church is the anticipation of the kingdom of God under the conditions of history, the vanguard of the new humanity (CPS 196). But anticipation involves representation. The Church is *pars pro toto:* a preliminary and fragmentary *part* of the coming *whole* (the universal kingdom), and so *representative* of the whole *for the sake of* the rest of the world whose future the whole is. Consequently, the Church can only prove itself as an anticipation of the coming kingdom 'through intervention and self-giving for the future of others' (CPS 194–195). This is why, in Moltmann's treatment of the way the Spirit anticipates the kingdom in the life of the Church (CPS V and VI), the mediations and ministries of the Spirit are always directed outwards and forwards. 'As the mediations and powers of the Holy Spirit, they lead the Church beyond itself, out into the suffering of the world and into the divine future' (CPS 198). The kingdom is anticipated in the Church only *as mission*, which is to say: only as the messianic fellowship of service for the kingdom of God in the world. This clarifies the sense in which, for Moltmann, the Church is a *provisional* reality, which at the end will have fulfilled its role and be superseded by the kingdom. Insofar as the Church anticipates the kingdom, it is continuous with the kingdom, although its necessarily imperfect anticipation of the kingdom under the conditions of history will be transcended in the perfection of the kingdom. But insofar as the Church anticipates the kingdom *in mission* it is provisional. Hence in Moltmann's discussion of the four marks of the Church (CPS VII), three are 'designations of the kingdom' which are applied to the Church as mediating the life of the kingdom in history, but the fourth mark, apostolicity, is not a characteristic of the kingdom in its eschatological fullness at all. It designates the Church in history precisely as a *missionary* anticipation of the kingdom:

> We can therefore say that the historical church *will* be the one, holy, catholic church through the apostolic witness of Christ, and in carrying out that witness; whereas the church glorified in the kingdom of God *is* the one, holy, catholic church, through the fulfilment of its apostolate. Historically the church has its being in carrying out the apostolate. In eternity the church has its being in fulfilment of the apostolate, that is, in the seeing face to face (CPS 358).

This passage also makes clear that the Church does not disappear at the end, but, its mission accomplished, finds its fulfilment in the kingdom. In its historical form, however, the Church's whole existence is characterised by the missionary mark of apostolicity, and this means that the other three marks take a missionary *form* in being directed outwards and forwards. The Church is not, for example, ' "one" for itself; it is one for the peace of divided mankind in the coming kingdom of God' (CPS 345).

None of this argument, however, seems to necessitate the kind of distinction Moltmann makes when he says that 'the real point [of the Church's mission within the mission of Christ and the Spirit] is not to spread the church but to spread the kingdom' (CPS 11), or that the aim of the Gospel which the Church proclaims 'is not to spread the Christian religion or to implant the church; it is to liberate the people for the exodus in the name of the coming kingdom' (CPS 84). Similarly, in criticising the ecclesiology of the Heidelberg Catechism, he objects that 'the whole human race only seems to be material for the election and gathering of the community of the saved, as if mankind were there for the church and not the church for mankind' (CPS 69). Yet, if the Church is the anticipation of the kingdom of God within history, it would seem natural to suppose that the way the Church serves the coming kingdom is by calling and gathering people into its own fellowship. The Church would then exist not for itself but for the world – in the sense that it exists not for the sake of those who are already its members but for the sake of extending its fellowship to others. This would not make the Church's mission self-serving, since it incorporates people not for its own sake but for theirs, and, as a fellowship continually turned outwards to the incorporation of others, for the sake of others too. In rejecting this way of thinking Moltmann is far from denying that the proclamation of the Gospel, which he consistently regards as the primary, though not the only, way in which the Church serves the kingdom, does create the Church. By liberating people from sin and calling them to discipleship it gathers the people of the eschatological exodus, the messianic fellowship (CPS 83–84). But the Church is not the goal. It is to Christ and his coming kingdom that people are converted, and it is on their way to the kingdom that they form the messianic fellowship. But is this materially different from saying that the aim of mission is the Church *as* a fellowship continually open to the inclusion of others? It is different, in Moltmann's thinking, because, although the Church has a centrally important role in preparing the way for the universal kingdom, it is not by the inclusion of the whole world in the Church that the universal kingdom will come.[12] There are movements towards the kingdom in world history independently of the Church, and the Church itself mediates the kingdom in history in other ways besides making disciples.

To take the latter aspect first, it is here that Moltmann's concept of multi-dimensional liberation comes into play (cf. CG 329–335; FC 109–114). The Gospel of Christ anticipates the kingdom by proclaiming and effecting liberation in all the inter-related spheres of life. 'Just as the coming kingdom is universal, so the gospel brings the liberation of men to universal expression. It seeks to liberate the soul and the body, individual and social conditions, human systems and the systems of nature from the closedness of reserve, from self-righteousness, and from godless and inhuman pressures' (CPS 223).

This means that the messianic fellowship spreads the liberation of the kingdom not only in every aspect of its own life and that of its members, but also through its members' influence in every aspect of society. The Gospel has its effect not only as people consciously respond to it in faith and discipleship, but also as it spreads freedom in the various dimensions of the life of secular society. In a hidden way and in anticipation of his presence at the end, God is present wherever people experience economic, political, cultural, ecological or personal liberation (HD 110–111). The dimensions are mutually interrelated and not reducible to one dimension which gives rise to the others, and so political liberation, for example, is not unilaterally dependent on the liberation experienced in Christian conversion. Thus the Church's influence for liberation may extend beyond its membership.

However, this need not invalidate the desire that all should join the messianic fellowship as Christian disciples: such a goal could remain desirable in addition to the Church's liberating activity of other kinds. At this point, therefore, we should consider a second relevant aspect of Moltmann's thought: the idea that the mission of the Son and of the Spirit towards the kingdom includes but is not confined to the Church. The Church is *one element* in the history of the Spirit's liberating activity, and there are 'saving efficacies of the Spirit outside the Church' (CPS 64–65). One might still ask whether it might not be desirable for the Church to include these in its own mission. Although Moltmann rejects Rahner's notion of anonymous Christianity, there is clearly a sense in which salvation outside the Church, which Moltmann believes to be the saving work of *Jesus Christ* (CPS 153), is 'anonymous' in not acknowledging Jesus Christ. Why should it not be desirable that this anonymous work of the Spirit come to explicit confession of Jesus Christ?

So, finally, we come to the uncrossable barrier which Moltmann attempts to erect in the way of any notion that the Church could ever become the universal kingdom: the Church has 'partners in history who are not the church and will never become the church' (CPS 134). These are Israel, which the Church cannot 'succeed' (CPS 148) or 'supplant' (CPS 351); the world religions, which will 'not be ecclesiasticized . . . nor will they be Christianized' (CPS 163); and the institutions and processes of secular life 'which can neither be ecclesiasticized nor Christianized' (CPS 163). Here Moltmann is especially concerned to guard against triumphalism (cf. HD 198): 'those enthusiastic dreams of realizing the universality of God's kingdom through a universal Christian state or by supplanting Israel' (CPS 351). Why are these only dreams? The case of Israel, the primary partner, is special but also, in a way, paradigmatic. For Moltmann, Israel and the Church have distinct divine callings in history, by which they complement each other and which they can only fulfil by not being each other (CPS 147–149; cf. HD 208–213). Each witnesses to the kingdom of God in its distinctive way which makes it a necessary 'thorn in the side' of the other (CPS 148). The point applies in a somewhat different way to the other partners. Because the Church is only an imperfect, fragmentary anticipation of the kingdom (CPS 167), it can only serve the truth of the whole by openness to partners who can open up potentialities for the kingdom not available to the Church in isolation (cf. CPS 163). It is Moltmann's profound belief in relationality and dialogue which is operative here. The Church can only fulfil its special role, as the messianic fellowship which confesses Jesus Christ, in relationship to other movements in history which have different potentialities for the kingdom. As a contemporary ecclesiological strategy this is convincing enough. But one is still bound to ask why theoretical and final limits must be placed on explicit response to the Gospel through confession of faith in Christ? Of the world religions, for example, Moltmann hopes that in dialogue with Christianity 'they will be given a messianic direction towards the kingdom. For this, people of other religions, and the other religions themselves, bring a wealth of potentialities and powers with them; and Christianity must not suppress these but must fill them with hope' (CPS 163). But in gaining this messianic direction, why should they not also, without forfeiting their distinctive potentialities for the kingdom, come to believe in Jesus as the Messiah of the kingdom? But then, as liberating movements of the Spirit, orientated to the kingdom and confessing Jesus Christ as Lord, they will, by Moltmann's definition, be his Church. It may well be that Moltmann's ecclesiological concerns can be maintained without setting any limits on the Church's mission to call people to faith in Jesus Christ.

# CONCLUSION

The adequacy of a contemporary Christian theology is tested in its ability to set the Christological centre of historic Christian faith in an illuminating, critical and effective relation to the characteristically modern experience of the world. This test is met neither by theologies which attempt to retain their Christian identity only by ignoring their context in the modern world nor by theologies which simply accept the modern world in a rationalistic and positivistic way. It is met neither by traditional fundamentalisms which sacrifice relevance to orthodoxy nor by traditional liberalisms which sacrifice orthodoxy to relevance. In neither case is there a critical inter-relationship from which an authentically Christian praxis can result. The greatest achievement of Moltmann's theology has been to open up hermeneutical structures for relating biblical faith to the modern world. The strength and appropriateness of these structures lie in their biblical basis, their Christological centre and their eschatological openness. They give Moltmann's theology a relevance to the modern world which is achieved not only without surrendering the central features of biblical and historic Christian faith, but much more positively by probing the theological meaning of these. By recovering a Christological centre which is both dialectical and eschatological, Moltmann's theology acquired an openness to the world which is not in tension with the Christological centre but is actually required by the Christological centre, and which is not an accommodation to conservative, liberal or radical values, but has a critical edge and a consistent solidarity with the most marginalised members of society. The addition, more recently, of a trinitarian ecclesiology has specified the ecclesiological mediation which such a theological structure needs in a church open in mission to the world and to the future.

To claim that Moltmann's most solid achievement lies in the hermeneutical structures of this theology is also to recognise that his theology is necessarily an unfinished project – not only in 1979, where this study breaks off, but even at the conclusion of the series of volumes on which he is currently engaged. This is because his theology is *structurally* open – to dialogue with and enrichment from all theological traditions and other academic disciplines, and to the world in its suffering and hope. The reader is not therefore required to admire and reflect – or to criticise and reject – a finished achievement, but to engage with Moltmann's work in a dialogue for the sake of the kingdom of God.

Ultimately, a theology is only open in a Christian way if it is primarily open to God and has been *opened by God* to the world. The dialectic of cross and resurrection needs to have left its mark on the theologian's own experience in his theological work. Moltmann aptly compares the true theologian to Jacob emerging from his wrestling match at the ford of the Jabbok, 'beaten and limping'. This is why our best theology is 'imperfect', shattered by that Greater One And that is why theology is at best only a directional indicator, pointing to the mysterious God who draws us to him, drives us on, and continually eludes all our concepts, images, and symbols.'[1] In view of Moltmann's conviction that the true situation of theology is in dialogue with God (HP 131) as well as in dialogue with all available human partners, it may be appropriate to conclude by quoting a prayer which Moltmann wrote towards the end of the period of his theological development which we have studied. It well expresses the eschatological trinitarianism, orientated both to praxis and to doxology, to which that development had led.[2]

FATHER IN HEAVEN
it is time you came.
For our time is running out
and our world is passing away.
You gave us our life with one another.
We have wrecked it by declaring war against one another.
You gave us trees and forests.

We have cut them down.
To the bird you gave the spring
and to the fish the rivers.
We have silenced spring and polluted the rivers.
To the work of your creation
you gave balance.
We have upset it and therefore come to grief.
Come, Creator of all,
renew the lifeless face of the earth.
Despite our unhappiness
give us hope for your Day
when, at peace with every creature,
we can laugh and praise you.

Jesus Christ, our Friend,
we cannot walk in your company
without our neighbours,
those near at hand and those far away,
friends and enemies.
Continue to be the friend of sinners,
poor with the poor,
weak with the weakly,
forsaken with those who are abandoned,
that they, and we with them, may have life.
We hope for the coming of your kingdom
as we hope for peace in this divided world.
We believe in your presence
just as we trust in meaningfulness,
even when faced with the meaninglessness of death.
We look for your coming
as we hunger for our daily bread.
Come, Lord Jesus, come quickly.

Holy Spirit, you are known to us
as power from on high,
as comforter in need.
We cry to you and our cry encourages us.
We call out to you and you call out with us.

We wait for you and you are in our hearts.
Open our eyes and we shall recognise
your footprints on our path.
Give us silence and we shall hear
your sighs in our prisons.
Take from us what you have to take
until we come to rest in you
and feel that we are resting,
aware of your life in us,
your burning love and your driving force,
your anguish and your happiness deep within us.
Come, Creator Spirit,
empty our heart of selfish anxiety,
fill our spirit with creative love.
Give us dreams and visions
of your kingdom of freedom.
Make us disconsolate if they are betrayed,
if they do not become a reality.

Father, Son and Holy Spirit.
The time has come, the time for the fulfilment of history,
the time for making all one with God and in God.

# NOTES

**Introduction**

1  M. D. Meeks, *Origins of the Theology of Hope* (Fortress Press, Philadelphia, 1974).

2  Throughout the book references to Moltmann's works are given in parenthesis in the text in the form of an abbreviation followed by page numbers (where upper case Roman numerals are used, they refer to chapters). A key to the abbreviations will be found in section A of the Bibliography.

**Chapter One**

1  C. Booker, *The Neophiliacs* (Fontana, London, 1970²), p. 12. The book is a disillusioned chronicle of the rise and fall of 60s optimism in Britain.

2  J. B. Metz (1966), quoted in G. C. O'Collins, 'Spes Quaerens Intellectum', *Interpretation* 22 (1968), p. 51; cf. RRF 3.

3  Cf. W. H. Capps, *Time Invades the Cathedral* (Fortress Press, Philadelphia, 1972), ch. 5, which is really against regarding Bloch, Metz and Moltmann as a school.

4  For Metz's theological development at this stage, see R. D. Johns, *Man in the World: The Theology of Johannes Baptist Metz* (American Academy of Religion Dissertation Series 16; Scholars Press, Missoula, Montana, 1976), ch. 4.

5  Cf. E. F. Tupper, *The Theology of Wolfhart Pannenberg* (SCM Press, London, 1974), pp. 25–26.

6  M. D. Meeks, *Origins of the Theology of Hope* (Fortress Press, Philadelphia, 1974), *passim*.

7  Moltmann, in *ibid.*, pp. xi-xii. For Moltmann's debt to Barth, see

also his 1965 letter to Barth, in K. Barth, *Letters 1961–1968*, ed. J. Fangmeier and H. Stoevesandt, tr. and ed. G. W. Bromiley (T. & T. Clark, Edinburgh, 1981), p. 349: 'It is far from my intention to try to replace [the *Church Dogmatics*] with anything else. From this castle I simply wanted to make a sortie into the lowlands of lesser conflicts.'

8   J. Moltmann, 'Die Wirklichkeit der Welt und Gottes konkretes Gebot nach Dietrich Bonhoeffer', in *Die mündlige Welt*, ed. E. Bethge, vol. III (Chr. Kaiser, Munich, 1960), pp. 42–67; 'The Lordship of Christ and Human Society', in J. Moltmann and J. Weissbach, *Two Studies in the Theology of Bonhoeffer* (Scribner's Sons, New York, 1967), pp. 19–94.

9   On Bonhoeffer's influence on Moltmann, see G. Hunsinger, 'The Crucified God and the Political Theology of Violence', *Heythrop Journal* 14 (1973), p. 392; Meeks, *op.cit.*, pp. 44–47; R. Gibellini, *La teologia di Jürgen Moltmann* (Queriniana, Brescia, 1975), pp. 16–30; and especially G. C. Chapman, 'Hope and the ethics of formation: Moltmann as an interpreter of Bonhoeffer', *Studies in religion/Sciences religieuses* 12 (1983), pp. 449–460.

10   Meeks, *op. cit.*, p. 30.

11   *Ibid.;* pp. 35–38. The quotation from Iwand on CG 36 is a good indication of the depth of Moltmann's indebtedness to Iwand's theology.

12   For Moltmann's estimate of the significance of von Rad's work for theology, see TGT 202.

13   K. Koch, *The Rediscovery of Apocalyptic* (Studies in Biblical Theology 22; SCM Press, London, 1972), ch. 2.

14   For a list of these historical-theological works, see P. F. Momose, *Kreuzestheologie: Eine Auseinandersetzung mit Jürgen Moltmann* (Herder, Freiburg, 1978), p. 24 n. 3, and for discussion of the extent to which Moltmann's theology of hope is developing in them, see *ibid.*, pp. 23–32; Gibellini, *op. cit.*, pp. 13–48; Meeks, *op. cit.*, pp. 22–23.

15   From the point of view of the debt which Moltmann's dialectical eschatology owes to Karl Barth's dialectical theology, it is worth noticing that the passage Moltmann quotes from Calvin's commentary on Hebrews (TH 18–19) is also quoted by Barth, in support of his dialectical theology, at the end of the preface to the third edition of his Romans: K. Barth, *The Epistle to the Romans*, tr. E. C. Hoskyns

(Oxford University Press, London, 1968), pp. 19–20. (I owe this observation to Dr. S. N. Williams.)

16   For a discussion of the beginnings of the theology of hope in Moltmann's dogmatic writings immediately before *Theology of Hope*, see Gibellini, *op. cit.*, pp. 49–76.

17   Moltmann in Capps, *op. cit.*, p. xiv.

18   The best study in English of Bloch's philosophy is W. Hudson, *The Marxist Philosophy of Ernst Bloch* (Macmillan, London, 1982), to which my accounts of Bloch's thought are frequently indebted. Cf. also R. M. Green, 'Ernst Bloch's Revision of Atheism', *Journal of Religion* 49 (1969), pp. 128–135; Capps, *op. cit.*, ch. 2; David Drew, 'Introduction', in E. Bloch, *Essays on the Philosophy of Music*, tr. P. Palmer (Cambridge University Press, Cambridge, 1985), pp. xi-xlviii. Studies especially relevant to Bloch's relation to Christian theology, including Moltmann's, are F. P. Fiorenza, 'Dialectical Theology and Hope', *Heythrop Journal* 9 (1986), pp. 143–163, 384–399; 10 (1969), pp. 26–42 (the promised concluding part of this study never appeared); G. G. O'Collins, 'The Principle and the Theology of Hope', *Scottish Journal of Theology* 21 (1968), pp. 129–144; H. Cox, Foreword to MHO, reprinted as 'Ernst Bloch and "The Pull of the Future" ', in *New Theology No. 5*. ed. M. E. Marty and D. G. Peerman (Macmillan, New York, 1968), pp. 191–203; Meeks, *op. cit.*, pp. 15–18, 80–89, 106–118; J. Bentley, *Between Marx and Christ: The Dialogue in German-Speaking Europe 1870–1970* (NLB, London, 1982), chs 5–6 (this replaces Bentley's earlier article in *Expository Times* 88 [1976], pp. 51–55); G. C. Chapman, 'Jürgen Moltmann and the Christian Dialogue with Marxism', *Journal of Ecumenical Studies* 18 (1981), pp. 435–450; P. R. Mendes-Flohr, ' "To Brush History Against the Grain": The Eschatology of the Frankfurt School and Ernst Bloch', *Journal of the American Academy of Religion* 51 (1983), pp. 631–650; F. Gradl, *Ein Atheist liest die Bibel: Ernst Bloch und das Alte Testament* (Beiträge zur biblischen Exegese und Theologie 12; P. Lang, Frankfurt am Main, 1979); P. Masset, 'Espérance marxiste, espérance chrétienne', *Nouvelle Revue Théologique* 99 (1977), pp. 321–339; *idem*, 'Une utilisation philosophique de la Bible: L'athéisme dans le christianisme d'Ernst Bloch', *Nouvelle Revue Théologique* 102 (1980), pp. 481–496; L. Hurbon, 'Théologie et politique dans l'oeuvre d'Ernst Bloch', *Études théologiques et religieuses* 49 (1974), 201–224; J.-R. Armogathe, 'Ernst Bloch, prophète marxiste? Promesse

et utopie', in J. Daniélou et al., *Espérance chrétienne et avenir humain (Les quatres fleuves* 2; Éditions du Seuil, Paris, 1974), pp. 108–114; P. Furter, 'L'espérance selon Ernst Bloch', *Revue de théologie et de philosophie* 15 (1965), pp. 286–301. (See also nn. 31, 47 below.)

Moltmann himself discusses Bloch's philosophy in RRF VIII (an essay first published in German in *Evangelische Theologie* 23 [1963], pp. 537–557, and appended, from the 3rd edition, to German editions of *Theologie der Hoffnung* [pp. 313–334], but not in the English translation); PT 174–188 (an essay which first appeared in the Bloch Festschrift in 1965); Moltmann's introduction to MHO; the essays collected in GEB (of which only ch. VI has appeared in English, as HD XI); EH III (an essay which first appeared in *Concilium* in 1966); and again recently in GC 42–45, 178–181.

19  Not until 1979 did Moltmann finally take up something of Bloch's eschatological mysticism of the 'darkness of the lived moment' (EG 76; though cf. already DTH 218), while in 1980 he was still seeking a doctrine of human freedom adequate to Bloch's protest against the oppressive divine Lord (TKG 203). In 1985 Bloch's views are again quite extensively discussed in GC.

20  For Moltmann's view of the stimulating quality of Bloch's work, cf. MHO 20; and for Moltmann's experience of the fruitfully provocative effect of conversation with Bloch, cf. GEB 63.

21  Cf Adorno's comment (quoted in Fiorenza, *art. cit.*, p. 390): 'Bloch is a mystic of the paradoxical unity of theology and atheism.'

22  With reference to the praise he had received from theologians, Bloch recalled an occasion in the Platonic dialogues when Socrates received praise from a sophist for a lecture he had given the day before and later remarked, 'He praised me! What did I say wrong last night?' (Fiorenza, *art. cit.*, p. 385).

23  For Moltmann's view of the question of Bloch's atheism, see GEB 66; MHO 24; HD 174.

24  In Capps, *op. cit.*, p. xiv, Moltmann rather plays down his debt to Bloch on the grounds that a theologian's 'philosophical expression' is 'a relatively incidental matter'. But he does not deny that his 'philosophical expression' derives from Bloch.

25  For Moltmann's use of Blochian language, see also G. Sauter in DTH 116.

26   Quoted in PH 275. For the controversy about Marx's attitude to philosophy and Bloch's position in it, see Fiorenza, *art. cit.*, pp. 31–37.
27   Cf. Moltmann's own statement of the parallel between the two: '*Das Prinzip Hoffnung* is no philosophical system, and the theology of hope is no *Summa Theologica*. Each is simply a critical stance, a polemical position, a controverted direction, taken within the conflicts of our time. Their purpose is to effect change: changes in consciousness and in our personal and political situation' (in Capps, *op. cit.*, p. xii).
28   Cf also the quotation from a letter from Moltmann (1980) in Chapman, *art. cit.*, p. 438: 'I discovered that not so much his neomarxism but his Jewish messianism brought me into friendship with Ernst Bloch.'
29   Moltmann himself was not especially fond of Bloch's favourite heretics: see RRF 171; GEB 61. But he developed a more appreciative view of the much misunderstood Joachim of Fiore by the time he wrote TKG 203–208, and 'Christliche Hoffnung: Messianisch oder transzendent? Ein theologisches Gespräch mit Joachim von Fiore und Thomas von Aquin', *Münchener Theologischer Zeitschrift* 33 (1982), pp. 241–260.
30   Cf TH 41: 'the loss of eschatology . . . has always been the condition that makes possible the adaptation of Christianity to its environment.'
31   For Bloch's interpretation of biblical religion, in addition to the literature cited in n. 18 above, see J. Niewiadomski, *Die Zweideutigkeit von Gott und Welt in J. Moltmanns Theologien* (Tyrolia, Innsbruck, 1982), pp. 21–28; and for discussions of Bloch's Old Testament interpretation by Old Testament theologians, see W. Zimmerli, *Man and his Hope in the Old Testament* (Studies in Biblical Theology 20; SCM Press, London, 1971), ch. XI; K. H. Miskotte, *Then the Gods are Silent*, tr. J. W. Doberstein (Collins, London, 1967), 295–302.
32   On Moltmann's criticisms of Bloch, see especially Chapman, *art. cit.*, pp. 444–448.
33   The phrase is Bloch's own (cf. O'Collins, *art. cit.*, p. 143). Moltmann's most extensive attempt at a positive Christian interpretation of Bloch's messianic atheism is HD 179–183, at the end of which he finds that in Bloch's Feuerbachian attempts to reduce God to nothing other than the hidden identity of humanity, 'he falls below the standard of messianic thought and of his own better insights.' If

Bloch's atheism were consistent, he would 'come out against "God" for God' (HD 176).

34   Cf one of the epigrams prefaced to AC 9: 'What is decisive: to transcend without transcendence.'

35   In TH 172, 197, however, Moltmann was still content to use the Blochian notion of the transformation of the negative into a 'not yet'.

36   On this critical question for Christian dialogue with Bloch's thought, see Mendes-Flohr, *art. cit.*, pp. 645–646.

37   For Bloch's view of death, see (in chronological order) MHO 41–69; PH 1103–1182; MHO 84–88; AC 255–263. For an interesting sidelight on Bloch's attitude to death, see Bentley, *op. cit.*, p. 96 n. 103.

38   There should never have been any doubt that Moltmann believes in the resurrection of individual persons to eternal life. The doubt which S. H. Travis, *Christian Hope and the Future of Man* (Inter-Varsity Press, Leicester, 1980), p. 94, shares with S. Sykes, 'Life after Death: the Christian Doctrine of Heaven', in *Creation, Christ and Culture: Studies in Honour of T. F. Torrance*, ed. R. W. A. McKinney (T. & T. Clark, Edinburgh, 1976), pp. 255–260, is based on a misunderstanding of CG 169–170, which is admittedly not very clear, but in the light of the rest of Moltmann's work must be interpreted as making his usual distinction between immortality as *survival* of death, which denies the real fatality of death and implies that the true spiritual self does not belong to this material and social world, and *resurrection* as God's new creation of life out of death, which corresponds, in Moltmann's view, to the fact that the risen Jesus is identical with the crucified Jesus solely by God's act of raising him from absolute death. For a passage which very clearly affirms personal resurrection and eternal life, see GK 101–102, where, as in his controversy with Bloch, Moltmann sees the distinctiveness of Christian eschatology in its hope for the dead. Hope for the kingdom of God offers a way of integrating individual and universal eschatology, whereas purely immanent eschatology (of the Marxist kind) for the kingdom without God can offer no personal hope. See also Moltmann's full recent discussion in GC X, especially pp. 268–270, 275.

39   In line with this trend of thought, Moltmann later takes ministry to the terminally ill as the paradigm of Christian ministry: HC 36, cf. 27–31.

40 Note how this topic emerges as the major point of disagreement in the discussion in GEB 55–62.

41 Cf PH 1196: 'God becomes the kingdom of God, and the kingdom of God no longer contains a god.' For Moltmann's later reflection on this saying of Bloch, see HD 179–183. For his use of 1 Cor. 1:28 in discussion with Bloch, see GEB 60.

42 On this reapplication of Bloch's terminology, see Meeks, *op. cit.*, pp. 106–113.

43 Fiorenza, *art. cit.*, pp. 40–42; Hudson, *op. cit.*, pp. 94–96, 138–139.

44 Cf Sauter's criticisms of Moltmann's use of Blochian terminology in DTH 116–120.

45 Gibellini, *op. cit.*, pp. 210–216, maintains that *The Crucified God* is throughout a response to the challenge of Bloch's attacks on the theology of the cross in AC.

46 He appears in HP 33, 43, 51; UZ 138; FH 5 n.; TKG 48; but scarcely in CG (cf. 274).

47 On Bloch's Job, see F. Chirpaz, 'Ernst Bloch and Job's Rebellion', *Concilium* 169 (1983) = *Job and the Silence of God*, ed. C. Duquoc and C. Floristan (T. & T. Clark, Edinburgh, 1983), pp. 23–29.

**Chapter Two**

1 Niewiadomski, *op. cit.*, p. 12, denies that Moltmann succeeds in doing without hermeneutical presuppositions.

2 See also HP III, VI.

3 Cf. J.-P. Thévenas, 'Vérité d'espérance ou vérité de connaissance? Les enjeux théoriques et politiques de la théologie de Jürgen Moltmann', *Études théologiques et religieuses* 49 (1974), pp. 233–40.

4 In the phrase *die Epiphanie der ewigen Gegenwart*, Moltmann exploits the ambiguity of *Gegenwart* (presence/present): the epiphany of the eternal present is also the presence of the eternal (*die Gegenwart des Ewigen*).

5 Moltmann here claims to be following 'the more recent theology of the Old Testament' (TH 42), and depends especially on von Rad and Zimmerli. The claim is reasonably justified (cf. C. Westermann, 'The Interpretation of the Old Testament', in C. Westermann ed., *Essays in Old Testament Interpretation* [SCM Press, London, 1963], pp. 46–49), though strongly rejected by A. H. J. Gunneweg, *Understanding the Old Testament* (SCM Press, London, 1978), pp. 199–200,

who regards Moltmann's interpretation of revelation in the Old Testament as 'an instance of excessively narrow-minded exegesis' (p. 201). Admittedly Moltmann leaves significant aspects of the Old Testament, such as the wisdom literature, out of account, but Gunneweg's excessive criticism (in which he makes little distinction between Moltmann and Pannenberg) is part of his thorough-going argument against history as the category for interpreting the Old Testament.

6  Moltmann's dependence in TH II on Victor Maag's account of the nomadic origin of Israel's religion of promise explains why he does not (as in EH 18; FH 17) follow Bloch in tracing Israel's religion of promise back to the historical event of the Exodus.

7  C. Morse, *The Logic of Promise in Moltmann's Theology* (Fortress, Philadelphia, 1979), p. 31.

8  Moltmann's exposition of this point (TH 105–106) owes a good deal to Bloch, PH 178–195.

9  In C. Westermann ed., *op. cit.*, pp. 89–122.

10  On Moltmann's approach to the problem of faith and history, posed by the resurrection, see also the illuminating discussion in FH 160–64, which is in part a spirited response to Van Harvey's criticism of Moltmann.

11  As John Macquarrie points out (FH 122; and *Thinking about God* [SCM Press, London, 1975] p. 229), this fails to explain how we can know of the reality of an event as yet unparalleled, but Moltmann does not intend it to explain this (cf. TH 82). As RRF 51 makes clear, he thinks that the resurrection is not historically, but only eschatologically, verifiable. In the meantime the effect of the resurrection, experienced as the power of the Spirit in Christian history (FH 163), saves resurrection faith from credulity.

12  Cf. also HP 106, in which this theme is related to Bonhoeffer's treatment of secularity.

13  For the argument against Pannenberg, see TH 276–79, 83–84.

14  Cf. Moltmann's account of the 'history of revolutions for freedom' in RRF 70–77.

15  Cf. Bloch's distinction between the historically varying content of social utopias and the invariant intention towards the utopian: PH 480.

16  Morse, *op. cit.*, pp. 65–67.

17   Cf. DTH 221: It is not, strictly speaking, creation *ex nihilo*, but creation from no-longer-being.

18   This sociological analysis first appeared in HP 131–39, and reappears in RRF 110–17.

19   R. A. Alves, *A Theology of Human Hope* (Corpus Books, New York/Cleveland, 1969), p. 61; cf. W. Pannenberg, *Christian Spirituality and Sacramental Community* (Darton, Longman & Todd, London, 1984), p. 51; L. Gilkey, *Reaping the Whirlwind: A Christian Interpretation of History* (Seabury, New York, 1979), p. 234.

20   Niewiadomski, *op. cit.*, pp. 10, 53, rather similarly considers 'the opposition between God and reality' to be the controlling idea of *Theology of Hope*.

21   On this claim, see Paul Ricoeur's interpretation of Moltmann, 'Freedom in the Light of Hope', *Essays on Biblical Interpretation*, ed. L. S. Mudge (S.P.C.K., London, 1981), pp. 163–4.

22   Against P. C. Hodgson, *Jesus – Word and Presence* (Fortress, Philadelphia, 1971), pp. 16–17, though his interpretation of Moltmann might be said to be one which Moltmann's language invites.

23   F. Kerstiens, 'The Theology of Hope in Germany Today', *Concilium* 9/6 (1970), p. 110, rightly refers to 'the confused concept of revolution' in the 'theology of revolution' of the late 1960s: 'Every author has his own version.'

24   E.g. E. Brito, *Hegel et la tâche actuelle de la christologie* (Lethielleux, Paris/Culture et Vérité, Namur, 1979), p. 79.

25   E.g. J. Míguez Bonino, *Revolutionary Theology Comes of Age* (S.P.C.K., London, 1975), pp. 139–42.

26   On the reasons why an eschatological theology must become a political theology, see also RRF 97–101, 200–2, 205; FH 45–48.

27   This to some extent meets the criticisms of *Theology of Hope* in Alves, *op. cit.*, pp. 56–68.

28   This translation of the German title occurs within the English edition (TJ 26), but the volume (with an introductory essay by David Jenkins) was given the title *Theology and Joy*. The American edition is called *Theology of Play*.

29   Cf. also Capps, *op. cit.*, pp. 140–46. On the origins of TJ, see also Gibellini, *op. cit.*, p. 185.

## Chapter Three

1 Cf. CG 204: 'The death of Jesus on the cross is the *centre* of all Christian theology. It is not the only theme of theology, but it is in effect the entry to its problems and answers on earth. . . . All Christian statements stem from the crucified Christ.'

2 Note how Moltmann's disagreement with Pannenberg focusses on the relation of the resurrection to the cross already in TH 83, and then again, much more fully, in CG 166–78.

3 For Moltmann's development towards a theology of the cross before CG, see Gibellini, *op. cit.*, ch. VII.

4 Cf W. H. Capps, *Hope Against Hope: Moltmann to Merton in One Theological Decade* (Fortress Press, Philadelphia, 1976), ch. 3.

5 Cf. HP 53 n.8; CG 111 n.51; CPS 380 n.16, for rare references to R. Rubinstein and E. Fackenheim.

6 For the steps in Moltmann's search for a way 'beyond theism and atheism', from TH to CG, see UZ 140–42.

7 For a synthesis, see Momose, *op. cit.*, ch. V.

8 The most debatable aspect of these chapters, in the light of more recent scholarship, is Moltmann's 'Lutheran' assumption that first-century Judaism interpreted the Law in terms of a legalism of works-righteousness.

9 Although Moltmann sometimes seems to attribute only a noetic significance to the eschatological reading of history backwards (HP 42; cf. CG 90–91, and in Momose, *op. cit.*, p. 177), he elsewhere bases it on a kind of ontological priority of the future, such as is also found in Pannenberg (DTH 215–22; cf. CG 184).

10 Moltmann said in 1971 that if he were writing *Theology of Hope* then he would call it *Theology of Liberation:* J.-P. Thévenaz, 'Vérité d'espérance ou vérité de connaissance? Les enjeux théoriques et politiques de la théologie de Jürgen Moltmann', *Etudes théologiques et religieuses* 49 (1974), p. 225.

11 On the Frankfurt School, see D. Held, *Introduction to Critical Theory* (Hutchinson, London, 1980); S. Buck-Morss, *The Origin of Negative Dialectics* (Harvester, Hassocks Sussex, 1977); G. Rose, *The Melancholy Science* (Macmillan, London, 1978); and on the relationship to theology, especially, R. J. Siebert, 'The New Marxist Conception of Christianity: Hope versus Positivism', *Anglican Theological Review* 59 (1977), pp. 237–259, 387–412; *idem, The Critical Theory of Religion: The Frankfurt*

*School: From Universal Pragmatic to Political Theology* (Mouton, Berlin/New York/Amsterdam, 1985).

12 On Luther's theology of the cross, see UZ 135–36; CG 70–73, 207–14; TC 135; and W. von Loewenich, *Luther's Theology of the Cross* (Christian Journals, Belfast, 1976); A. E. McGrath, *Luther's Theology of the Cross* (Blackwell, Oxford, 1985).

13 With Moltmann's use of Schelling here there is a significant parallel (and perhaps source) in K. Kitamori, *Theology of the Pain of God*, tr. M. E. Bratcher (SCM Press, London, 1966), p. 26.

14 The correction indicates Moltmann's desire to avoid the implication that evil is necessary for the sake of good: see DGG 144 (where Kasper interprets the quotation from Schelling in this way) and 151 (where Moltmann rejects this implication).

15 The trio is intended only as a summary of the many explicitly and implicitly religious idols which humanity constantly creates.

16 This is one of the complaints in the exaggerated criticism of Moltmann in A. R. Eckhardt, 'Jürgen Moltmann, the Jewish People, and the Holocaust', *Journal of the American Academy of Religion* 44 (1976), pp. 675–91. Eckhardt's standard of judgment is indicated by his concluding claim (p. 691) that the only adequate Christian response to the Holocaust is to give up the confession of Jesus as the Christ. This amounts to saying that the Christian faith is *by definition* anti-Semitic – a curious conclusion for a post-Holocaust theologian determined to avoid even innocent complicity with Nazi ideology!

17 For a summary of this critique, cf. G. Hunsinger, 'The Crucified God and the Political Theology of Violence', *Heythrop Journal* 14 (1973), pp. 383–385.

18 For Moltmann's treatment of the theodicy problem, with reference to Dostoyevsky, Camus and Wiesel, see also R. Bauckham, 'Theodicy from Ivan Karamazov to Moltmann', *Modern Theology* (1987), forthcoming.

19 Since the English translation of this work (*The Rebel* [Hamish Hamilton, London, 1953/Penguin, Harmondsworth, 1971]) omits material which is important in Moltmann's use of Camus, references in the text are to the French original.

20 Moltmann already refers to Camus' book in the context of a discussion of theodicy in 1968 (HP 34). In CG, the relevant explicit

references to Camus are on pp. 221–22, 226, 252. Cf. also FC 171, 193 n.28; EH 116, 142.

21 This surprisingly harsh judgment on Bloch is somewhat offset by the observation (CG 5) that 'Bloch too is becoming more and more disturbed by the power of evil.'

22 Cf. CG 223: 'what keeps Ivan Karamazov's protest alive?'

23 M. Horkheimer, *Die Sehnsucht nach dem ganz Anderen* (Furche-Verlag, Hamburg, 1970). For a useful summary, see Siebert, *art. cit.*, pp. 404–11. For the broader context of Horkheimer's thought, cf. also *idem, op. cit.*, pp. 128–146.

24 CG 178 takes up this form of the theodicy question with the important qualification that the righteousness of grace in the cross and resurrection gives it: 'The message of the new righteousness which eschatological faith brings into the world says that in fact the executioners will not finally triumph over their victims. It also says that in the end the victims will not triumph over their executioners.'

25 For Camus's interpretation of the cross, see J. Onimus, *Albert Camus and Christianity* (Gill and Macmillan, Dublin, 1970), pp. 48–50.

26 Cf. Onimus, *op. cit.*, p. 49.

27 A. Camus, *The Fall* (Penguin, Harmondsworth, 1963), pp. 83–84.

28 HR 34 n.; cf. Onimus, *op. cit.*, p. 49.

29 This seems also to be the point of Moltmann's reference to Camus (CG 80 n.65) as one of those 'outsiders and atheists' who can remind Christians of 'the alien nature of the crucified Christ in a "Christian" culture' (CG 68).

30 This is because the resurrection is itself a matter of the divine righteousness in the history of the suffering of this world (CG 166–78).

31 Against H. Blocher, 'Christian Thought and the Problem of Evil', *Churchman* 99 (1985), pp. 119–21, 128. Cf. RRF 168: 'Maidanek and Hiroshima find no soothing dialectical answer.'

32 Cf J.-B. Metz, 'Facing the Jews: Christian Theology after Ausch-witz', *Concilium* 175 (5/1984) = *The Holocaust as Interruption*, ed. E. S. Fiorenza and D. Tracy (T. & T. Clark, Edinburgh, 1984), p. 29: 'The text has become prototypical.' For Christian theological interpretation of this passage of Wiesel, see also D. Soelle, *Suffering* (Darton, Longman & Todd, London, 1975), pp. 145–150; K. Surin, 'The Impassibility of God and the Problem of Evil', *Scottish Journal of Theology*

35 (1982), pp. 111–112; *idem*, 'Theodicy?', *Harvard Theological Review* 76 (1983), pp. 240–243.

33 DGG 115–116; Soelle, *op. cit.*, pp. 26–27. A similar criticism is made, in milder terms, by M. L. Cook, *The Jesus of Faith* (Paulist Press, New York, 1981), pp. 74–76.

34 On this point, see J. J. O'Donnell, *Trinity and Temporality* (Oxford University Press, Oxford, 1983), pp. 153–156. As O'Donnell points out there and in *idem*, 'The Doctrine of the Trinity in Recent German Theology', *Heythrop Journal* 23 (1982), pp. 157, 163, in Hans Urs von Balthasar's understanding of the cross, which is closely akin to Moltmann's, the self-surrender of the Son in loving surrender to his Father's will is rather more prominent, while von Balthasar also explicitly points out that the death of Jesus involves both this active self-surrender and the passivity of being left to die. Von Balthasar's treatment thus resists Soelle's criticism more clearly than Moltmann's, but with considerations which are nevertheless present in Moltmann's treatment.

35 G. M. Jantzen, 'Christian Hope and Jesus' Despair', *King's Theological Review* 5 (1982), p. 5.

## Chapter Four

1 For Moltmann's recent trinitarian thought, see also MF; HG 70–106; FHS; IU.

2 K. Barth, *Letters 1961–1968*, ed. J. Fangmeier and H. Stoevesandt, tr. and ed. G. W. Bromiley (T. & T. Clark, Edinburgh, 1981), pp. 175–176 (cf. also DTH 215).

3 *Ibid.*, p. 348.

4 W. Pannenberg, *Theology and the Kingdom of God* (Westminster Press, Philadelphia, 1971), especially pp. 51–71; 'The God of Hope', in *Basic Questions in Theology*, vol. 2 (SCM Press, London, 1971), pp. 234–249.

5 On which, see E. F. Tupper, *The Theology of Wolfhart Pannenberg* (SCM Press, London, 1974), pp. 247–249; W. J. Hill, *The Three-Personed God: The Trinity as a Mystery of Salvation* (Catholic University Press of America, Washington, D.C., 1982), pp. 155–166; R. Olson, 'Trinity and Eschatology: The Historical Being of God in Jürgen Moltmann and Wolfhart Pannenberg', *Scottish Journal of Theology* 36 (1983), pp. 213–227.

6 For a basic survey, see J. Thompson, *Christ in Perspective: Christolog-*

*ical Perspectives in the Theology of Karl Barth* (Saint Andrew Press, Edinburgh, 1978), chaps 3–4.

7   K. Rahner, 'Remarks on the Dogmatic Treatise "De Trinitate" ', in *Theological Investigations*, vol. 4 (Darton, Longman, and Todd, London, 1966), pp. 77–104; *The Trinity* (Burns & Oates, London, 1970).

8   See, briefly, J. J. O'Donnell, 'The Doctrine of the Trinity in Recent German Theology', *Heythrop Journal* 23 (1982), pp. 156–160; and, for a fine study of Jüngel, J. B. Webster, *Eberhard Jüngel: An Introduction to his Theology* (Cambridge University Press, Cambridge, 1986), especially chaps 6–7.

9   Cf. K. Barth, CD IV/2, p. 252: 'In the deepest darkness of Golgotha He enters supremely into the glory of the unity of the Son with the Father. In that abandonment by God He is the One who is directly loved by God.'

10   Thus the term 'crucified God' is itself entirely orthodox and traditional: e.g. Gregory of Nazianzus, *Orat.* 45:29; M. Luther (*W.A.* I, 614); C. Wesley, Methodist Hymn Book 457, quoted by G. Wainwright, *Doxology: The Praise of God in Worship, Doctrine and Life* (Epworth Press, London, 1980), p. 208. Moltmann's innovation lies in making the cross an inner divine experience.

11   Moltmann does not seem to acknowledge the origin of this idea of the differentiated suffering of the Father and the Son in Barth's talk of the 'fatherly fellow-suffering of God' (CD IV/2, p. 357).

12   Cf. TKG 25: 'We *can* only talk about God's suffering in trinitarian terms. In monotheism it is impossible.'

13   TKG 23–25; R. Bauckham, ' "Only the suffering God can help": divine passibility in modern theology', *Themelios 9/3* (1984), p. 8 and n. 23.

14   K. Barth, CD IV/1, pp. 186–188.

15   For a bibliography of this tradition from 1890 to the present, see Bauckham, *art. cit.*, p. 6 nn. 3, 4.

16   On this see, briefly, Bauckham, *art. cit.*, pp. 9–10; more fully, J. C. Merkle, 'Heschel's Theology of Divine Pathos', in *Abraham Joshua Heschel: Exploring His Life and Thought*, ed. J. C. Merkle (Macmillan, New York/ Collier Macmillan. London, 1985), pp. 66–83; J. C. Merkle, *The Genesis of Faith: The Depth Theology of Abraham Joshua Heschel* (Macmillan, New York/Collier Macmillan, London, 1985), pp. 130–135.

17   A. J. Heschel, *The Prophets* (Harper & Row, New York/Evanston, 1962), p. 235.

18   G. O'Collins, 'Towards a Theology of the Cross', in G. O'Collins, R. Faricy, and M. Flick, *The Cross Today: An evaluation of current theological reflection on the Cross of Christ* (E. J. Dwyer, Rome/Sydney, 1977), p. 37, complains that *The Crucified God* does not follow the example of *Theology of Hope* 'by sufficiently linking the events of Good Friday and Easter Sunday back to the suffering history of Israel.' I made a similar criticism in 'Jürgen Moltmann', in *One God in Trinity: An analysis of the primary dogma of Christianity*, ed. P. Toon and J. D. Spiceland (Bagster, London, 1980), pp. 130–131, and whereas I now think that Moltmann's account of Heschel's interpretation of the prophets meets the need rather more adequately than I then recognised, I still consider it insufficient to function as chap. II does in *Theology of Hope*.

19   Hill, *op. cit.*, p. 154.

20   Cf. the problems raised in response to Moltmann by A. Chapelle in L. Rumpf *et. al.*, *Hegel et la théologie contemporaine: L'absolu dans l'histoire?* (Delachaux & Niestlé, Neuchatel/Paris, 1977), pp. 222–225.

21   W. Kasper in DGG 144–146.

22   W. Kasper in DGG 146; H. H. Miskotte in DGG 83–86.

23   J. Milbank, 'The Second Difference: For a Trinitarianism Without Reserve', *Modern Theology 2* (1986), pp. 223–224: D. Wiederkehr, 'Neue Interpretation des Kreuzestodes Jesu. Zu J. Moltmanns Buch »Der gekreuzigte Gott«', *Freiburger Zeitschrift für Philosophie und Theologie* 20 (1973), p. 262.

24   Cf. W. Kasper, *The God of Jesus Christ* (SCM Press, London, 1984), p. 193.

25   Cf. Moltmann's criticism of Hegel in CG 90–92; TKG 17–18.

26   The German original of this is 'Gesichtspunkte der Kreuzestheologie heute', *Evangelische Theologie* 33 (1973), pp. 346–365.

27   So Hill, *op. cit.*, p. 170; cf. Bauckham, *art. cit.*, p. 124.

28   Cf. Moltmann's obvious sympathy for C. E. Rolt's theology of eternal divine suffering: TKG 31–34. At times Moltmann seems to approach the view that God's creative love for his other is inevitably contradicted and so must suffer: TKG 59. However, his speculative accounts of creation in relation to nothingness (FC 119–124; GC 86–93) are careful to avoid the implications that God creates evil or that evil is necessary.

29   From this position Moltmann later develops the view that the creation of the world is a necessity of God's love (TKG 105–108), revoking his earlier adherence to the traditional view that God 'did not have to create something to realise himself' (TJ 42; cf. LF 80–81). 30   G. Hunsinger, 'The Crucified God and the Political Theology of Violence', *Heythrop Journal* 14 (1973), p. 278; cf. DGG 181; Bauckham, *art cit.*, p. 130. For the basis of this statement, see especially CG 244; FH 27; GTT 34; CPS 62.

## Chapter Five

1   For Moltmann's view of confessional traditions in theology, see TKG xiv–xv; and, with special reference to the Protestant-Roman Catholic distinction, his 'Nachwort' in P. F. Momose, *Kreuzestheologie: Ein Auseinandersetzung mit Jürgen Moltmann* (Herder, Freiburg, 1978), pp. 174–176.
2   For Moltmann's use of the notion that life exists in *open relationship* to other life, while to close oneself within oneself is to atrophy, see also CPS 194; OC 35; CG 11; EH 13.
3   Moltmann uses the term 'poor' in a very broad sense. Poverty is a 'multi-dimensional' concept, which 'extends from economic, social and physical poverty to psychological, moral and religious poverty' (CPS 79).
4   Moltmann finds Christ's promise to be present in the poor in Matt. 25:31–46 (so also CCR 43–45; PR 156). However, exegetical opinion is divided on the identity of 'the least of Christ's brethren' in this passage, and, as M. Tripole, 'A Church for the Poor and the World: At Issue with Moltmann's Ecclesiology', *Theological Studies* 42 (1981), pp. 646–650, points out, they are more plausibly understood, in their Matthean context, as Christian missionaries. (For a recent study which surveys the spectrum of interpretations of the passage – though oddly without mentioning Moltmann – and reaches a conclusion which, while not supporting Moltmann's idea of Christ's presence in the poor, is in a general way compatible with Moltmann's ecclesiology, see J. R. Donohue, 'The "Parable" of the Sheep and the Goats: A Challenge to Christian Ethics', *Theological Studies* 47 (1985), pp. 3–31.) But if the specific idea of Christ's promise to be present in the poor cannot be derived from Matt. 25, Moltmann's more general notion of the Church's necessary solidarity with the poor is Christologically based

on Jesus' fellowship with the poor in his ministry (CPS 78–80) and his identification with the godforsaken on the cross.

5  For Moltmann's view of the significance of Israel for Christian theology's own health and integrity, see also TGT 203–204; HG XII.

6  Moltmann is here more accurate than in his odd claim that 'the system of voluntary religion originated in the American republic' (TGT 190) – which, incidentally, inverts the historical relationship between ecclesiology and political democracy in a way one would not expect of Moltmann.

7  The Confessing Church in Germany under the Nazis also has a special importance for Moltmann, since it discovered the Church's own free identity and critical distance from civil society: TGT 198–201; CPS 334; CR 111.

8  Moltmann's account of the charismatic structure of the Church is indebted to Käsemann, usually his principal guide in Pauline exegesis, and to Küng's rather similar account: H. Küng, *The Church* (Search Press, London, 1968), section C.II.

9  It could be said that by extending the concept of friendship in this way, Moltmann is diluting the real quality of friendship, which is dependent on its being 'preferential' and 'reciprocal' (according to C. G. Meilaender, *Friendship: A Study in Theological Ethics* [University of Notre Dame Press, Notre Dame/London, 1981], chs 1, 2). This would not mean that friendship has to be love of like for like, but only that it is by its nature restricted and cannot be a principle of general social relationships. What Moltmann is really doing, however, is finding in certain aspects of 'preferential friendship' a model for relating to people in a 'friendly' way: these aspects can be extended more widely than 'preferential friendship' without necessarily (though this is not explicit in Moltmann's argument) invalidating the special quality of 'preferential friendship' which must remain restricted.

10  S. Sykes, *The Identity of Christianity: Theologians and the Essence of Christianity from Schleiermacher to Barth* (SPCK, London, 1984), p. 297 n. 61.

11  For criticism, see Tripole, *art. cit.*, pp. 656–658: I am taking up some of his points in what follows.

12  Nor is it by the exclusion of those who do not belong to the Church. Moltmann apparently never envisages that eschatological salvation will be less than fully universal.

## Conclusion

1  Moltmann in W. H. Capps, *Time Invades the Cathedral* (Fortress Press, Philadelphia, 1972), pp. xiv-xv; cf. EH 13–14.

2  Published anonymously in D. Cremer, *Sing me the Song of my World*, tr. B. Davies (St Paul Publications, Slough, 1981), pp. 140–141.

# BIBLIOGRAPY

## A. Abbreviations

In the text and notes the following abbreviations are used for Moltmann's works and some other books. Where no author's name is given, the work is by Moltmann and full bibliographical details will be found in section B of this Bibliography. In the case of other works, bibliographical details are given here.

AC     E. Bloch, *Atheism in Christianity: The Religion of the Exodus and the Kingdom*. Tr. J. T. Swann. New York: Herder & Herder, 1972.

AH     'L'Absolu et l'Historique dans la doctrine de la Trinité'.

CCR    'The Cross and Civil Religion'.

CD     K. Barth, *Church Dogmatics*, ed. G. W. Bromiley and T. F. Torrance (Edinburgh: T. & T. Clark, 1936–1969).

CG     *The Crucified God*.

CJC    'The Confession of Jesus Christ: A Biblical Theological Consideration'.

CPS    *The Church in the Power of the Spirit*.

CR     'The Challenge of Religion in the '80s'.

DGG    M. Welker ed., *Diskussion über Jürgen Moltmanns Buch »Der gekreuzigte Gott«*. Munich: Chr. Kaiser, 1979. (This includes J. Moltmann, '»Dialectik, die umschlägt in Identität« – was ist das? Zu Befürchtungen Walter Kaspers'; and 'Antwort auf die Kritik an »Der gekreuzigte Gott«'.)

DTH    W.-D. Marsch ed., *Diskussion über die »Theologie der Hoffnung« von Jürgen Moltmann*. Munich: Chr. Kaiser, 1967. (This includes J. Moltmann, 'Antwort auf die Kritik der »Theologie der Hoffnung«'.)

EC      'The Expectation of His Coming'.

EG      *Experiences of God.*

EH      *The Experiment Hope.*

FC      *The Future of Creation.*

FH      F. Herzog ed., *The Future of Hope: Theology as Eschatology.* New York: Herder & Herder, 1970. (This includes J. Moltmann, 'Theology as Eschatology'; and 'Towards the Next Step in the Dialogue'.)

FHS      'The Fellowship of the Holy Spirit – Trinitarian Pneumatology'.

FTO      'The Future as Threat and as Opportunity'.

GC      *God in Creation.*

GEB      *Im Gespräch mit Ernst Bloch.*

GK      'God's Kindgom as the Meaning of Life and of the World'.

GTT      'The "Crucified God": God and the Trinity Today'.

HC      T. Runyon ed., *Hope for the Church: Moltmann in Dialogue with Practical Theology*, Nashville: Abingdon, 1979. (This includes J. Moltmann, 'The Diaconal Church in the Context of the Kingdom of God'; and 'Response'.)

HD      *On Human Dignity.*

HFM      E. H. Cousins ed., *Hope and the Future of Man.* London: Teilhard Centre for the Future of Man, 1973. (This includes J. Moltmann, 'Response to the Opening Presentations'; and 'Hope and the Biomedical Future of Man'.)

HG      *Humanity in God.*

HR      A. Camus, *L'Homme Révolté.* Paris: Gallimard, 1951.

IU      'The Inviting Unity of the Triune God'.

JM      *Jewish Monotheism and Christian Trinitarian Doctrine.*

LF      'The Liberating Feast'.

M      *Man.*

MF      'The Motherly Father: Is Trinitarian Patripassianism Replacing Theological Patriarchalism?'

MHO      E. Bloch, *Man on his Own: Essays in the Philosophy of Religion.* Tr. E. B. Ashton. New York: Herder & Herder, 1970. (This includes J. Moltmann, 'Introduction'.)

MSM      'Man and the Son of Man'.

OC      *The Open Church.*

| PH  | E. Bloch, *The Principle of Hope*. Tr. N. Plaice, S. Plaice and P. Knight. Oxford: Blackwell, 1986. |
| PP  | *Prädestination und Perseveranz.* |
| PPL | *The Power of the Powerless.* |
| PR  | 'Die politische Relevanz der christlichen Hoffnung'. |
| PT  | *Perspektiven der Theologie.* |
| RRF | *Religion, Revolution, and the Future.* |
| SB  | *Die Sprache der Befreiung.* |
| T   | 'Theodicy'. |
| TA  | 'Teresa of Avila and Martin Luther: The turn to the mysticism of the cross'. |
| TC  | 'Cross, Theology of the'. |
| TGT | 'Theology in Germany Today'. |
| TH  | *Theology of Hope.* |
| TJ  | *Theology and Joy.* |
| TKG | *The Trinity and the Kingdom of God.* |
| TTC | 'The "Crucified God": A Trinitarian Theology of the Cross'. |
| UZ  | *Umkehr zur Zukunft.* |
| VZ  | 'Verschränkte Zeiten der Geschichte: Notwendige Differenzierungen und Begrenzungen des Geschichtsbegriffs'. |

Moltmann's Works

Those of Moltmann's works which have been consulted in the preparation of this book are here listed in alphabetical order. Whenever available, the English translations are given in preference to the German originals. Articles which have been subsequently reprinted in the volumes of collected essays are not listed separately.

A fairly complete bibliography of Moltmann's works (including translations) up to 1974 appears in R. Gibellini, *La teologia di Jürgen Moltmann* (Brescia: Queriniana, 1975), pp. 343–76; while the bibliography (confined to works in German) in P. F. Momose, *Kreuzestheologie: Ein Auseinandersetzung mit Jürgen Moltmann* (Freiburg: Herder, 1978), pp. 186–190, goes up to 1976. There is no published bibliography of Moltmann's later work.

'Antwort auf die Kritik an »Der gekreuzigte Gott«' In *Diskussion über Jürgen Moltmanns Buch »Der gekreuzigte Gott«*, ed. M. Welker (Munich: Chr. Kaiser, 1979), pp. 165–190.

'Antwort auf die Kritik der »Theologie der Hoffnung«'. In *Diskussion über die »Theologie der Hoffnung« von Jürgen Moltmann*, ed. W.-D. Marsch (Munich: Chr. Kaiser, 1967), pp. 201–237.

'Christliche Hoffnung: Messianisch oder transzendent? Ein theologisches Gespräch mit Joachim von Fiore und Thomas von Aquin'. *Münchener Theologischer Zeitschrift* 33 (1982), pp. 241–260.

'Christologie – die paulinische Mitte: Bemerkungen zu Georg Eichholz' Paulus interpretation'. *Evangelische Theologie* 34 (1974), pp. 196–200.

'Cross, Theology of the'. In *A New Dictionary of Christian Theology*, ed. A. Richardson and J. Bowden (London: SCM Press, 1983), pp. 135–137.

'Commentary on "To Bear Arms" '. In R. A. Evans and A. F. Evans, *Human Rights: A Dialogue between the First and Third Worlds* (Maryknoll, New York: Orbis Books/ Guildford: Lutterworth Press, 1983), pp. 48–52.

'»Dialektik, die umschlägt in Identität« – was ist das? Zu Befürchtungen Walter Kaspers'. In *Diskussion über Jürgen Moltmanns Buch »Der gekreuzigte Gott«*', ed. M. Welker (Munich: Chr. Kaiser, 1979), pp. 149–156.

'Die Bibel und das Patriarchat: Offene Fragen zur Diskussion über "Feministische Theologie" '. *Evangelische Theologie* 42 (1982), pp. 480–484.

'Die politische Relevanz der christlichen Hoffnung'. In *Christliche Freiheit im Dienst am Menschen* (Martin Niemöller Festschrift), ed. K. Herbert (Frankfurt am Main: Otto Lembeck, 1972), pp. 153–162.

*Die Sprache der Befreiung: Predigten und Besinnungen.* Munich: Chr. Kaiser, 1972.

'Editorial: Can there be an Ecumenical Mariology?' *Concilium* 168 (1983) = *Mary in the Churches*, ed. H. Küng and J. Moltmann (Edinburgh: T. & T. Clark, 1983), pp. xii-xv.

*Experiences of God.* Tr. M. Kohl. London: SCM Press, 1980.

*God in Creation: An Ecological Doctrine of Creation.* Tr. M. Kohl. London: SCM Press, 1985.

'God's Kingdom as the Meaning of Life and of the World'. *Concilium* 117 (8/1977) = *Why did God make me?*, ed. H. Küng and J. Moltmann (New York: Seabury Press, 1978), pp. 97–103.

'Hope'. In *A New Dictionary of Christian Theology*, ed. A. Richardson and J. Bowden (London: SCM Press, 1983), pp. 270–272.

'Hope and the Biological Future of Man'. In *Hope and the Future of Man*, ed. E. H. Cousins (London: Teilhard Centre for the Future of Man, 1973), pp. 89–105.

*Humanity in God.* By E. Moltmann-Wendel and J. Moltmann. London: SCM Press, 1984.

'Ich glaube an Gott den Vater: Patriarchalische oder nichtpatriarchalische Rede von Gott?' *Evangelische Theologie* 43 (1983), pp. 397–415.

*Im Gespräch mit Ernst Bloch: Eine theologische Wegbegleitung.* (Kaiser Traktate 18.) Munich: Chr. Kaiser, 1976.

'Introduction'. In E. Bloch, *Man on his Own: Essays in the Philosophy of Religion,* tr. E. B. Ashton (New York: Herder & Herder, 1970), pp. 19–29.

*Jewish Monotheism and Christian Trinitarian Doctrine.* A Dialogue by Pinchas Lapide and Jürgen Moltmann. Tr. L. Swidler. Philadelphia: Fortress Press, 1981.

'L'Absolu et l'Historique dans la doctrine de la Trinité'. In L. Rumpf et al., *Hegel et la théologie contemporaine: L'absolu dans l'histoire?* (Neuchatel/Paris: Delachaux & Niestlé, 1977), pp. 190–204.

*Man: Christian Anthropology in the Conflicts of the Present.* Tr. J. Sturdy. London: SPCK, 1974.

'Man and the Son of Man'. In *No Man is Alien: Essays on the Unity of Mankind,* ed. J. R. Nelson (Leiden: E. J. Brill, 1971), pp. 203–224.

'Messianismus und Marxismus'. In *Über Ernst Bloch: Mit Beiträgen von Martin Walser, Ivo Frenzel, Jürgen Moltmann, Jürgen Habermas, Fritz Vilmar, Iring Fetscher und Werner Maihofer* (Frankfurt am Main: Suhrkamp, 1968), pp. 42–60.

'Nachwort'. In P. F. Momose, *Kreuzestheologie: Eine auseinandersetzung mit Jürgen Moltmann* (Freiburg/ Basel/ Vienna: Herder, 1978), pp. 174–183.

*On Human Dignity: Political Theology and Ethics.* Tr. M. D. Meeks. London: SCM Press, 1984.

'Perseverance'. In *A New Dictionary of Christian Theology,* ed. A. Richardson and J. Bowden (London: SCM Press, 1983), pp. 441–442.

*Perspektiven der Theologie: Gesammelte Aufsätze.* Munich: Chr. Kaiser/ Mainz: Matthias Grünewald, 1968.

*Prädestination und Perseveranz: Geschichte und Bedeutung der reformierten Lehre "de perseverantia sanctorum".* (Beiträge zur Geschichte und Lehre der Reformierten Kirche 12.) Neukirchen: Neuchirchener Verlag, 1961.

*Religion, Revolution, and the Future.* Tr. M. D. Meeks. New York: Charles Scribner's, 1969.

'Response'. In J. Moltmann with M. D. Meeks, R. J. Hunter, J. W. Fowler, N. L. Erskine, *Hope for the Church: Moltmann in Dialogue with Practical Theology*, ed. and tr. T. Runyon (Nashville: Abingdon, 1979), pp. 128–136.

'Response to the Opening Presentations'. In *Hope and the Future of Man*, ed. E. H. Cousins (London: Teilhard Centre for the Future of Man, 1973), pp. 55–59.

'Teresa of Avila and Martin Luther: The turn to the mysticism of the cross'. *Studies in Religion/ Sciences Religieuses* 13 (1984), pp. 265–278.

'The Challenge of Religion in the '80s'. In *Theologians in Transition: The Christian Century 'How My Mind Has Changed' Series*, ed. J. M. Wall (New York: Crossroad, 1981), pp. 107–112.

*The Church in the Power of the Spirit: A Contribution to Messianic Ecclesiology.* Tr. M. Kohl. London: SCM Press, 1977.

'The Confession of Jesus Christ: A Biblical Theological Consideration'. *Concilium* 118 (8/1978) = *An Ecumenical Confession of Faith?*, ed. H. Küng and J. Moltmann (New York: Seabury Press, 1979), pp. 13–19.

'The Cross and Civil Religion'. In J. Moltmann, H. W. Richardson, J. B. Metz, W. Oelmüller, M. D. Bryant, *Religion and Political Society*, ed. and tr. in the Institute of Christian Thought (New York: Harper & Row, 1974), pp. 9–47.

'The "Crucified God": A Trinitarian Theology of the Cross'. *Interpretation* 26 (1972), pp. 278–299.

'The "Crucified God": God and the Trinity Today'. *Concilium* 8/6 (1972), pp. 26–37.

*The Crucified God: The Cross as the Foundation and Criticism of Christian Theology.* Tr. R. A. Wilson and J. Bowden. London: SCM Press, 1974.

'The Diaconal Church in the Context on the Kingdom of God'. In J. Moltmann with M. D. Meeks, R. J. Hunter, J. W. Fowler, N. L. Erskine, *Hope for the Church: Moltmann in Dialogue with Practical Theology*, ed. and tr. T. Runyon (Nashville: Abingdon, 1979), pp. 21–36.

'The Expectation of His Coming'. *Theology* 88 (1985), pp. 425–428.

*The Experiment Hope.* Ed. and tr. M. D. Meeks. London: SCM Press, 1975.

'The Fellowship of the Holy Spirit – Trinitarian Pneumatology'. *Scottish Journal of Theology* 37 (1984), pp. 287–300.

*The Future of Creation.* Tr. M. Kohl. London: SCM Press, 1979.

'The Future As Threat and As Opportunity'. In *Contemporary Religion and Social Responsibility*, ed. N. Brockman and N. Piediscalzi (New York: Alba House, 1973), pp. 103–117.

'The Inviting Unity of the Triune God'. *Concilium* 177 (1/1985) = *Monotheism*, ed. C. Geffré and J.-P. Jossua (Edinburgh: T. & T. Clark), pp. 50–58.

'The Liberating Feast'. *Concilium* 2/10 (1974) = *Politics and Liturgy*, ed. H. Schmidt and D. Power (London: Concilium, 1974), pp. 74–84.

'The Life Signs of the Spirit in the Fellowship Community of Christ'. In J. Moltmann with M. D. Meeks, R. J. Hunter, J. W. Fowler, N. L. Erskine, *Hope for the Church: Moltmann in Dialogue with Practical Theology*, ed. and tr. T. Runyon (Nashville: Abingdon, 1979), pp. 37–56.

'The Lordship of Christ and Human Society'. In J. Moltmann and J. Weissbach, *Two Studies in the Theology of Bonhoeffer* (New York: Charles Scribner's, 1967), pp. 19–94.

'The Motherly Father: Is Trinitarian Patripassianism Replacing Theological Patriarchalism?' *Concilium* 143 (1981) = *God as Father?*, ed. E. Schillebeeckx and J. B. Metz (Edinburgh: T. & T. Clark, 1981), pp. 51–56.

'Theodicy'. In *A New Dictionary of Christian Theology*, ed. A. Richardson and J. Bowden (London: SCM Press, 1983), pp. 564–566.

'Théologie et droits de l'homme'. *Revue des Sciences Religieuses* 52 (1978), pp. 299–314.

*Theology and Joy.* Tr. R. Ulrich. London: SCM Press, 1973.

'Theology as Eschatology'. In *The Future of Hope: Theology as Eschatology*, ed. F. Herzog (New York: Herder & Herder, 1970), pp. 1–50.

'Theology in Germany Today'. In *Observations on 'The Spiritual Situation of the Age': Contemporary German Perspectives*, ed. J. Habermas, tr. and intro. A. Buchwalter (Cambridge, Mass./ London: MIT Press, 1984), pp. 181–205.

*Theology of Hope: On the Ground and the Implications of a Christian Eschatology.* Tr. J. W. Leitch. London: SCM Press, 1967.

*The Open Church: Invitation to a Messianic Lifestyle.* Tr. M. D. Meeks. London: SCM Press, 1978.

*The Power of the Powerless.* Tr. M. Kohl. London: SCM Press, 1983.

*The Trinity and the Kingdom of God: The doctrine of God.* Tr. M. Kohl. London: SCM Press, 1981.

'Towards the Next Step in the Dialogue'. In *The Future of Hope: Theology as Eschatology,* ed. F. Herzog (New York: Herder & Herder, 1970), pp. 154–164.

*Umkehr zur Zukunft.* Munich: Chr. Kaiser, 1970/ Gütersloh: Gerd Mohn, 1977.

'Verschränkte Zeiten der Geschichte: Notwendige Differenzierungen und Begrenzungen des Geschichtsbegriffs'. *Evangelische Theologie* 44 (1984), pp. 213–227.

'Warum "Schwarze Theologie"? Einführung'. *Evangelische Theologie* 34 (1974), pp. 1–3.


C. Studies of Moltmann's Theology

Alves, R. A. *A Theology of Human Hope.* New York: Corpus, 1969. (Pp. 56–68 on Moltmann.)

Arts, H. *Moltmann and Tillich: Les fondements de l'espérance chrétienne.* Gembloux: J. Duculot, 1973.

Attfield, D. G. 'Can God be Crucified? A Discussion of J. Moltmann'. *Scottish Journal of Theology* 30 (1977), pp. 47–57.

Balthasar, H. Urs von. 'Zu einer christlichen Theologie der Hoffnung'. *Münchener Theologische Zeitschrift* 32 (1981), pp. 81–102.

Basset, J.-C. 'Croix et dialogue des religions'. *Revue d'histoire et de philosophie religieuses* 56 (1976), pp. 545–558.

Bauckham, R. J. 'Bibliography: Jürgen Moltmann'. *Modern Churchman* 28 (1986), pp. 55–60.

—— 'Jürgen Moltmann'. In *One God in Trinity,* ed. P. Toon and J. D. Spiceland (London: Bagster, 1980), pp. 111–132.

—— 'Moltmann's Eschatology of the Cross'. *Scottish Journal of Theology* 30 (1977), pp. 301–311.

—— 'Theodicy from Ivan Karamazov to Moltmann'. *Modern Theology* (1987), forthcoming.

Blanchy, A. 'Lire Moltmann'. *Études théologiques et religieuses* 46 (1971), pp. 355–383.

—— 'Théologie trinitaire et éthique sociale chez J. Moltmann'. *Études théologiques et religieuses* 2 (1982), pp. 245–254.

Blaser, K. 'Les enjeux d'une doctrine trinitaire sociale: A propos du dernier livre de Jürgen Moltmann'. *Revue de théologie et de philosophie* 113 (1981), pp. 155–166.

Borowitz, E. B. *Contemporary Christologies: A Jewish Response.* New York: Paulist Press, 1980.

Braaten, C. E. 'A Trinitarian Theology of the Cross'. *Journal of Religion* 56 (1976), pp. 113–121.

—— 'Toward a Theology of Hope'. In *New Theology* No. 5, ed. M. E. Marty and D. G. Pearman (New York: Macmillan/ London: Collier-Macmillan, 1968), pp. 90–111.

Bühler, P. 'Existence et histoire: Quelques éléments de réponse à Jean-Pierre Thévenaz'. *Revue de théologie et de philosophie* 115 (1983), pp. 209–214.

—— *Kreuz und Eschatologie: Eine Auseinandersetzung mit der politischen Theologie, im Anschluss an Luthers theologia crucis.* (Hermeneutische Untersuchungen zur Theologie 17.) Tübingen: Mohr (Siebeck), 1981.

Capps, W. H. *Hope Against Hope: Moltmann to Merton in One Theological Decade.* Philadelphia: Fortress, 1976.

—— *Time Invades the Cathedral: Tensions in the School of Hope.* (With a Foreword by J. Moltmann.) Philadelphia: Fortress, 1972.

Chapman, G. C., Jr. 'Black Theology and Theology of Hope: What Have they to Say to Each Other?' *Union Seminary Quarterly Review* 29 (1974), pp. 107–129.

—— 'Hope and the ethics of formation: Moltmann as an interpreter of Bonhoeffer'. *Studies in Religion/ Sciences religieuses* 12 (1983), pp. 449–460.

—— 'Jürgen Moltmann and the Christian Dialogue with Marxism'. *Journal of Ecumenical Studies* 18 (1981), pp. 435–450.

—— 'Moltmann's Vision of Man'. *Anglican Theological Review* 56 (1974), pp. 310–330.

Cook, M. L. *The Jesus of Faith: A Study in Christology.* New York: Paulist Press, 1981.

Dillistone, F. W. 'The Theology of Jürgen Moltmann'. *Modern Churchman* 18 (1974–75), pp. 145–150.

Dumas, A. *Political Theology and the Life of the Church*. Tr. J. Bowden. London: SCM Press, 1978. (Ch. 5 on Moltmann.)

Eckhardt, A. R. 'Jürgen Moltmann, the Jewish People, and the Holocaust'. *Journal of the American Academy of Religion* 44 (1976), pp. 675–691.

Eyt, P. 'La réévaluation de l'espérance selon J. Moltmann'. *Bulletin de littérature ecclésiastique* 72 (1971), pp. 161–186.

Fiorenza, F. P. 'Dialectical Theology and Hope'. *Heythrop Journal* 9 (1968), pp. 143–163, 384–399; 10 (1969), pp. 26–42.

Gibellini, R. *La Teologia di Jürgen Moltmann*. (Giornale di Teologia 89.) Brescia: Queriniana, 1975.

Gilkey, L. *Reaping the Whirlwind: A Christian Interpretation of History*. New York: Seabury, 1976. (Pp. 226–238 on Moltmann.)

—— 'Reinhold Niebuhr's Theology of History.' In *The Legacy of Reinhold Niebuhr*, ed. N. A. Scott (Chicago: University of Chicago Press, 1975), pp. 63 ff. (= *Journal of Religion* 54/4, 1974).

Grässer, E. '»Der politisch gekreuzigte Christus«: Kritische Anmerkungen zu einer politischen Hermeneutik des Evangeliums'. *Zeitschrift für die neutestamentliche Wissenschaft* 62 (1971), pp. 260–294.

Hedinger, U. 'Glaube und Hoffnung bei Ernst Fuchs und Jürgen Moltmann'. *Evangelische Theologie* 27 (1967), pp. 36–51.

Henke, P. *Gewissheit vor dem Nichts: Eine Antithese zu den theologischen Entwürfen Wolfhart Pannenbergs und Jürgen Moltmanns*. Berlin/ New York: de Gruyter, 1978.

Herzog, F. ed. *The Future of Hope: Theology as Eschatology*. New York: Herder & Herder, 1970.

Hill, W. J. *The Three-Personed God: The Trinity as a Mystery of Salvation*. Washington, D. C.: Catholic University Press of America, 1982. (Pp. 166–175 on Moltmann.)

Hodgson, P. C. *Jesus – Word and Presence: An Essay in Christology*. Philadelphia: Fortress, 1971. (Pp. 9–20, 220–241 on Moltmann.)

Hryniewicz, W. 'Le Dieu souffrant? Réflexions sur la notion chrétienne de Dieu'. *Église et théologie* 12 (1981), pp. 333–356.

Hunsinger, G. 'The Crucified God and the Political Theology of Violence'. *Heythrop Journal* 14 (1973), pp. 266–279, 379–395.

Irish, J. A. 'Moltmann's Theology of Contradiction'. *Theology Today* 32 (1975–76), pp. 21–31.

Jantzen, G. M. 'Christian Hope and Jesus' Despair'. *King's Theological Review* 5 (1982), pp. 1–7.

Kerstiens, F. 'The Theology of Hope in Germany Today'. *Concilium* 9/6 (1970), pp. 101–111.

Küng, H. 'Die Religionen als Frage an die Theologie des Kreuzes'. *Evangelische Theologie* 33 (1973), pp. 401–423.

Lavalette, H. de. 'Ambiguïtés de la théologie politique'. *Recherches de science religieuse* 59 (1971), pp. 545–562.

McGrath, A. E. *The Making of Modern German Christology: From the Enlightenment to Pannenberg.* Oxford: Blackwell, 1986. (Ch. 8 on Moltmann.)

Mackey, J. P. *The Christian Experience of God as Trinity.* London: SCM Press, 1983. (Pp. 202–209 on Moltmann.)

Macquarrie, J. *Christian Hope.* London/ Oxford: Mowbrays, 1978. (Pp. 47–49, 101–103 on Moltmann.)

—— 'Theologies of Hope: A Critical Examination'. In *Thinking about God* (London: SCM Press, 1975), pp. 221–232.

—— 'Today's Word for Today: I. Jürgen Moltmann'. *Expository Times* 92 (1980), pp. 4–7.

Marsch, W.-D. ed. *Diskussion über die »Theologie der Hoffnung« von Jürgen Moltmann.* Munich: Chr. Kaiser, 1967.

Matic, M. *Jürgen Moltmanns Theologie in Auseinandersetzung mit Ernst Bloch.* (Europäische Hochschulschriften 23/209.) Frankfurt am Main: P. Lang, 1983.

Meeks, M. D. *Origins of the Theology of Hope.* Philadelphia: Fortress, 1974.

—— 'Trinitarian Theology: A Review Article'. *Theology Today* 38 (1981–82), pp. 472–477.

Migliore, D. L. 'Biblical Eschatology and Political Hermeneutics'. *Theology Today* 26 (1969–70), pp. 116–132.

Miguez Bonino, J. *Revolutionary Theology Comes of Age.* London: SPCK, 1975. (Pp. 144–150 on Moltmann.)

Momose, P. F. *Kreuzestheologie: Eine Auseinanderseztung mit Jürgen Moltmann.* Mit einem Nachwort von Jürgen Moltmann. Freiburg/ Basel/ Vienna: Herder, 1978.

Mondin, B. 'Theology of Hope and the Christian Message'. *Biblical Theology Bulletin* 2 (1972), pp. 43–63.

Morse, C. *The Logic of Promise in Moltmann's Theology*. Philadelphia: Fortress, 1979.

Mottu, H. 'L'espérance chrétienne dans la pensée de Jürgen Moltmann'. *Revue de théologie et de philosophie* 17 (1967), pp. 242–258.

Müller, D. 'Résumé des débats'. In L. Rumpf et al., *Hegel et la théologie contemporaine: L'absolu dans l'histoire?* (Neuchatel/ Paris: Delachaux & Niestlé, 1977), pp. 219–225.

Muller, R. A. 'Christ in the Eschaton: Calvin and Moltmann on the Duration of the *Munus Regium*'. *Harvard Theological Review* 74 (1981), pp. 31–59.

Niewiadomski, J. *Die Zweideutigkeit von Gott und Welt in J. Moltmanns Theologien*. (Innsbrucker theologische Studien 9.) Innsbruck/ Vienna/ Munich: Tyrolia, 1982.

O'Collins, G. 'Spes Quaerens Intellectum'. *Interpretation* 22 (1968), pp. 36–52.

—— 'The Principle and Theology of Hope'. *Scottish Journal of Theology* 21 (1968), pp. 129–144.

O'Donnell, J. J. 'The Doctrine of the Trinity in Recent German Theology'. *Heythrop Journal* 23 (1982), pp. 153–167.

—— *Trinity and Temporality: The Christian Doctrine of God in the Light of Process Theology and the Theology of Hope*. Oxford: Oxford University Press, 1983.

Olson, R. 'Trinity and Eschatology: The Historical Being of God in Jürgen Moltmann and Wolfhart Pannenberg'. *Scottish Journal of Theology* 36 (1983), pp. 213–227.

Pannenberg, W. *Christian Spirituality and Sacramental Community*. London: Darton, Longman & Todd, 1984. (Ch. 3 on Moltmann.)

Pawlikowski, J. 'The Holocaust and Contemporary Christology'. *Concilium* 175 (5/1984) = *The Holocaust as Interruption*, ed. E. S. Fiorenza and D. Tracy (Edinburgh: T. & T. Clark, 1984), pp. 43–49.

Preston, R. H. 'Reflections on Theologies of Social Change'. In *Theology and Change: Essays in Memory of Alan Richardson*, ed. R. H. Preston (London: SCM Press, 1975), pp. 143–166.

Ricoeur, P. 'Freedom in the Light of Hope'. In *Essays on Biblical Interpretation*, ed. L. S. Mudge (London: SPCK, 1981), pp. 155–182.

Runia, K. *The present-day Christological debate*. Leicester: Inter-Varsity Press, 1984. (Pp. 38–46 on Moltmann.)

Sobrino, J. *Christology at the Crossroads: A Latin American Approach*. Tr. J. Drury. London: SCM Press, 1978. (Pp. 28–33 on Moltmann.)

Strunk, R. 'Diskussion über "Der gekreuzigte Gott." ' *Evangelische Theologie* 41 (1981), pp. 89–94.

Sykes, S. W. 'Life After Death: the Christian Doctrine of Heaven'. In *Creation Christ and Culture: Studies in Honour of T. F. Torrance*, ed. R. W. A. McKinney (Edinburgh: T. & T. Clark, 1976), pp. 250–271.

Thévenaz, J.-P. 'Le Dieu crucifié n'a-t-il plus d'histoire?' *Revue de théologie et de philosophie* 115 (1983), pp. 199–208.

—— 'Vérité d'espérance ou vérité de connaissance? Les enjeux théoriques et politiques de la théologie de Jürgen Moltmann'. *Études théologiques et religieuses* 49 (1974), pp. 225–247.

Thils, G. '»Soyez riches d'espérance par la vertu du Saint-Esprit« (Rom 15,13): La théologie d'espérance de J. Moltmann'. *Ephemerides Theologicae Lovanienses* 47 (1971), pp. 495–503.

Tripole, M. R. 'A Church for the Poor and the World: At Issue with Moltmann's Ecclesiology'. *Theological Studies* 42 (1981), pp. 645–659.

—— 'Ecclesiological developments in Moltmann's Theology of Hope'. *Theological Studies* 34 (1973), pp. 19–35.

Vignaux, P. 'Conditions d'une théologie d'espérance'. In J. Daniélou et al., *Espérance chrétienne et avenir humaine (Les quatres fleuves 2)* (Paris: Éditions du Seuil, 1974), pp. 82–96.

Walsh, B. J. 'Theology of Hope and the Doctrine of Creation: An Appraisal of Jürgen Moltmann'. *Evangelical Quarterly* 59 (1987), pp. 53–76.

Webster, J. B. 'Jürgen Moltmann: Trinity and Suffering'. *Evangel* 3/2 (1985), pp. 4–6.

Welker, M. ed. *Diskussion über Jürgen Moltmanns Buch »Der gekreuzigte Gott«*. Munich: Chr. Kaiser, 1979.

Widmer, G.-P. 'Le nouveau et le possible: Notes sur les théologies de l'espérance'. *Revue d'histoire et de philosophie religieuses* 55 (1975), pp. 165–175.

Wiebe, B. 'Interpretation and Historical Criticism: Jürgen Moltmann'. *Restoration Quarterly* 24 (1981), pp. 155–166.

—— 'Revolution as an Issue in Theology: Jürgen Moltmann'. *Restoration Quarterly* 26 (1983), pp. 105–120.

Wiederkehr, D. 'Neue Interpretation der Kreuzestodes Jesu: Zu J.

Moltmanns Buch »Der gekreuzigte Gott«'. *Freiburger Zeitschrift für Philosophie und Theologie* 20 (1973), pp. 441–463.

Winling, R. 'Futur et Avenir: à propos d'une mise au point de J. Moltmann'. *Recherches de science religieuse* 53 (1979), pp. 180–184.

Young, N. *Creator, Creation and Faith*. London: Collins, 1976. (Chap. 8 on Moltmann.)

## EYES THAT SEE: The Spiritual Gift of Discernment

*Douglas McBain*

The first of a new series, Renewal Issues in the Church, which examines the effects of charismatic renewal on corporate church life and individual Christian experience from a biblical perspective.

Douglas McBain, a leading figure in renewal first in the Baptist Church and now on a wider basis, provides a comprehensive and thorough scripture-based guide to the gift of discernment; which, with the resurgence of emphasis on signs and wonders, healing and deliverance, is 'the most necessary gift for the present day church'.

## ISSUES FACING CHRISTIANS TODAY

*John Stott*

A major appraisal of contemporary social, moral, sexual and global issues, combined with one man's attempt to think 'Christianly' on this broad spectrum of complex questions, make ISSUES FACING CHRISTIANS TODAY a *best-seller*.

'This is powerful stuff. Highly contemporary . . . awkwardly personal . . . thoroughly biblical.' *Baptist Times*

'A valuable resource for Christians responding to the huge needs to seek the renewal of society.' *Buzz*

'It stands alone as a scholarly, scriptural and profoundly well-argued and researched authority on many of the most perplexing and intractable problems of the present day.' *Renewal*

# CHOICES . . . CHANGES

*Joni Eareckson Tada*

Joni has inspired millions with her courage and faith in dealing with her quadriplegia. In her third book, she writes revealingly of her life, her ministry and her marriage. 'I've sat in on bridal showers for so many others; it seems odd that it should be my turn. In my wheelchair with its dusty gears and squeaky belts, I seem slightly out of place among the delicately wrapped gifts and dainty finger sandwiches.'

This warm, honest, sometimes funny and often poignant autobiography shows us vividly that though life is full of changes – wanted and unwanted – God uses each one of them to make us more like Him. Illustrated.


# TWO MILLION SILENT KILLINGS: the Truth about Abortion

*Dr Margaret White*

Essential, informed reading for all Christians on this critical contemporary issue; likely to engender wholehearted and healthy controversy.

GP Margaret White exposes the deliberate attempt to confuse the public over the issue of abortion by the use of euphemistic language and the minimizing of its harmful side-effects. She traces the history of abortion from legal, medical and religious perspectives, describes the clinical methods used to terminate pregnancies, and answers the various arguments put forward by the pro-abortionists in terms of God's basic rules for life. At the heart of these is the Creator's desire for his creation's health, stability and well-being. Dr White demonstrates that the extent of the damaging effects of abortion on women and society is one of today's best-kept secrets.

# THE GOSPEL COMMUNITY

*John Tiller*

An important and timely call to the established churches to rediscover the distinctive life of the Spirit and to become true 'gospel communities' – attractive, authoritative and relevant.

Neither the experience of renewal nor nationwide evangelistic missions resulted in a mass return to the churches. Instead, the house church seems to promise a better future for Christianity. Can revival still come through the established churches? John Tiller, Chancellor and Canon Residentiary of Hereford Cathedral, looks at Jesus' radical definitions of the temple, priesthood and sacrifice, and outlines the style of leadership which will enable the church to become again a 'living temple'. A critical book practically showing the way ahead for the established church.


# THE INFINITE GUARANTEE: A Meditation on the Last Words from the Cross

*Andrew Cruickshank*

A profound and thoughtful series of reflections on Jesus' seven sayings from the Cross by one of TV's most familiar and favourite actors. Andrew Cruickshank's deeply challenging study provides ideal devotional reading material, which encourages us to establish their significance of Jesus' words for us today.

'. . . a very remarkable book . . . quite outstanding. It demands to be read, re-read and read again. I can only describe it as *a little masterpiece . . .*'                    Rev Dr William Neil

If you wish to receive *regular information* about *new books,* please send your name and address to:

London Bible Warehouse
PO Box 123
Basingstoke
Hants RG23 7NL

Name......................................................................

Address.................................................................

............................................................................

............................................................................

............................................................................

I am especially interested in:
☐ Biographies
☐ Fiction
☐ Christian living
☐ Issue related books
☐ Academic books
☐ Bible study aids
☐ Children's books
☐ Music
☐ Other subjects